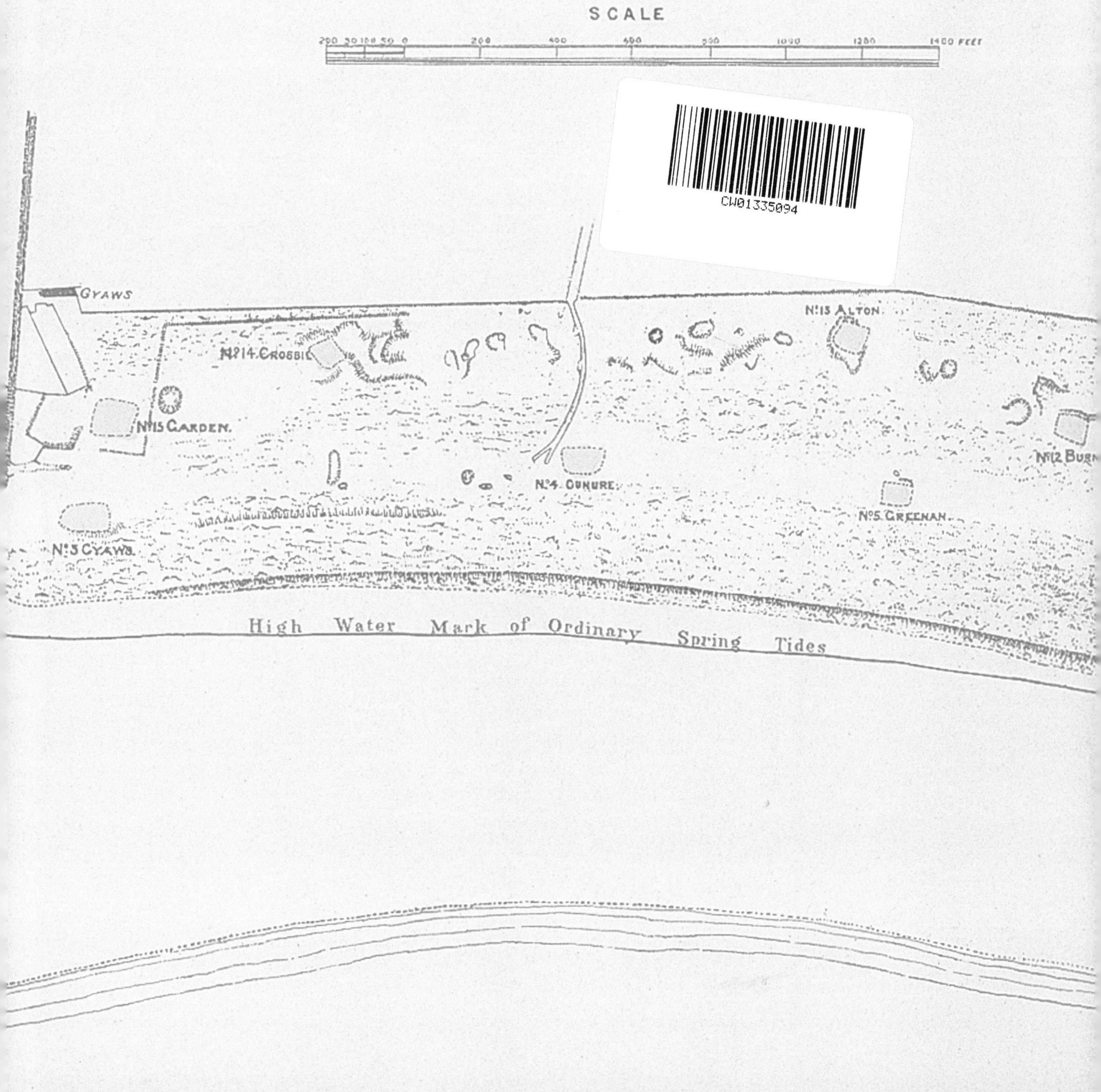

THE BREEZY LINKS O'TROON

A HISTORY OF ROYAL TROON GOLF CLUB

James Dickie
The Club's First Captain, 1878-82

The Breezy Links o'Troon

A HISTORY OF ROYAL TROON GOLF CLUB
1878-2000

by R. A. Crampsey

PUBLISHED BY ROYAL TROON GOLF CLUB
2001

Photographic Credits

Allsport UK Ltd pages 93, 104; *Allsport UK Ltd photographs by David Cannon* pages 135, 136; *Allsport UK Ltd/Hulton Deutsch* page 38; *Bara, Troon* page 18; *Caithness Brothers, Kirkcaldy* page 85; *Douglas Studio, Troon* page 97, 103 upper; *The Field* pages 45 upper, 46; *Kenneth Ferguson Photography* pages 102 lower, 108, 115, 141, 143, 145, 146, 147, 148, 154, 156, 157, 158, 159, 160, 164, 166, 171, 172, 174, 175, 185, 189, 193, 199, 220 lower; *Donald Ford Images* page 153; *Alistaire Gilchrist* pages 149, 150; *Tom Gilfillan* page 101; *Robin Gray* pages 103, 106; *Dr. L. A. Hardie* pages 86, 92, 94, 96, 102 upper, 105 upper, 119 upper and lower, 123; *Michael Joy, St Andrews* pages 120, 169; *Little Brown Publishing* pages 21, 50, 180; *James Macartney, Troon* page 16 upper; *Mayall & Co* page 144; *Derek M. McCabe* page 196; *Wm McCallum, Ayr* page 113 middle; *Karen Murray* pages 101 lower, 151; *Wm S. Paton, Kilmarnock* pages 90 upper, 112 upper and lower, 122, 125, 126, 127, 133, 134, 138, 139, 191; *Prestwick Golf Club* page 5 lower; *R. Rankine, Glasgow* page 9 upper and lower; *Royal Liverpool Golf Club* page 32, 33 upper; *SMG Newspapers Ltd* page 34, 39, 40 upper & lower, 48, 55, 75 lower, 76, 81, 83, 91, 98, 186; *Sport & General Press Agency, London* page 41 Upper; *Sportsprint Publishing, Edinburgh* page 100; *St. Andrews University Library* pages 71, 72, 74, 152.

© Copyright

The text of book is the property of Royal Troon Golf Club.
No part of it may be reproduced, in any manner whatsoever,
without the written permission of the Committee.

ISBN 0-9541542-0-7

Contents

Foreword	VI
Acknowledgements	VIII

The Early Years
First Beginnings	2
The Ladies Championship of 1904	20
1904-1914	23
J. L. C. Jenkins and the Amateur Championship of 1914	25
The Great War of 1914-18	29

The Club Becomes a Championship Venue
After the War	32
The Open Championship of 1923	34
The Amateur Championships of the Twenties	47
The 1938 Amateur Championship	54
The Second World War	61

Back to Normality
Post War Years	68
The Open Championship of 1950	69
Back with the Club	74
The Amateur Championships of 1956	76
Ayrshire Golfers 1930-60	82
The Open Championship of 1962	86
A Time to Reflect	92

The Years of Expansion
The Amateur Championship of 1968	94
An Outside View	98
The Seventies	100
The Open Championship of 1973	103
The Scottish Amateur Championship of 1977	110

The Club Becomes Royal
100 Up	112
The Club Becomes Royal	114
The Amateur Championship of 1978	118
Being a Member of Royal Troon	120
The 1980s	121
The Open Championship of 1982	124
Colin S. Montgomerie	131
The Open Championship of 1989	133
James D. Montgomerie	141

The 1990s
The 1990s	144
Major Developments	146
The Post-war Green Superintendents	151
The Open Championship of 1997	159
New Arrival, Senior Member	172
The Ladies' Golf Club	176
Troon Portland Golf Club	183
Clubmasters and Caddie Masters	189
Old Course Championship Guide	193

The New Millennium
The Millennium Year	196
Might I Suggest?	200
Envoi	203

Appendix I
Honorary Presidents, Captains, Secretaries and Treasurers	205

Appendix II
The Origin of the Hole Names	207

Appendix III
Course Records	209

Appendix IV
The Club's Principal Medals and Trophies with their Winners	210

Foreword
Colin S. Montgomerie, MBE

I AM honoured to be asked to write this foreword for the new history of Royal Troon Golf Club. Royal Troon played an important part in my development as a golfer and I have always felt proud and privileged to be associated with the Club, first as an Ordinary Member and more recently as an Honorary Life Member. The more senior members of the Club will be well aware that I have had a long association with Royal Troon which started as a four year old playing the Par 3 Course with my brother. However, my real enthusiasm for the game began when my father, James, a Country Member at the time, brought me and the rest of the family to watch Tom Weiskopf's Open in 1973.

At that time, I was a 10 year-old schoolboy with limited experience of golf but watching Weiskopf, Johnny Miller, Jack Nicklaus, Gary Player and all the other leading stars in action made a massive impact on me and the visit also heightened the emotion I felt when membership of the Club was conferred on me in 1984.

Having left Strathallan School to go to Houston Baptist University in America, it was not always possible to be in Troon as much as I would have liked, but despite frequent absences I still played an active role in club life and would like to think that I made some impact.

In those days I had the good fortune to win the Summer Meeting scratch prize in 1987 and various other club medals but one of my biggest regrets was that I was never able to compete in the Club Championship. This was staged between the months of May and September when I was over in the States. That is an omission from my record I will always regret but it was not the only disappointment I suffered while I was a young member at Royal Troon because I can recall in 1986 being disqualified from my first competition. I thought I had won the Summer Meeting when I recall holing a bunker shot on the last for what I thought was a winning birdie only to be told when I handed in my card that I had been disqualified because I had not signed in before I had gone out! What made it worse was that I had been playing with the gentleman who preceded my father as Club Secretary. Not unnaturally, we were both embarrassed, but at least it did instil in me the importance of checking the paperwork, both before and after a round.

Happily, however, that was one bad moment amongst many happy ones I can recall during my youth at Royal Troon and it was soon all but forgotten as I developed as a golfer, earning a plus-three handicap, winning the Scottish Stroke-Play and Scottish Amateur Championships, and then representing Great Britain and Ireland in two Walker Cups before turning professional towards the end of 1987.

Prior to that, whilst still an amateur, one of my proudest moments came when I was selected to represent Scotland in the 1984 Home Internationals, an event staged over Royal Troon. Fortunately, that week, I found an excellent vein of form and I emerged undefeated, a performance that won me a place in the subsequent Eisenhower Trophy in Hong Kong, in a Great Britain and Ireland team that was captained by another Scot, Charlie Green, and also included David Gilford, Peter McEvoy and Garth McGimpsey.

To this day, I can still remember the support I received from the local members that week and it was the same 13 years later when I made my one, and to date only, appearance in an Open Championship at Royal Troon.

In 1989, the year Mark Calcavecchia won the Open at Royal Troon, I had to sit on the sidelines because I failed by one shot to come through the Final Qualifying tournament at Barassie. That, as you can imagine, was a terrible disappointment but, if nothing else, it made me doubly determined to give my best when The Open returned in 1997. Sadly, it was not to be. Plagued by the strong winds that hampered all the late starters that afternoon, I opened with a disappointing 76 that left me nine shots behind the leaders and in danger of missing the cut. Fortunately, that fate did not befall me and although I hit back with rounds of 69, 69 and 70, I still could finish no better than a tie for 24th place, a distant 12 shots behind the winner, America's Justin Leonard, who tied an Open record when he came from five shots behind to win the title with a closing 65. Leonard, it has to be said, deserves enormous credit for that performance because, like Arthur Havers, Bobby Locke, Arnold Palmer, Tom Weiskopf, Tom Watson and Mark Calcavecchia before him, he prevailed on a course that takes no prisoners, even on the odd occasions when the weather is benign.

As a local member, and someone who knows the course better than most, I am often asked how I rate Royal Troon alongside the other classic Scottish links. I tend to respond by suggesting that it is right up there alongside Carnoustie as the toughest links course in the country. Certainly, I have always felt that if I can get round in par or better off the back tees, particularly when the wind is blowing, then I know there is nothing much wrong with my game. However, it would be wrong to suggest that Royal Troon is nothing more than a brute because, as successive generations of Open competitors have found, you need finesse and touch as well as strength to play it well.

The Club's motto is "Tam Arte Quam Marte", which translates "As Much By Skill As By Strength", and I cannot help but feel it is an excellent description of how the course plays. True, you need strength to compile a score, particularly on the 6th, the longest hole in Open Championship golf, and on most of the back nine, but at other times a marvellous touch is required as well. Royal Troon has some wonderful holes, but arguably my favourite is the Postage Stamp, the par-3 8th, which at 126-yards might be the shortest hole on the Open Championship rota, but is also one of the most demanding, particularly if the wind is swirling and you cannot quite decide what club to hit from the tee.

The biggest compliment I can pay the Postage Stamp is to say that it is a bit like the Road Hole at St. Andrews, the 12th at Augusta National, and the 17th at Sawgrass – in a competition your score is never safe until you have got through the hole, something German amateur, Herman Tissies, found to his cost during the Open in 1950 when he succumbed to a 15 on that one hole. Fortunately, the Postage Stamp has never been quite so cruel to me but it is still a formidable test which is why it was fitting that in the 1973 Open, the legendary Gene Sarazen, the oldest competitor in the field, and a man making an emotional return to a Championship he won at Prince's in 1932, should have a hole-in-one there in front of the BBC TV cameras.

That remains one of the highlights in Royal Troon's rich history but it is by no means alone as, I am sure, this fine volume will indicate.

Colin Montgomerie

Acknowledgements

I have an infinite number of people to thank and really should mention the total membership of Royal Troon Golf Club but inevitably I had to work more closely with some than with others.

First and foremost I must mention the Captain, Bryan Boucher-Myers and the Golf Club History Committee under the dynamic chairmanship of David Smyth. The Committee was just what any writer of a club history would want, supplying a constant stream of information and possible illustrations for the book and reading the written work with a vigilant though never uncharitable eye.

David Smyth and Ian Valentine drew on their unrivalled knowledge of the workings of the Open Championship, Andrew Taylor is unsurpassed in his awareness of what illustrations might be available, Sir James Armour contributed his experiences of top level golf over half a century. Brian Anderson who has played the course as much as any man also revealed his love for the artefacts of the game, in particular the old hand-made clubs and also the golf ball at every stage of its development. Phil Martin and John Greene were unfailingly supportive and Jan Chandler took notes with an efficiency which left no doubt as to what we had actually said.

Outwith the Committee I must render personal thanks to Dr Leslie Hardie who gave unstinted access to his fine and numerous photographs which were invaluable information on the Club at various stages of its development. In the area of photography one must also mention Ken Ferguson whose skilful and painstaking work has rendered even the most creased and crumpled pictures suitable for reproduction.

The co-operation of the older members is vital in such a book and the late H.V.S. Thomson did us an enormous favour in taking us back to those pre-war days of which so few golfers now have personal remembrances. Dr. Willie Somerville contributed some diverting recollections of the Old Course during the war years. Often the view from outside is the more penetrating and Jack Cannon recalled some Troon 'greats' while Sandy Sinclair testified to his pride in being an Honorary Life Member.

Troon is of course the links where the great golfers play, that is the public perception of it. It is very gratifying that every living champion who had gained success at Troon has seen fit to commemorate his achievement in his own words and the pride they display in their success, the enjoyment of the welcome afforded them and what they clearly felt is the enormous honour done to those who were given Honorary Life Membership, all these aspects shine out from the pieces they have written.

It was gratifying too to read the reflections of such as Charlie Yates who won the first Amateur at Troon, John Beharrell, Amateur Champion at 18, Michael Bonallack, a Colossus of amateur golf in the 1960s and Peter McEvoy, who would go the distance in the Masters at Augusta.

The greatest professional golfer in Europe for the last decade, Colin Montgomerie, has close links with Royal Troon, indeed perhaps the most hopeful lines in the book for the foot-soldiers will be his admission that, in his time as amateur, he never broke par in a Troon medal. Equalled yes, broke no.

Norman Fergusson made himself available for a lengthy interview in which he showed himself master of the laconic observation. I have the House Staff and the Office Staff to thank for their warm and unvarying welcome. One would have thought that I had come to confer benefit rather than to disrupt their normal routine.

There were times when it was important to write about all three clubs. The Captain of the Ladies' Golf Club and the Secretary, Valerie Laidlaw, were kindness itself. They made the Minute Books freely available to me and, an even greater treasure, their marvellous Cuttings Book than which it would be difficult to find a better guide to Ladies' inter-war golf. In like manner the Portland Club with the aid of their Captain, Tom Irvine, placed their Minutes at my disposal and this was crucial for getting the hosts' view of the arrival of the Old Course members in the depths of World War Two.

All of which tends to reinforce my initial impression that the list of acknowledgements exactly corresponds with the list of members. I thank all such for their unflagging courtesy and express the hope that between us we have produced a book that will convey some of the individuality of the Club and record the remarkable part it has played in the development of the game in Scotland.

Throughout the work of preparation of this book, the previous History of the Club, that of I.M. Mackintosh, has been an invaluable source of reference and I am grateful to Mrs Patsy Patterson, his daughter, for allowing me to quote from it.

I would also like to thank Siobhan Crampsey for her meticulous work in preparing a fair copy of the original draft.

Finally David Smyth's drive was welcome and invaluable. Rome, they say, was not built in a day but had David been Clerk of Works it might well have been!

Dr. John Highet MB

CHAPTER ONE
The Early Years

First Beginnings

IT was the coming of the railway that made golf courses in general and Troon Golf Club in particular viable. Had it not been for the railway speculators it is fair to say that golf's arrival as a major pastime would have occurred a good half-century later.

There is some evidence, although not much, that there was a golf course of sorts in Troon about 1870 but it was far from being a properly constituted Club. Such a Club would require a structure and a system of governance formed as the result of an inaugural meeting.

As things stood then, golf was very much an East of Scotland game. It was firmly rooted in those small Fife towns such as St. Andrews, Crail and Burntisland where a walk of a few hundred yards would bring merchant and artisan to the course. This set-up stretched on both shores of the Forth and Leven, Lundin and Scotscraig had their counterparts in Dunbar, North Berwick and Musselburgh.

Things were very different in the more congested West. The venerable Glasgow Golf Club had been driven from Glasgow Green by increasing public usage and the fact that merchants now lived out in the suburbs, too far away in the absence of mechanised transport. The Glasgow Golf Club had in fact only just emerged in 1870 from a thirty-five year hibernation. What the Victorians called "the encroachments of the avaricious building fiend" were playing havoc with the city courses. It may be remarked here that of all the Glasgow courses which have celebrated their centenary only Cathkin Braes still plays on its original ground. In the West, Prestwick was indeed a lonely beacon.

We are mainly concerned with a meeting in Troon in 1878 but all over Scotland such meetings were taking place. In Glasgow one such led to the formation of the Queen's Park Football Club, another

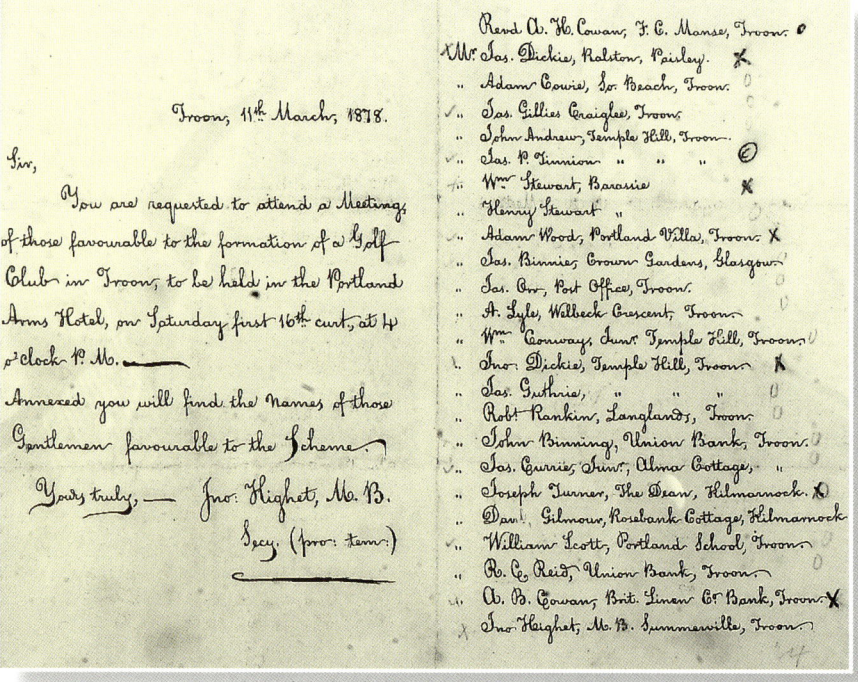

Letter of March 11th 1878, proposing formation of Golf Club

to the emergence of the Glasgow Academical Rugby Football Club. Railways had made this possible. Glasgow was probably never more prosperous than in the third quarter of the nineteenth century and her wealthy city merchants could now have houses at the

Some of the original members and their caddies, 1878

coast. Even from the city they could get down to Ayrshire on the short winter days, let alone the long summer evenings. To be on a railway line was to travel at 50 m.p.h., to be off it was to be confined, like one's grandfathers, to the speed of the fastest horse available.

Early Days

As *Golf* stated in its edition of July 31 1891 the Troon Golf Club had an unpromising beginning with certain things counting against it. There was the apathy of the local population towards the game, an apathy which an early Secretary, Dr John Highet, attempted to counteract by engaging a local brass band to play at one of the fledgling club's competitions! How successful this venture was remains uncertain.

Certainly at first there was no great enthusiasm for the game, the second phase, railway-led, would come a little later. The Club began with fewer than fifty members and it took some time to nudge this number up to the 100 mark.

More serious was the fact that Prestwick had got the start and all but cornered the market in this part of Ayrshire. But as six holes trebled in number the Club began to gain a better conceit of itself and this coincided with a sudden upsurge in the game of golf among the businessmen of Glasgow so that the Troon clubhouse which had been thought adequate at least for the coming generation had to be doubled in size within two or three years.

The writer, J. McBain, writing in 1891 has no doubt of the happy future awaiting Troon Golf Club. He has this to say:

"There are a few places whose names have become synonymous with Golf, St. Andrews, Prestwick, Musselburgh, North Berwick. Troon has not attained to that distinction yet but it is safe to say that the name is now better known from its connection with Golf than from any other connection. That such a flourishing institution as Troon Golf Club should have sprung up among the sand hills of Troon, the most sanguine of its promoters could hardly have dreamed. It is a striking and let us hope, lasting monument to the perseverance of a few determined men fighting against adverse circumstances."

There were of course other reasons why the game began to spread like wildfire in the West. On the Ayrshire coast there was an abundance of that flat, scrub land so unfit for cultivation yet so uniquely suited for the playing of what would come to be called links golf. There were economic factors at work too. One of these was the appearance of the gutta percha or "gutty" ball. Its predecessor, the "feathery" had been extremely expensive and above all non-durable. The gutta percha ball was a massive improvement and the rubbercored Haskell ball was even better. Clubs became easier to acquire and within a generation some of them at least would be factory-made.

We have a meeting to attend. There was a comparatively small and unattractive piece of ground to lay out. It would start with (sources vary) five or six holes only but that mattered little. It was a while before eighteen became the sacrosanct figure and well into the twentieth century – and not a hundred miles away – Skelmorlie in Ayrshire and Port Bannatyne in Bute managed perfectly well with thirteen holes apiece.

From this modest start with a handful of holes came first a sturdy, well-doing, local club which in less than half a century would open on the world as an internationally famous course so that the name Troon would be immediately recognised wherever golfers convene. It is a redoubtable bastion of the game that Scots play to a better standard than any other and it all began with a meeting.

Call to Arms

On a spring Monday morning in March 1878 certain gentlemen in Troon and the surrounding district received a circular letter among the other items of their post.

Troon, 11th March 1878

Sir,

You are requested to attend a Meeting of those favourable to the formation of a Golf Club in Troon to be held in the Portland Arms Hotel on Saturday first, 16th curt. at 4 o'clock p.m.

Annexed, you will find the names of those gentlemen favourable to the scheme.

Yours truly
(Signed.) Jno. Highet M. B.
Secy. (Pro tem).

Of the 24 names attached, one signatory came from Paisley, one from Glasgow and the rest from Kilmarnock or Troon. The Glasgow element was to increase very significantly before much time had elapsed.

The letter was a second attempt at getting things started. There had been a previous venture that ended in failure the month before, when a survey revealed that land allocated by the owner, the Duke of Portland, was deemed unsuitable for the purpose. The parcel of land allocated lay between the Pow Burn and Craigend but beyond the Gyaws Burn the ground would have cost a small fortune to make playable.

This letter, confessing inability to proceed, had been sent to the Duke's agent, Mr Frederick J. Turner by James Dickie who was to be the Club's first Captain when it got under way. The circular letter, calling the meeting, was sent out over the signature of John Highet who as Secretary would play such a leading part in the formative years. Highet, a medical doctor, was nothing if not decisive as the following extract from the *Ayr Advertiser* of Thursday 19 August 1886 shows:

"On Tuesday morning at half past eight William McKay, a labourer, was observed from the Golf Clubhouse to rush into the sea at Seal Rock. George Strath and Lorimer the golf club steward immediately proceded to the spot and, with difficulty, frustrated the man in his intentions. Dr. Highet was shortly afterwards on the spot and, after using restoratives, ordered his removal to the County Asylum, Ayr."

What the circular was after was approval of the plan to start with a small course, a "round of the green" as it was then called, which would consist of either five or six holes and the players would do circuits of the course until the necessary number of holes had been completed.

The Club was blessed from the outset by having friends in high places. The Duke of Portland exercised a benign interest and for the next forty years or so the ducal agents, Frederick J. Turner and later his son, J. Harling Turner, busied themselves to work in the Club's interests.

Evolution of the golf ball

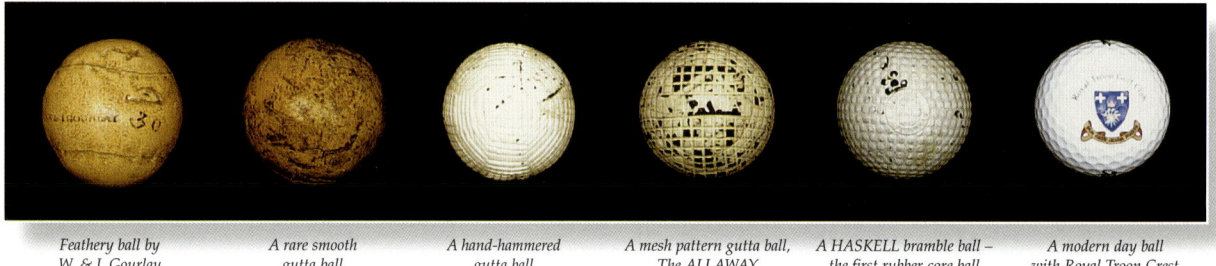

Feathery ball by W. & J. Gourlay circa 1840
A rare smooth gutta ball circa 1849
A hand-hammered gutta ball circa 1852-55
A mesh pattern gutta ball, The ALLAWAY circa 1890
A HASKELL bramble ball – the first rubber core ball introduced in 1898
A modern day ball with Royal Troon Crest circa 2000

THE EARLY YEARS

The Club's first honorary president, His Grace William John Arthur Charles James, 6th Duke of Portland K.G. P.C. G.C.V.O.

The ground which the newborn club was about to inhabit had nothing of the spectacular about it, if one discounts the majestic background of Arran on the other side of the Firth of Clyde. The terrain was scrubby and scattered with whin bushes, unsuitable for raising crops, indifferent for grazing, in fact pretty useless for anything except, by a marvellous dispensation of Providence, the playing of golf.

The meeting which Dr Highet's circular had called had, as the Club's first Minute declared, "resolved to form themselves into a Golf Club". The resolution, once taken was acted upon with speed and the first Committee Meeting took place on the 21st March in the Free Church Manse. Mr. James Dickie of Ralston, near Paisley, was elected as Captain and Dr John Highet filled the dual role of Secretary/Treasurer.

No time was lost in drawing up the Club Rules. Together with the Captain and the Secretary/Treasurer there were to be five Committee members of whom three would constitute a quorum. Admission to membership would be in the hands of the committee. In the ballot, three black balls would ensure the rejection of the applicant.

It was necessary to get the infant Club on a firm financial footing and the annual subscription was fixed at one guinea (£1.05 in present day terms). Life members would pay five guineas when they took such membership out and then, after five years, another five guineas. This was a more realistic concept of Life Membership than some other clubs had at the time but even then it was seriously underselling the value of a perpetual membership.

A special working party was created for the purpose of getting the new ground into a playable state and professional help was sought on clearing the course from Charles Hunter who was Keeper of the Green at Prestwick.

The course was rudimentary, accounts vary as to whether there were five or six holes at the outset, there were certainly no more. The clubhouse by all accounts seems to have been a converted railway carriage and for the first two years Troon Golf Club appears to have subsisted quite happily without a lavatory. But with each month that passed the Club seemed more confident, more deeply rooted.

Charles Hunter

In September 1878 Captain James Dickie presented a gold cross for annual competition, the winner to hold the trophy in perpetuity if he achieved the customary three consecutive successes. Of almost equal antiquity is the W. Stewart Handicap Medal, which was awarded to the most frequent Medal winner over the year.

At the first Annual General Meeting of 1879 the

Committee announced that the Clubhouse had been insured for a rather surprising £200, a figure which surely must have reflected the inconvenience of a possible replacement rather than any assessment of the building's appointments. There was a cheerful note of optimism, as this from the Minutes of the first Autumn General Meeting: *"There being no business of importance, all were anxious to proceed to the links and do battle for the Maltese Cross presented last year by the Captain for annual competition".*

The five holes seem to have become six in December 1879 when mention is made in the Minutes of the construction of a new hole to be called Dunure.

The Captain, James Dickie, appears to have lent the Club £50 to get started, and, moreover, to have declined the first offer of repayment. By now the Club was sufficiently well established to invite the Duke of Portland to become a member, an invitation that was accepted.

The expansion of the course seems to have been in carefully planned stages, six holes to twelve to eighteen. By 1883 there were eighteen holes, six of which were described as "new" and by 1885 the work was virtually completed according to an article by Rockwood in the *Illustrated Sporting and Dramatic News* of 17th October 1885.

"The Craigend hole, which is the opening one, and goes seaward (the original first) is halved in four and then we strike along the out-going line of the course straight for Ayr steeple. The Seal hole is the next and is followed by the Black Rock hole, both having nice golfing ground intervening and calling forth much dextrous play with the cleek, more particularly when getting slightly off the line amongst the bent. The Gyaws hole requires one to be exceedingly careful as there is a burn fringed with the nearest thing to an English oxer fence possible and the timber stops a badly played ball.

The Dunure follows still on the straight line out and allows for a couple of full drives and some clever work in the grass hollows at times with the spoon. From Greenan we proceed to Ailsa where there is a nicely-prepared putting green which reflects indeed much credit on Strath, the greenkeeper. From Ailsa we drive quite hard on to what looks quite a mountaineering course to Turnberry the turning point of the round. The putting-green is beautifully situated and a capital view of the Prestwick Links just over the Pow Burn is obtained. Across the links to Tel-el-Kebir is quite a desert march indeed, the ground being wild and the hill faces steep and sandy. Lost balls are at present common occurrences in this part but by and by this will be remedied.

The Sandhills hole, next the Railway follows and then come the Burmah, Alton, Crosby (sic) and the Well holes, all over ground which bring into play every club and every art of the players. The latter have numerous hazards and patience and skill are well brought out. Altogether, the new course at Troon is one which, when there has been a little more trampling, will prove one of the best in Scotland as no doubt the place will prove one of the most fashionable of West coast resorts."

Things were going well. In the summer of 1880, the Club's most distinguished member, the Duke, donated a Medal for a Scratch Competition. The following February brought the first mention of an inter-club match. The opponents were to be the Glasgow Golf Club and there would be twelve players a side. An early match of which we have

Dickie Cross, Spring Meeting – Scratch

George Strath long nosed woods

information was a meeting between the same two clubs on July 17 1886 noticed in the benevolent columns of the *Ayr Advertiser*: "A match between Troon and Glasgow Golf Clubs was played on Saturday. Nineteen couples took part and as the green was in good condition several of the players registered low figures. The game however was very one-sided, only three of the Troon players managing to score and on the cards being examined it was found that Glasgow won by 66 holes. A number of interesting matches, singles and foursomes, were afterwards played."

Duke of Portland Gold Medal, Summer Meeting – Scratch

More important in the long run was that the Club was in funds to the extent of £40 and in a position to contemplate the employment of a professional. The Club aimed high in its choice and George Strath became the first of only five professionals who span the 123 years of Troon's existence. He came from a well-known golfing family in St. Andrews as one of his brothers, Andrew, was Open Champion in 1865 and another was employed for several years by the Glasgow Golf Club when it played over Alexandra Park in the east end of the city.

Strath gave the Club six years service but although a very fair golfer his talents lay more in club-making, particularly he was famous for the making of long-nosed woods, and as a greenkeeper. This would be borne out by the fact that at the same time as he arrived James Gow was employed by Troon to coach new players.

The Club was ever anxious to do the right thing. It wrote to the R&A "to ask the proceedings for allowing valuable medals temporarily out of the possession of the club into that of the current winners". This may have

George Strath, Club Professional 1881-88

been connected with the fact that it had recently been decided to make the Dickie Cross a handicap event. It may equally have been the decision by several Edinburgh gentlemen to give a medal which would always be Club property but a small trinket would be given to the winners at the Club's expense.

As in every Golf Club there were the few who were dilatory in the matter of their subscriptions. The Committee strove for a form of words that would neither be over-peremptory nor give the impression that they did not mean business. In the event the well-tried formula of "Your early attention will oblige" was thought to be the most appropriate.

There were some peculiarly local difficulties in the upkeep of the course. Several of the holes on the outward half were so close to the sea that when there were severe storms, as was the case in April 1888, it required several carts to remove the heavy deposits of sand, especially between the Seal and Black Rock holes. Then the farmers who were allowed to collect the wrack from the seashore had an annoying habit of driving their carts over fairways and in some extreme examples, across greens.

Despite these minor irritations the game continued to grow in popularity, not least with the ladies. In May 1882 it was proposed that the Craigend hole and the ground behind it be set apart for their exclusive use. This was turned down but the ladies were to be given use of a section between Seal and Rabbit,

Edinburgh Medal, Summer Meeting – Handicap

indeed a separate course would be constructed for them.

More serious was the claim of some non-member males to have an immemorial right to play over the ground on which the Troon course was laid out. This kind of claim had been upheld on some of the great old East Coast courses such as St. Andrews and Musselburgh and the Committee were worried that there could be considerable encroachment by non-members. Shortly after Strath's appointment as professional/greenkeeper he was charged to keep a vigilant lookout for "strange golfers", the strangeness relating to their identity rather than their swing.

The situation was complicated by the fact that such artisan clubs were by no means unknown in other parts of Scotland. Courses such as Edzell in Angus had an artisan section where for a few shillings a year the course could be enjoyed although of course clubhouse facilities were withheld. Very often as in the case of Edzell, it was the wish of the landlord that such artisan societies should exist and certainly in the case of Troon the Duke was anxious that there should be the possibility of play for the working man.

The position of George Strath appears to have been a little unusual about this time. He is described in the Minutes as "the Professional without salary" which must have been very self-denying on his part and a little later he is referred to as "Collector of the Club in the matter of refreshments". In these references there is more than a hint of Strath's impending departure.

In May 1882 the first-ever Captain of Troon, James Dickie, intimated his resignation as he was moving to London. He had been an admirable servant of the Club and his last official action was typically selfless. He took the money which he had loaned to the Club but absolutely declined to receive any interest on the loan. His place was filled by Robert Easton.

The farmers with their carts were still a source of bother. In June 1882 the Committee felt constrained to make representations to the Duke's agent, J. H. Turner, about the incidence of wheeled traffic on the old road which ran by the Gyaws Burn out to the hole called Dunure. Mr Turner had a knack of combining business and enjoyment and he requested a "play of the links" so that he might see for himself. He thought the Club's position justified, and addressed this note to an offender. We have the note but not the name of the addressee:

"I'd strongly advise you to tell The Higgler, or whoever it is that crosses along this road that he'd better go quietly away or he will get himself in a hole he will not be played out of!"

The Club added action to precept by cutting a bunker across the old road. They also used a little

The Gyaws cottages

diplomacy to break the nuisance of carting and dumping seaweed and running carts across the green. They hinted ever so delicately to Mr Turner, and through him of course to the Duke, that it would be much easier for His Grace to feu the land if there were a golf course in good order adjacent. The upshot was an edict that no seaweed was to be dumped on the links south of the Craigend Burn.

Troon Golf Club was becoming known and they received a rather strange invitation from Prestwick St.

THE EARLY YEARS

The 10th hole Sandhills bunker

and green circa 1898

Nicholas to play in a match Glasgow v. Ayrshire (Old Prestwick to be excepted). It is unclear whether Old Prestwick had refused a similar invitation or had simply not been asked although the latter scenario seems unlikely. At all events Troon declined to take part for the Club seems to have been still fairly inward looking. This would soon change.

A knowledge of Latin appears to have been an essential for the ambitious committee man in the 1880s. When in 1883 the weather for the Dickie Gold Cross was especially foul it was cheerfully stated that *"Jupiter Pluvius reigned supreme"*. When in the same month an inter-club match against Glasgow Golf Club did go ahead there was a skittish reference to the expenses raised for the meal *"to provide creature comforts for the strangers ad libitum"*.

Caddies have played their part in the history of Troon, none more so than the one who spent the whole of the Second World War refugeeing in a bunker out on the course. We will hear more of him later. They are first mentioned and rated in the summer of 1882 when their payment is fixed at 4d a round (1.5p). Members were on no account to pay more as it caused discontent and the idea of a competition for the caddies found little favour.

Meanwhile the ladies were given the use of The Links "for the duration of the season" (sic). It was stressed that this was only a temporary arrangement and that they would get a separate course as soon as maybe. There would be a Ladies Course, there would be a separate course for what would have been Extraordinary Members and the Old Course, as it was coming to be called, would be extended to the full eighteen holes. The cost would be £200 and the caddies could now look forward to eightpence (3p) for the round.

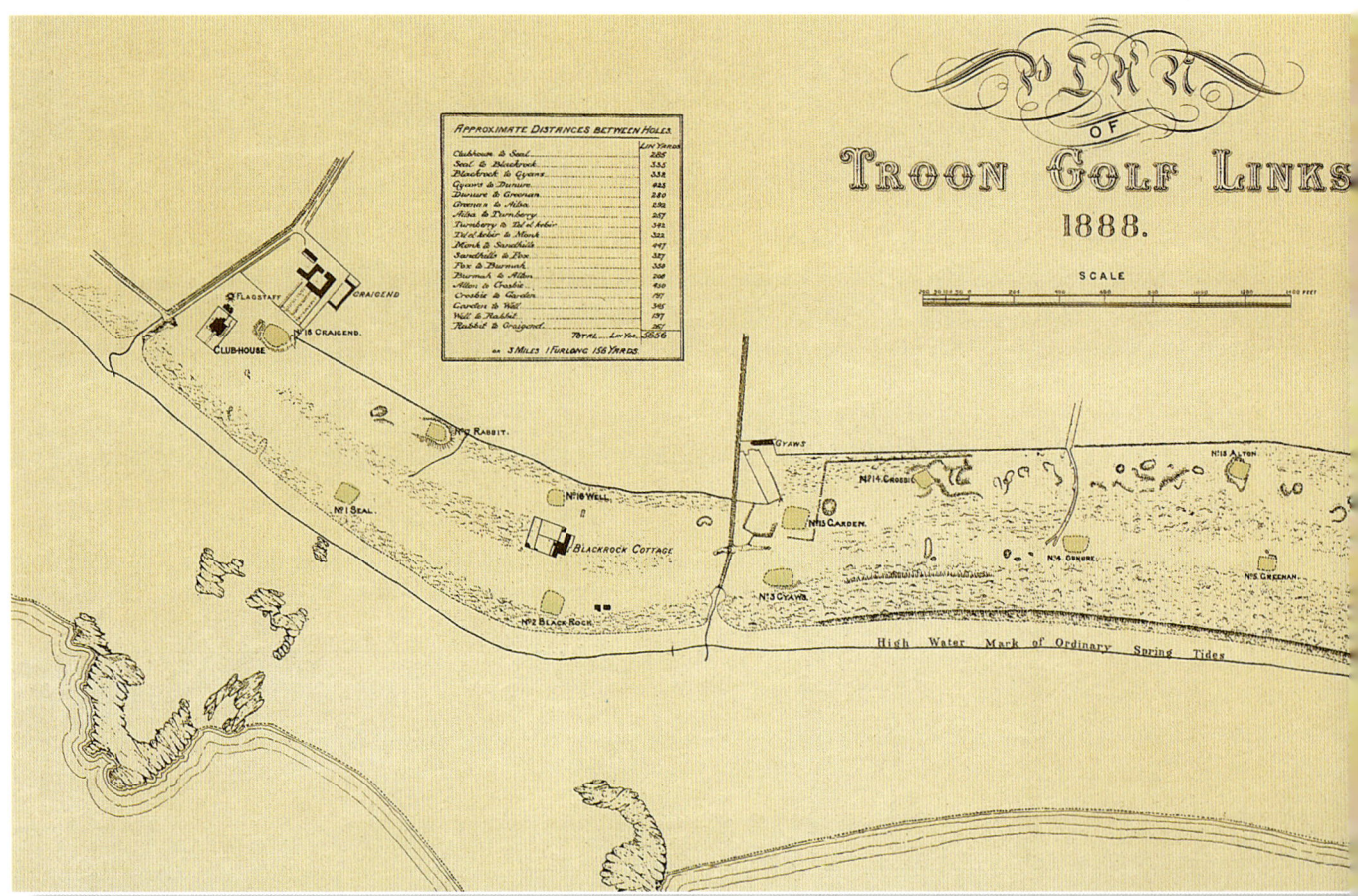

The Victorians were not as mealy-mouthed as has been supposed. Sometimes they made little attempt to wrap things up. Thus a new foursomes competition was described as "A strong man with a weak against the same". If this seems faintly wounding international football trials for matches against England were advertised as Probables v Improbables.

By the autumn of 1893 the course was at full stretch and all competitions were over a conventional 18-hole layout. An entry fee of one guinea was now required but if the course was satisfactory the old original Clubhouse was decidedly less so. A new one was essential and a local architect, Mr G. Andrew, was invited to draw up plans.

In the event the plan submitted and accepted almost a year later was that of a Glasgow architect, Henry Clifford. Ground was to be acquired and the edifice was not to cost more than £1500. The building of the new Clubhouse was in a very real sense a leap of faith since the club neither owned the ground nor had the comparative security of a long lease.

Up to £1000 of this money would if necessary be borrowed and the Club took the chance to augment its own subscription income. From now on the entry fee would be three guineas, a very sharp rise, and the annual subscription would be twenty-five shillings. The possibility of the Duke building the Clubhouse and then leasing it back to the Club was discussed but did not get far. At a Special General Meeting in April 1895 a proposal to double the sum for life membership from ten guineas to twenty went down but a compromise was achieved on fifteen guineas. It was important to have done this for by offering life memberships absurdly cheaply some Clubs had made very bad bargains indeed.

The question of tenure was to be solved in the creation of The Portland Club. From the very start the question of non-members playing over the original links had been a bone of contention. They, the non-members, would cite some non-existent historical precedent which allowed them to play, the Committee would issue a rebuttal along the lines that *"the golfing course was strictly for the members of the Club"*.

There was the additional complication that the Duke of Portland was anxious to provide golfing facilities for the non-members and it would be impolitic, to put it mildly, to antagonise needlessly a landlord who was almost always well disposed.

The solution adopted was the formation in 1894 of a new course (The Relief Course, as it was first known) and a separate Club to play on it. The Portland Club would be a self-standing club in all respects, except that admission to membership would come under the scrutiny of the Troon Club.

I. M. Mackintosh in the previous Club History has rightly pointed out that few of the membership of the new course (it would not become the Portland course formally until 1924) would have easily fitted into the class of artisan since most were small businessmen.

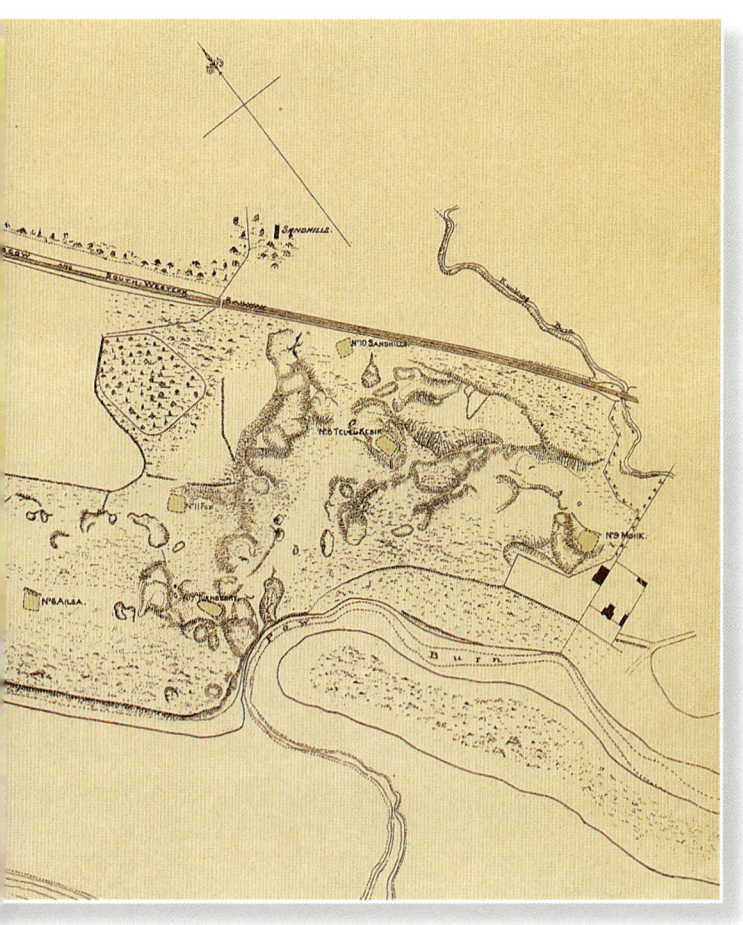

Map of Course 1888

It is fair to say that the Troon Club could restrict membership of the Portland (150 was the maximum) and that their agreement to take over the supervision of the Relief Course was greatly to the benefit of all. The Duke was pleased with the outcome and agreed not only to subscribe £20 per annum but also to let the Club have a 20-year lease of both links for a paltry £5 per year.

There was mixed news on the staff front. The professional, Strath, had come back to the payroll and was in receipt of 25 shillings per week for looking after both greens and Clubhouse. That militant race, the caddies, had hoisted the standard of revolt against an attempt to reduce their fees. They simply refused to work. A disgruntled member noted: *"the radical cure for such a state of affairs is for members to carry their own clubs and thus rob these extortionate representatives of the caddy species of their legitimate income"*. A touch of muddled thinking here, it seems, if the income was legitimate, could it be extortionate? Anyway, life soon resumed its normal tenor and the caddies appear to have won this one.

On matters financial the Committee had been empowered to borrow between £500 and £1000 for the building of the Clubhouse. In the event most of the money was raised by interest-bearing debentures, the rate fixed at 4½% and, as was usual if the debentures were being sold, then the first offer should be to the Club. The issue was a great success with over £1000 being taken up.

As with every other construction since the Tower of Babel, costs soon exceeded estimates and the Committee agreed to go to £1594 or even £1856. The great work was done at last and the new Clubhouse prepared for occupancy. In the midst of rejoicings there was a farewell to an old friend for the original first hole had disappeared in the preparation of the new building.

A new Clubhouse called for a special tournament and it was decided that it should be a professional one. The prize money of £26 was considerable for the time and the winner would receive £10, the runner up £5, third place would bring £3 while there were various lesser prizes. There was a very strong entry

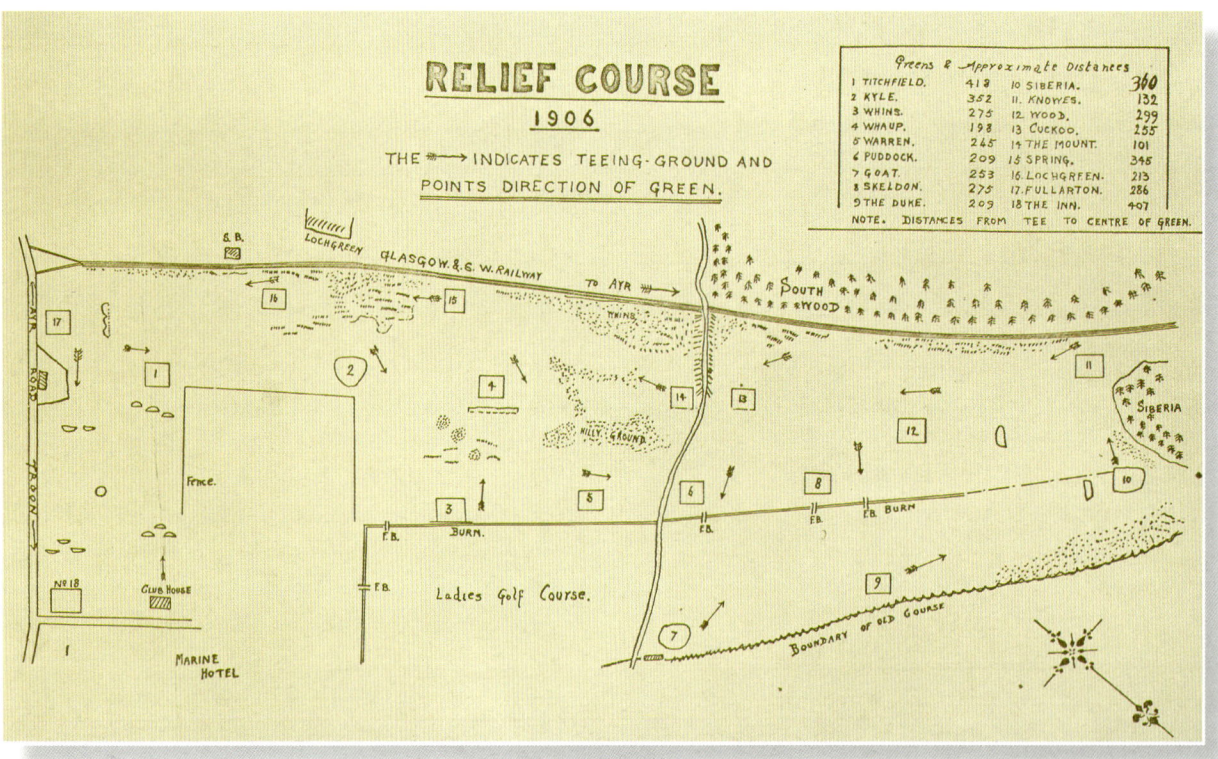

The Relief Course 1906

THE EARLY YEARS

and the winner, Willie Park Jr. had two Open Championships to his credit. Just as remarkable was his aggregate of 148 with 74's morning and afternoon, truly remarkable scoring in those pre-Haskell days of the "gutty".

The best individual round was returned by Bob Ferguson of Musselburgh whose 73 was a marvellous score for the time. The professional tournament had been a great success, so too was the dinner which followed it. The toast list was awe-inspiring and only after the Loyal Toast, The Duke, Other Clubs, The Prizewinners, The Guests, The Committee, The Ladies, Troon Golf Club and The Chairman did the company run out of ideas.

If such exhibition matches added glamour, the day to day business of running the Club had to go on. The posts of Club Master and Club Mistress were advertised in the national newspapers. The basic wage was £52 p.a. plus all profits on food and one third of those on liquor. It was estimated that the profit on liquor would be worth £18 per year. In addition, as was customary, there would be a free house and free gas, water and coal. The appointees were Mr and Mrs Fleming with experience of London and Edinburgh.

It was an era of predominantly low prices which

Professional tournament, Troon, August 27th 1886

reflected the comparative prosperity of the last years of Victoria's reign. A glass of whisky cost fivepence and sevenpence would purchase half a pint of claret. There was one area where prices were felt to be too high and that was the carriage fee charged by William Robertson for conveying golfers from the railway station to the Clubhouse. The single fare was sixpence and the Committee asked that this be halved. Robertson came back with an offer of ninepence return, sixpence one way and the Committee held out for the fourpenny single. Within a few weeks the matter was resolved in Robertson's favour.

The Duke was still taking a benevolent interest in things and in September 1886 he agreed, possibly on the prompting of the Turners, to donate £5 towards the prize fund. The Ladies were thriving and they asked for ground beyond the Gyaws Burn on which two more holes could be laid out, a request that met with approval.

There was the occasional rebuff. It was regarded as "disappointing" that the Glasgow and South Western Railway Company could not see their way clear to construct a railway halt near the Clubhouse. It was pointed out quite acidly that two neighbouring clubs, Glasgow Gailes and

The clubhouse circa 1900

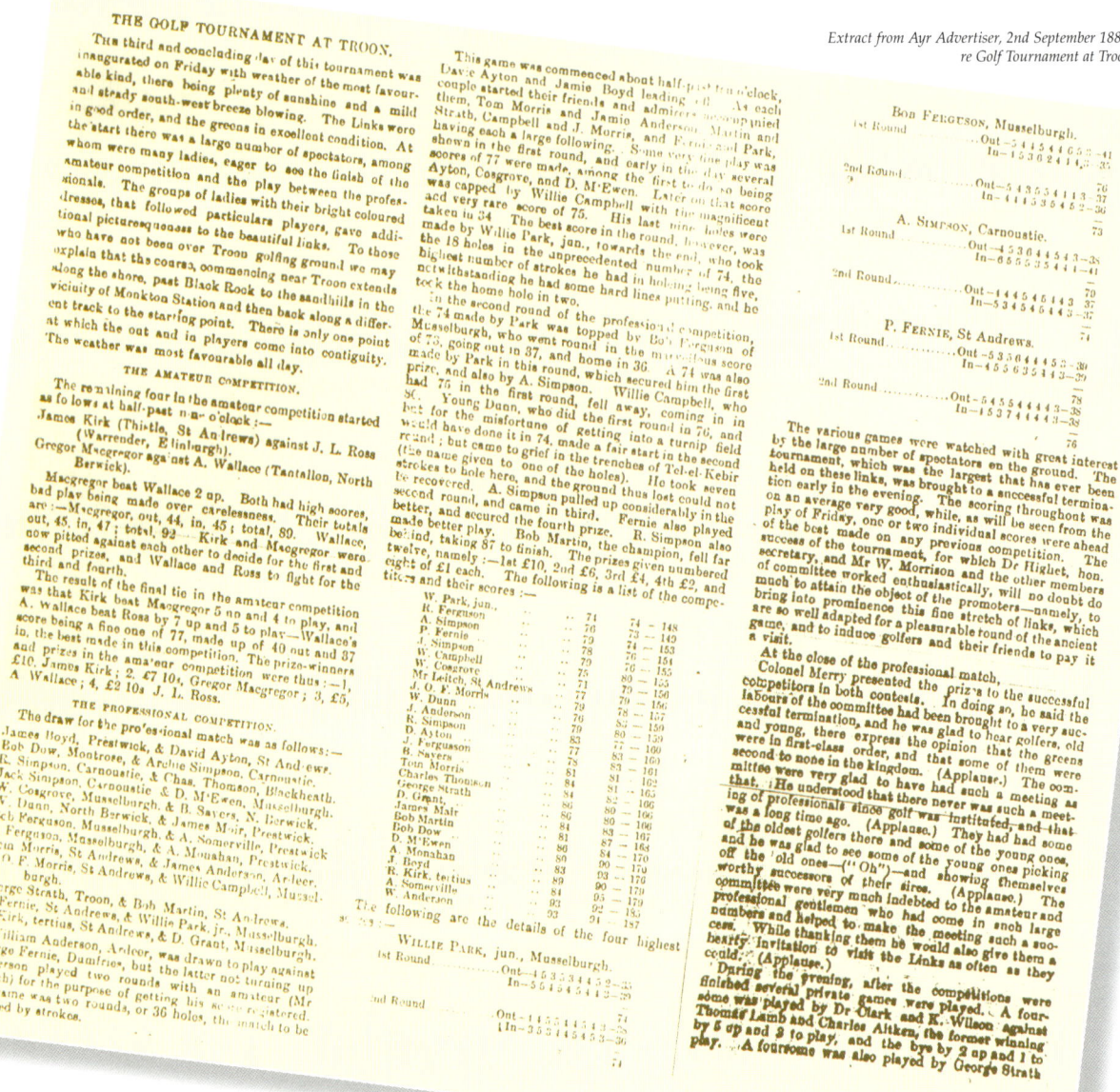

Extract from Ayr Advertiser, 2nd September 1886, re Golf Tournament at Troon

Barassie had been furnished with just such a facility in the near past.

There was too a strong Glasgow component in the membership. Indeed in 1887 so many men were members of both clubs – Troon and Glasgow – that the Engagement Card was drawn up as a joint venture. With the coming of summer the course was heavily played over and in the short term ladies were not allowed to lunch or dine in the Clubhouse.

On the election of William Morison as Captain in May 1887, the membership stood healthily at 246. A suggestion that to slow the rate of increase, the entry fee should be increased did not find favour with the membership. As the Club grew in size administrative duties inevitably became more onerous and the time had come to separate the offices of Secretary and Treasurer. Dr Highet continued in the former post with John Andrew as the new Treasurer. The new man was on the ball as he demonstrated when a member, John Wallace, complained that one of his friends, a non-member, had been overcharged for lunch. Mr Wallace was laconically informed (a) that his friend had had a second helping and therefore had not been overcharged and (b) as a non-member there should have been no question of his having paid for anything, anyway.

Around this time the Club conferred the great honour of Honorary Membership on the Duke's agent Frederick J. Turner. It would bestow this honour on others in the coming years but it is fair to say that no one would ever deserve the recognition more. He consistently took the part of the Club in local arguments and he constantly exerted a wise and moderating influence.

The caddies were not extinguished, they were merely smouldering. In July 1887 there was what the Minutes describe as a caddie strike. It petered out, as such things do, but the ringleaders, caddies McGhee, Affleck and Hastings were suspended for a fortnight. It was decided that at busy times, Strath would be given assistance by Robert Guthrie but such assistance would be paid for by Strath himself. Although there was a rethink and the Club itself met the payment it was clear that Strath's days in the land were finite. He was dismissed with effect from April 2nd 1888. Some of the members mounted a defence in a "Save Our Strath" campaign but at a Special General Meeting it was decided by an emphatic 84 votes to 24 that he had to go.

Willie Fernie

The identity of Strath's successor, Willie Fernie, caused a great stir when it was revealed. It became evident that two things had happened. First, the Club had aimed high and hit its mark. Second, Troon had grown fast in reputation indeed when a professional such as Willie Fernie would consider joining it.

Professionals had to be versatile in those days and Fernie was employed as greenkeeper, clubmaker, ballmaker and player. Open Champion in 1883 after a tie with Bob Ferguson (he prevented Ferguson taking the title four times in a row) he came second in the competition on four other occasions. Although he would spend almost forty years at Troon, retiring just after the first Open Championship had been held there in 1923, he was by origin a Fifer, coming from a well-known golfing family in St. Andrews.

Morison Medal, Autumn Meeting – Scratch

There is no doubt that he was a catch for the young club. He was in great demand as a layer-out of courses and honoured for giving an honest and sometimes caustic appraisal of the land he was being asked to survey. The average "Scotch" professor, as they were called, was apt to bear in mind his fee and declare that surely the Creator had this tract of land (unpromising though it looked) destined for no other purpose than the playing of golf. Fernie supervised the laying-out of a course in Phoenix Park, Dublin and one on the Duke of Portland's estates in the Midlands of England. He also had at least one Continental course to his name, that of Spa in Belgium and was responsible for Turnberry. Fernie was engaged by the Marquis of Ailsa to design the first course there. He laid out the course and supervised its construction, the course being opened for play in August 1901. Over the next five years Fernie also supervised the maintenance of the new Turnberry course.

As a player he was resilient, had he not been he would not have recovered from a 10 to tie for the Open and win the play-off. In four-cornered matches he played the best of his day, Taylor, Braid, Vardon and Duncan and was not remotely out of place in such company. In an age of craftsmen his club making was legendary, especially his long-nosed woods and his bulgers (a variation on the niblick). He knew his worth and his reluctance to devalue his own clubs led to a few members berating his "Buchanan Street prices". The majority of members knew a good thing when they saw it and gladly paid the going rate. In the teaching sphere he could command three shillings per non-teaching round, a lesson being a shilling more. It was the great age of challenge matches and on August 28 1890 a very famous one took place at Troon.

It was a foursome match played between Willie and George Fernie of Troon against the brothers Kirkaldy, Jack and Andrew. Two days before Andrew had played Willie Park junior over the same course. On that occasion he had the better of things but in the meeting of the brothers the St. Andrews men were put to the sword. At the end of the first round they had given up the match and would not, as it were, answer the bell for the second round.

Willie Fernie playing 1st hole

The Fernie brothers had a very fine 76 made up of 38 out, 38 in. Willie Fernie was a man who liked his golf and, deprived of his arranged second round against the Kirkaldys he fixed up a game in the evening with a Mr A. Adams of London and went round again in 76.

The Fernies' first round of 76 had been a very fine one but should not have produced quite such a crushing lead. There were rumours of fraternal differences on the defeated side. Andra Kirkaldy, later for many years the Starter at the Old Course at St. Andrews, could be pernickety about many things, not least the spelling of his name. Woe to the golf writer who furnished Andra's surname with the superfluous letter "c". This invariably drew a plaintive and indignant; "Kirkcaldy? Whit dae they think I am? A bluidy toon?"

Willie Fernie had started at Dumfries and Galloway and, apart from a short and not particularly happy spell at Felixstowe, he was Scottish-based for the remainder of his career. He wrote an excellent little booklet on how to play Troon for the Open Championship of 1923, an event in which his own sons, one of whom at least was an excellent golfer, would play a key role though not exclusively on the links.

Sometimes in Golf Clubs trouble with the catering staff is all too easily predictable. In March 1888, the Clubmaster's son-in-law decided to open a large new hotel on South Beach. The Club declared itself enthusiastic although it did not say why and the Clubmaster was given permission to help in the hotel provided there was no conflict of interest. It was stressed that the new hotel was non-licensed but before long, Mr Fleming had taken over the running of the hotel himself and applied for a licence. The Troon Club declared itself "disappointed" which it was entitled to be and "surprised" which perhaps it should not have been.

There was a move just about then that the Club should have a uniform such as that still worn in Epping Forest with the special coats that were in favour with the old Edinburgh links. A crested button was designed and samples made of scarlet tail coats with dark blue facings but perhaps robust Scottish egalitarianism reasserted itself for the projected garments never saw the light of day in any numbers.

Vardon, Braid, Fernie and Taylor, four Open Champions at Troon, August 1901

It seemed that no sooner had the new Clubhouse been built than it required extension. The Debenture scheme, which had been so successful before, was repeated and to make assurance doubly sure entry money was increased to six guineas at the same time as the number of Treasurers was increased to two.

It was not forgotten that the most important events were those which took place out on the course. There was a heated debate as to what should constitute first class. Many members felt that scratch to four, inclusive, was much too rigid a definition. Rigid, or careful? Probably that was what W. J. N. Cowan asked himself when he was disqualified from the St. Andrews Cross for having played round without a caddy.

If Willie Fernie was not weaned with a cleek in his hand he came fairly close for he describes himself as having been *"hard at the golf at the age of five"* and when he was fifteen he won his first professional prize from a highly respectable field at St. Andrews. Between his sixteenth and twenty-third birthdays he won the St. Andrews Mechanics' Club medal six times and this is a remarkable record in a town where almost every working man was a golfer. When he won the Open Championship from Bob Ferguson in 1883 he did so with a two at the last hole against the senior man's four and he won despite having the wrong sort of albatross hung around his neck when he ran up a ten at one hole.

At a time when nobody broke 70 he had a 68 over Troon. He was tall by the standards of the day and, at just over 13 stones, he was heavy although muscular. Like many of his era he was a highly skilled club-maker and always willing to test new developments which might improve the game. *Golf Magazine* thought this to be greatly to his credit and expressed its approval in the high-flown language common to such publications at the time: *"He thinks that in the multitude of inventions wisdom shall surely be found and that in many patents shall be discovered the price of understanding; hence he tries them all, one after another, as fast as they come out, from which it will be seen that he is progressive in his policy and exhibits a laudable catholicity and breadth of view".*

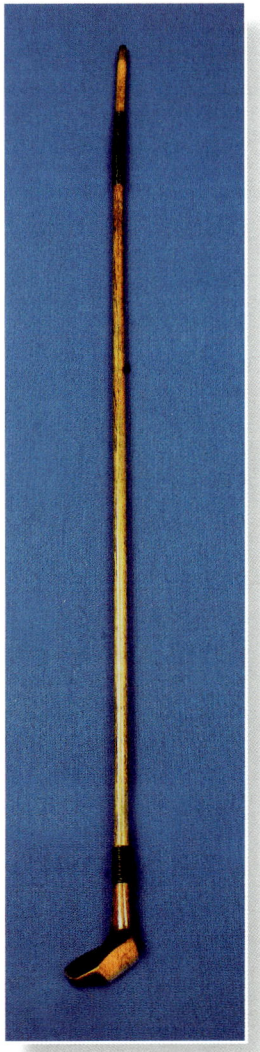

Sabbath Wood by Willie Fernie

The Club Thrives

Not all of the Club's money raising was self-centred for they promised to give financial help to the Ladies who were also building a Clubhouse. The entry fee was rocketing upwards at a surprising rate; by 1890 it stood at ten guineas. There may have been the odd member who questioned the need for a page boy who would cost £30 a year plus two sets of uniform. One of his duties now was to pass on telephone messages since the Clubhouse was now connected with the great world beyond. This put paid to the custom of telegraphing the weather conditions at Troon to Glasgow on a Saturday morning. By coincidence two of the great names of the Scottish textiles industry joined the club at almost the same time and the Clarks of Paisley and the Coats of Paisley were now represented.

The Club ran happily enough but there was a feeling that perhaps it was just a touch over-cosy and certainly the Committee seems to have been taken aback by the strength of feeling shown at the Annual General Meeting of 1891 when it became clear that the system of the Committee's virtually perpetuating itself from year to year should cease and that henceforth nominations for Committee should be voted upon from the floor.

By the beginning of 1893 the Club had a new secretary, William Mackie, who would replace one of the early giants, Dr J. Highet. At the same time, the Clubmaster, W. Fleming, surprisingly restored to favour, left for good this time to become the manager of the Eglinton Arms in Ardrossan. The emoluments offered to his successor showed how the Club had grown in size and the increased usage of it made by members. The new appointee would receive £230 for himself and wife, plus profits on food and the usual free perquisites of office. To assist him he would have two page boys which even across the years seems rather lavish and two female servants.

William Mackie predictably ended up doing both jobs, Treasurer and Secretary. By October 1894 the Club had acquired new ground for a Relief Course which would eventually become the Portland Course. Less important but more noticeable was the new flag pole which the Club now had, fifty feet high and made by the Ailsa Shipbuilding Company. The Troon Club turned down a Cabinet Minister, not for the last time, when it was suggested by a member that A. J. Balfour was coming to the district and, a keen golfer, might be asked to play over the links. There was no enthusiasm for the notion.

By now the Relief Course had come into being and a highly satisfactory settlement arrived at from the Club's viewpoint. There would be a combined rental for the two courses of £85, of which £50 would be for the New or Relief Course. The Club felt able to contribute ten guineas to the testimonial to Old Tom Morris. Their own professional, Willie Fernie, had just given up his greenkeeping responsibilities. This was at his own request and from now on he would be exclusively a professional and clubmaker.

At the Annual General Meeting of 1896 there was more animated debate than was customary. There was considerable opposition to the fact that a previous Clubmaster, William Fleming, had been elected to membership. There was a proposal that from this time Captains should not hold office for more than a year but the general feeling was that the disadvantages of a lack of continuity more than outweighed the risks of a Bonaparte. There was an unsuccessful proposal to limit membership to 200 but perhaps the raising of the entry fee to ten guineas and the new Life Members rate of 20 guineas were meant to deter indirectly.

In May 1897 a link with the Club's very first days was severed by the resignation of Dr John Highet who had been Secretary for the first fifteen years of Troon's existence and who had also discharged the duties of Treasurer. He was a colourful figure who affected a solar topee and after his resignation he saw service in South Africa during the Boer War. Like another great sporting doctor, W. G. Grace, his attention to the game he loved was so total that one wondered how he found time to visit his patients. He had offered a large portrait of himself to the Club which initially declined it on account of its size but on the Doctor's death in 1906 it was presented by his widow and today impressively dominates the Dining Room.

William Mackie, Secretary 1893-1909

Dr. Highet's caddy in the painting is a local lad Joe McMorran, who later achieved fame by emigrating to the United States where he became a professional golfer and golf course designer.

Willie Fernie was still reckoned to be a formidable golfer. He had entered for the Open at Hoylake and the Club agreed to help him with his expenses. This was only done when the event fell due to be played in England. There had been a testimonial raised for him and this produced an awkward moment when the cash in the box was some five pounds short of what it should have been according to the Subscription List. The Club agreed to make good the deficiency. They did more. They arranged a match between Fernie and Sandy Herd of Huddersfield, the winner to get £20 and any surplus to be held in trust for future matches.

In 1899 an event was set in motion which was to become very much part of the Club's social tradition. This was the Caddies' Treat and on this occasion two members entertained 70 caddies, appropriately enough in the Portland Arms Hotel. In later years there would be buses to go to Ayr for a meal and a visit to the Gaiety Theatre and not even World War Two could put a stop to this celebration.

In 1899 the Club acquired another 36 acres of land on a 14-year lease. The rent would be £100 per annum and the Golf Club agreed to keep up the houses and fences within the new area after they had been made tenantable by the Duke.

The Troon Links had become a much sought-after place on which to play and there were many applications from various societies and clubs. The construction of the Relief Course meant that it was possible to entertain more of such requests. In the space of a month there were applications from Fettesians-Lorettonians, the Shipping Trade and Albany Academicals.

There was a world outside. The club secured a photograph of the great young amateur golfer, Freddie Tait, who had been killed in action in the Boer War. As a young subaltern he had incurred the wrath – and admiration – of his C.O. by driving a ball from the highest point of Edinburgh Castle, the Rookery, in a match against another officer to hole out in the fountain in Princes Street Gardens some 350 feet below. Now he was dead, aged 30, when the whole golfing world lay before him.

It was a more innocent age, an age in which the Committee could complain to the Portland

Troon clubhouse circa 1900. James Dickie, Dr. John Highet, Mr Murray, Mr Fullarton and caddies

Club about "promiscuous play" by the Ladies and make a later observation that one of the greenkeeping staff, Claude Haldane, "seems quite taken over by the Ladies' Club".

The Club was approaching its Silver Jubilee and the pioneers were going. In April 1902 the original Captain, James Dickie, died. He would have been well pleased in his work of foundation. The Club was now in negotiations which would see it secure a 50 year lease over its ground to commence at Martinmas 1904. Before that would happen, a major championship would be held at Troon which would enable the Club to burst upon an astonished world.

Dr. John Highet MB

Ladies' Championship of 1904

IT was thanks to the Ladies' Golf Union that the spotlight of public scrutiny was first turned upon Troon Golf Club. Their decision to hold the Ladies' Championship there in 1904 was a bold one, given that the course in its recognisable modern form had been in place for scarcely a decade. The L. G. U. were rewarded for their courage by a remarkable final.

Golf at this stage was almost exclusively a middle-class sport, as far as women were concerned and it is easy to forget just how much time women of that

Ladies Championship, 1904

stratum of society had for the playing of sport between leaving school and marriage since very few went to University and to work was in many cases held to be unthinkable, often by the girl's family rather than by the girl herself. As we shall see, the eventual winner was an arch exemplar of this.

There was a good entry, 95 in all, of whom almost exactly one third were described by the newspapers and golf magazines of the day as "Scotch". There was even one intrepid American, Miss Higgins. Miss Higgins was to go down in golfing history as the originator of a device which enabled women to play golf in the voluminous clothes they wore at the start of the twentieth century. The well-known golfer of the time, Mabel E. Stringer, describes it thus:

"Miss Higgins" (named after the American golfer) was indispensable on account of the width of the skirts. 'Miss Higgins' was an elastic band which was slipped round the knees as the player was addressing her ball and it was the most useful as well as the most unsightly of the many inventions to counteract the vagaries and the inconsistencies of la mode. The golfing girl of today should indeed be grateful that she need not play golf in a sailor hat, a high stiff collar, a voluminous skirt and petticoats and a motoring veil."

The championship proved the start of a strangely enduring connection between Troon and Royal Portrush in Northern Ireland.

The eventual champion, Lottie Dod, was almost a parody of the successful Victorian sportswoman. She had won the Ladies Singles at Wimbledon before she was sixteen and would go on to take the title five times in all. She then abandoned lawn tennis because no one could give her a game – she was in her fifth championship before she even lost a set – and turned her attention to golf. She was already a fine skater and the best female archer in England.

She had the tenacity which marks the great sportsman or woman and in an early round at Troon

THE EARLY YEARS

she fought back from four down at the turn to take six successive holes and eventually win on the home green. As she worked her way through one half of the draw, May Hezlet was quietly moving through the other.

The early twentieth century was an age of golfing dynasties and none of these was more remarkable than the Hezlet family. In this very championship there were five Hezlet ladies – Mama and the Misses May, Emmie, Florence and Violet. Three daughters would figure in Ladies' Finals, finalist and semi-finalists, indeed three years after this Miss May and Miss F. would provide an all-Hezlet final. Even in 1904 three Hezlet girls made it to the third round and in the fourth Miss M. knocked out Miss V.

There was a strong public for ladies' sports at that time, indeed Association Football for ladies was disappearing not because it did not attract large crowds but precisely because it did. The *Glasgow Herald* admired the size of the golfing crowd but hinted at problems: *"A numerous company – around 4000 we would guess – witnessed the final and so unruly did they become that threats were made that play would have to be stopped. Afterwards a little better order was kept"*.

The paper was perfectly prepared to admit that the problems were caused by excessive enthusiasm rather than for any more sinister reason but it was a warning that the staging of major events did not come trouble-free. As to the final itself, it was expected that May Hezlet, who had already won the title twice, would prevail against Lottie Dod. Lottie was admitted to be a phenomenon but she had gained her fearsome reputation in other sports, notably tennis as we have seen. She proved however to be the Babe Zaharias of her day. In the final she was two up at the eleventh but then allowed the lead to dribble away and on the seventeenth she stood one down. In a delightful phrase the *Glasgow Herald* then said:

"Miss Dod took the two final holes to win 1 up although the weather was on the North side of friendly".

If the name of Hezlet seems vaguely familiar to members of Royal Troon it should be. Some ten years later a noted Troon golfer, James Jenkins would bring tremendous honour to the Club by winning the Amateur Championship and in the final he would meet up with Charles Hezlet, brother of the formidable girls. The connection between the families went even further since in the Ladies' Championship of 1904 Dora Jenkins, sister of James, did well, and she would later be Irish champion.

Despite the occasional carping observation from the *Glasgow Herald*, the course had passed its first big test successfully. Many of the spectators had come down by rail from Glasgow – it would have cost them five shillings

Charlotte (Lottie) Dod, Dorothy Campbell, May Hezlett and Miss M. A. Graham, finalists and semi-finalists 1904 Ladies Championship, won by Lottie Dod

return, first class. Of course, in August Troon was full of holidaymakers anyway. The rubber-cored balls which were to bring about the beginning of modern golf had come into use a couple of years beforehand and there were local varieties on sale such as the Allaway and the Scotch Haskell, each of which could be purchased for one shilling.

If the ladies permitted themselves a quiet smile of satisfaction, it may have enabled them more easily to control their temper after reading 'Hints To Young Golfers' by Dr. J. G. McPherson. He spoke from on high as follows:

"Ladies are indispensable in a Young Club. So much is expected of them in the raising of that necessary element – money ... On the principal meeting day of the week afternoon tea should be served in the Clubhouse (however primitive) by the Ladies' Committee...A small amount should be charged for the tea from the participants and the surplus, after clearing expenses, should be given to the cleaning of the Clubhouse and the general funds of the Club.

Of course if the first subscription efforts have not been able to secure a humble Clubhouse as well as the Green Keeper's wages, a bazaar must be got up for providing one and for bettering the course.

If the ladies work well – and who is to say they will not – the most skilful gentlemen golfers should play mixed foursomes with them. You have no idea how much the ladies improve in their game in this way. And they soon enjoy it when they can see the ball rise after weeks of topping and can hole out decently on the putting green."

Lottie Dod may well have read this as she sat in the train on her way to her next hockey international. She played that game as well.

1904-1914

THE Ladies' Championship had been by any standards a great success. It lingered in the collective Troon memory despite the passage of twenty years and the intervention of a World War. When eventually the event returned in 1925, the burgh marked it by the closing of the schools and the shipyard so that there might be a maximum gallery to appreciate the play. Much would happen before that.

There was a feeling that there were too many external competitions held under the auspices of visiting clubs. The Committee promised to hold them to one a week but the general feeling was they should be done away with altogether. There was not felt to be any great need of external financial input, the Club was thriving with 700 members and 90 potential members on the waiting list. William Mackie retired as Secretary at this time. He had been diligent and thorough but he possessed one of the most indecipherable hands in the Western world and no historian of the Club could but welcome his demitting office.

His successor was to be very influential in the affairs of the Club. H. Ross Coubrough came to Troon from Buxton and perhaps more than anyone else interested himself in the history and background of the Club. The fact that we know as much as we do about the early days of Troon is largely due to him.

The Club brushed shoulders with the world of politics on two separate occasions. As the skies of the Edwardian late afternoon darkened, so did the military presence increase. The coast at Barassie and Gailes was great Territorial Army country and much drilling and exercising went on. There was a move to grant Territorial Army officers the courtesy of the course but it was decided not to extend the privilege beyond regular officers for the time being.

There had been another, potentially more embarrassing situation at much the same time. It would appear that on a day in May 1910, the Prime Minister, Mr H. H. Asquith, appeared at the Clubhouse accompanied by two ladies. One has by indirection to find direction out. It seems that he may well not have been recognised (much more likely then than now) and may have been offered the prospect of play over the Relief Course. What is certain is that a directive was issued to the Secretary subsequently that he should receive distinguished visitors personally and, if accompanied by ladies, the latter should be allowed to play over the Old Course.

At the A.G.M. of 1910 an attempt to create a two-tier system of subscriptions came before the meeting, as it did every now and then. The effect of it was that those who had joined post-1902 should pay a higher subscription than those who had been in membership at that time. As usual, debate generated more heat than light, the motion failed and those who had backed it could console themselves with the notion that it would crop up again at no great distance in time.

H.R. Coubrough, Secretary 1909-1929

Occasionally decisions were arrived at that could best be described as baffling. It was decided that those members living in Glasgow should, on medal days in the winter months be given alternate ballot numbers between 1.30pm and 2pm.

Most equitable, is the first thought, until one remembers that in those months it is dark along the

Ayrshire Coast by 4pm. Even George Duncan could not have completed a medal round in the time available.

Suddenly the Club was running at a loss. At a Special General Meeting of March 1911 it was revealed that there was a deficit of £362 from the previous year. Ten shillings per member would realise £350 but it was clear that sterner measures were needed and the Committee went away to consider them.

The detailed but essential work of administration went on, growing with the Club. A new caddiemaster, Manson, was engaged on the understanding that he would be strictly teetotal while on duty. The Club sent two guineas to the Silloth Golf Club in Cumberland, which was engaged in a most important joust with the Inland Revenue. That body wished golf clubs to pay tax on green fees received from visitors and had chosen Silloth as the battleground. The case was protracted and bitterly fought but the golfers triumphed at length and two guineas had been well expended. It would raise its head again in 1996.

On the Portland Course a new Clubhouse was going up. Troon Golf Club underwrote the building and gave the Portland Club a cheque for £100 to get the new venture going. And so the last days of peace slipped away. Some of the more bellicose locals seemed to have anticipated the outbreak of hostilities. A Mr Tod, whose wife had been reprimanded for taking dogs on the course, called to see the Secretary. He informed the unfortunate Mr Coubrough that "he did not care a damn for the links or the Committee" and would use the links as he thought fit.

The Club appeared to have much to look forward to in 1914. They had a golfer, James Jenkins who was as good as anyone not only in Scotland but in Great Britain. And for the first time the Old Course would be used as a Qualifying Course for the Open Championship, due to be played at Prestwick. The local School Board was leant upon to give the schoolboys a holiday to enable them to caddy. Only the Marine Hotel spoiled the party mood by declining to tender for the catering.

It was a fine summer and with the Club's attentions firmly fixed on Sandwich, where the Amateur would be held and on its own course (which would soon be put to the test), it was easy enough to overlook the fact that the numbers of Terriers on the nearby beaches seemed to be increasing with every day.

The clubhouse in the early 20th century

J. L. C. Jenkins and the Amateur Championship of 1914

OF all those members who over the years have played the great bulk of their golf over Royal Troon the name of James Lawrence Christie Jenkins must stand pre-eminent. By British standards, let alone Scottish, he was an outstanding player and to his artistry was added a fiery and indomitable toughness in match-play. He was the player you very much wanted on your side in a competitive match but he would not necessarily be first choice for a social round.

His triumph at Sandwich in 1914 was an epic feat of golfing mastery and physical endurance. There had been a huge entry of 232 golfers and the organisers had been rather caught on the hop as, after all, Sandwich was not the most accessible of venues. The result was that a championship which was scheduled to end on the Friday carried over to the Saturday with all the administrative inconvenience which that entailed.

Seven golfers lay directly in his path and it may be instructive to give their names. In order of dismissal they were Horace Castle, O. L. Smith, O. Martin Smith, Captain E. H. Hambro, the Hon. Michael Scott, Norman Hunter and E. Martin Smith.

There is a dash of mystery here. The reader will have noticed an abundance of Smiths but a look at the golfing magazines of the time will show that the first of those, O. L. Smith, is coyly referred to as "the ghostly Mr Smith" and indeed one of the magazines carried scepticism to extremes by putting O. L. Smith in inverted commas. This ethereal golfer was widely held to be a well-known Irish golfer Lionel Munn and the change of name was unusual but until the First World War not unique. Before the days of widespread filming, televising and even comprehensive press photography, there were not infrequently young men playing international association football or rugby ... and, yes, golf ... who thought it better if their employers were in blissful ignorance of their being so engaged.

All sources agree that the word which epitomised Jenkins was "combative". He feared no one and golfing reputations meant nothing to him. Having removed the seven golfers mentioned above he found himself in the final up against Major Charles Hezlet of Portrush, whose sisters had figured so prominently in the Ladies Championship at Troon back in 1904.

It was just about this time that the fashion reached its peak for golfers to be given convenient tags or nicknames. Thus a phenomenally long University player in the championship, R. P. Humphries, was known as "the great Cambridge swiper" and Hezlet, at 23 much the younger of the finalists, was painted as "the smiling young Irishman'". Significantly, Jenkins was described by William Reid of Golf Monthly as "a nailing good golfer" and throughout the championship, the *Glasgow Herald* saw him as "the plucky little Troon crack".

The championship in that last pre-war summer was played in baking heat, tempered only by a couple of sporadic thunder showers. The players sweltered in the conditions and the two rounds per day was a most gruelling imposition. There were many who thought that youth would prevail given the conditions of the week.

Jenkins was ready for his big chance. Of the five male members of his family he himself had been plus five, two other brothers were plus two, one was scratch and the last unfortunate played off two, something which most mortals would be delighted with but which in the Jenkins household must have been a wounding badge of inferiority. And if one adds to that the fact that a sister, Dora, would win the Irish championship then Hezlet would need all his dynastic qualifications to survive.

On the eve of the final there was a brisk dash of thundery rain and again during the opening holes but it was dry by the fourth. Jenkins strove to establish an early mastery, his iron play was of its usual high standard, the crisp noise that his iron clubs made at impact was described as resembling the snapping shut of a penknife blade.

There was never much in the first round of the final, followed by "a small but enthusiastic crowd". If the sparse attendance strikes one as strange in the heyday of amateur golf it has to be remembered that no play had been originally scheduled for the Saturday and that already the winner with his trophy should have been on his way home.

Jenkins was one up at the turn and by the end of the first round had improved that to three. He was much shakier on the outward half the second time round and indeed had a most indifferent 40 to the 35 of Hezlet. However as included among the 40 was a wretched 6, the difference of 5 strokes was only worth 2 holes to Hezlet who was therefore still one down.

The decisive hole proved to be the eleventh in the afternoon. Both men were on the green, Jenkins at fifteen feet, Hezlet at four feet and Jenkins then two up. Jenkins holed his putt, Hezlet missed his and suddenly a probable one down had become three down. Jenkins was not the kind of man to let such a development go. The end came at the sixteenth where he laid a dead stymie and Hezlet lived up to his sobriquet of "smiling young Irishman" by deliberately knocking his own ball well wide of the hole in symbol of surrender.

Now it was back to Scotland and the pulling along of the car in which Jenkins was seated by teams of willing Troon townsfolk and his fellow members.

Before that, fog signals had been placed under the wheels of his railway carriage and let off in token of celebration.

There seemed to be no fields in which he might not conquer. In the Open, held at Prestwick in that last long pre-war summer he did very well. He finished as the top Scottish player of either description professional or amateur and indeed for a fleeting moment had been third. After the war he remained a very fine player indeed but the indefinable something that distinguishes the great from the very good was now less in evidence. In the international field he remained a daunting adversary and he had proved during his time on service that his courage was not confined to the links. *The Glasgow High School Magazine* of March 1918 reports as follows:

J. L. C. Jenkins

"Second Lieutenant (Acting Captain) James Lawrence Christie Jenkins, Cameron Highlanders, was awarded the Military Cross on September 26th 1917 for conspicuous gallantry and devotion to duty when commanding two companies in a raid on enemy trenches. Although there had been no chance of examining the ground beforehand he showed a fearless disregard of danger and by his splendid leadership he ensured the success of the raid. He was the last to leave the enemy lines and personally assisted in carrying back our wounded thus preventing any of them falling into the hands of the enemy. Second Lieutenant Jenkins is the son of James G. Jenkins of Cambuslang. He won the Amateur Golf Championship in 1914 and his old school is proud that he has proved himself as good a soldier as he is a golfer."

He would perhaps have himself admitted that he was not the easiest of men. That noted journalist and fine golfer Sam McKinlay recounted on Jenkins' death an encounter he had had with him. In the 1938 Amateur Championship at Troon, McKinlay was drawn against Hector Thomson with Jenkins as referee. Either of these players was a very plausible winner at that stage and a large crowd collected for the late afternoon tie. He informed the players that he hoped matters would be conducted briskly as he had a dinner engagement for seven o'clock.

With the usual perversity of things his soup must have got cold for the match went to the twentieth before Thomson snatched victory and it was nearer nine than eight o'clock when they finished. Incidentally it was the first of three consecutive times that Thomson had, as it were, to go into extra time and in the clutch against Charlie Yates in the semi-final that might just have tipped the scales.

James Jenkins was still representing his country at golf in the mid-1940's and he was the club's first post-World War Two Captain. There is little doubt that the almost immediate breaking out of World War One diverted attention from almost all sports and that history has underestimated the very real qualities of this "nailing good golfer".

One would therefore have to say that it was a foolhardy and ill-advised burglar who one night broke into the Jenkins' house and the felon might well have admitted this himself after he had been pursued down the street by the "plucky little Troon ace" and been soundly hammered into the bargain.

James Jenkins would return from the wars with almost half a century of service still to give the Club. He would be a distinguished Captain after World War Two but before that he was instrumental in bringing the 1923 Open championship to his home course. He was a member of the Championship Committee of the Royal & Ancient almost from its inception and he was present at a very early meeting on May 19th 1922

Amateur Championship Medal J. L. C. Jenkins, 1914

when the Honourable Company of Edinburgh Golfers wrote to say that Muirfield would be unavailable.

Strangely, although there was extensive course reconstruction going on at Muirfield, the reasons the club itself gave for being relieved of its obligations were *"that there is no suitable accommodation near the course and it would be too expensive for participants to travel"*. James Jenkins – presumably already sure of his answer – undertook to speak to the Committee at Troon and enquire whether they would be prepared to stage the 1923 Open.

There were a few signs that the Championship Committee realised that they were giving Troon rather short notice for this same meeting resolved that clubs should henceforth be given two years warning and the Open Championship should always be staged on seaside courses. A hint of the informality which still pervaded things was the note that *"the exact dates of the Championship should be left to the Championship Clubs but that they should correspond as closely as possible to that of 1923"*.

James Jenkins had been a golfer of the highest calibre playing as he did when the gap between the top-class amateurs and the leading professionals had not become insurmountable. In the 1914 Open at Prestwick he finished eighth overall and first amateur. But there was more. He had finished ahead of such titans as James Braid, Ted Ray, the Frenchman Arnaud Massy and George Duncan who scorched round courses and not infrequently burned them up. In the entire Championship, his 73 in the third round was only equalled by Harry Vardon in his first.

There was no doubt at all that J. L. C. Jenkins was a great occasion player. *Golf Illustrated* was resounding in its praises: *"The first notable score to be returned was a most brilliant 73 by Mr. Jenkins. It was a great pleasure to his many local adherents to find the Amateur Champion in such splendid form. He reached the turn in 35, aided by a lovely two at the 2nd and 7th holes.*

This brought his aggregate to 232 and put him well in the running."

He was to slip seriously in the last round with an 83 – as did J. H. Taylor – but he finished in eighth spot ahead of James Braid and George Duncan and was comfortably the leading amateur. The same magazine predicted great things ahead of him:

"At Prestwick Mr. Jenkins in every way confirmed his form in the Amateur at Sandwich. It was a great feat on his part to pull himself into third position at the end of the morning round on Friday. And, whatever may happen for the remainder of the season, he has already accomplished sufficient to earn for himself the distinction of being considered the premier amateur of the year. As I have before suggested in these columns he is a thoroughly accomplished little player who is not in any way likely to lose his form as many amateurs are not a little prone to do after winning one of the big events".

J. L. C. Jenkins playing out of a bunker in the 1914 Open Championship at Prestwick

The Great War of 1914-18

THERE was a certain irony in the fact that at the moment that the lights were going out all over Europe, almost the last peacetime Minute noted that it had been decided that the Clubhouse should be electrically lit. The project was not proceeded with immediately, there were now more pressing problems.

The running of a Golf Club during a war is never easy. The First World War did not impinge on the day to day life of civilians as its successor did but the problems arising from it were multifarious. From the very outset there were severe financial constraints since patriotism dictated that every member on active service should be relieved of the necessity of paying a subscription. The drawback to this commendable attitude only appeared later in the war when it was estimated that at least one third of the membership was by then in the Forces.

The problem was further compounded by the offer of free playing facilities to commissioned officers in His Majesty's Forces, and there were many of them stationed on the Ayrshire coast. Add to that the fact that the number of visiting parties would dwindle almost to vanishing point and it is easy to see that the Club would have to prepare itself for difficult times.

There were other threats to golf courses. Troon was fortunate in that it was laid out on poor land and therefore the risk of government occupation was reduced. But the beaches and sandy wastes might well be required for military exercises and a well-equipped Clubhouse had its attractions as temporary military quarters.

What little the Club could do to improve the financial position was done. Fifteen extra members were admitted to take the places of those who had volunteered, since almost incredibly and in marked distinction to 1939, conscription was not introduced until much later in the war.

In a rare event the Committee got ahead of the members, too far ahead. At the Annual General Meeting of 1915 it was proposed to impose a levy to meet the substantial deficiency on the year's working. The Captain, Sir Frederick N. Henderson, was strongly in favour of this and stated that: *"It would be the feelings of the Club that when the young members of the Club who were doing their bit returned home they should find the Club in a healthy financial position"*.

An admirable sentiment, but, by this time there were 186 members already in the services. There may well have been the feeling that, should another levy be required, there would not be members enough at home to fund it. It was felt that the idea had not been sufficiently thought through and the committee was asked to ponder further.

The expected inroads on the course soon arrived. Much of the New Course was taken over by a Grenade School. The War Department would eventually pay compensation by way of War Damage Settlement but this might be long enough in coming.

The toll of members would indeed be heavy – there were 41 deaths – and, in the Committee meeting which followed immediately on the Battle of the Somme in 1916, the Captain had the melancholy task of intimating that three members had been killed outright and a further three had subsequently died of wounds.

By 1917, a levy was deemed essential, 30 shillings per head being the sum and the number on service was just short of 200. Food rationing was not a great problem and there was no blackout to contend with as Scotland was outwith the range of air attack but there were minor pinpricks. By the close of the war the Club was no longer serving dinners and the shortage of manpower led to the unthinkable with women occasionally working on the greens.

The Armistice

At last the war was over and things began to approach normality. One could think about electrifying the Clubhouse. Officers could be taken off the courtesy list where they had been since 1914. There was a payment of £371-3-6d – the War Department was admirably precise in these matters – for damage to the New Course by the Grenade School. This was followed in short order by a final settlement of £2112-4-11d for all remaining war damage. The Amateur Championship trophy which James Jenkins had won in 1914 and which had stayed at Troon all during the war could at last move on to Muirfield where the next championship would be held.

Smoke Room War Memorial 1914-1919

J. E. "Teddy" Dawson

CHAPTER TWO

The Club becomes a Championship Venue

After the War

THE first major job to be done was the reconstruction of the New Course which at the end of the makeover would be referred to as the Portland. There was much else to do for the Club had operated on a care and maintenance basis for four years but the absolute priority was the New Course reconstruction.

The total expenditure would cost £5000 and the money would be raised in two ways.

i) Life membership would be offered at a fee of fifty guineas

ii) There would be a Debenture issue (for 14 years at 3½%)

These financial arrangements proved totally satisfactory.

Until this time, Troon Golf Club had on leases from the Duke of Portland, the Old Course, the Relief (Portland) Course, and the Ladies' Course, (now the Par 3 Course). But in 1921, the Club negotiated the purchase of these courses from the Duke, for the sum of £5000, the area being slightly over 335 acres. This did not include the three Clubhouses, which were on separate feus.

On one occasion and on one occasion only the strange blend of fierceness and coolness which made James Jenkins such a formidable match-play opponent deserted him. It was at a bad time, for the match between Great Britain and the U.S.A. at Hoylake in 1921 was the precursor of the official Walker Cup matches which were soon to follow.

In the singles Jenkins's opponent was a man who would have a strong Troon connection, – Francis Ouimet – who could fairly be reckoned as the first great native-born American golfer. Common ties went for nothing as the American won the first six holes and there was no way back. The final margin of defeat was 6 and 5 and the reporting golfing correspondent, safely shrouded in anonymity dismissed the Scot with *"Mr. Jenkins appeared uncertain of which end of the putter he was using and the result confirmed this supposition"*.

The U.S.A. took the match 9-3 at the end of what, with a nice line in understatement, the writer described as "a very imperfect day for Britain". As so often would happen in Walker Cup matches it was not so much a case of the Americans playing superlative golf as of nerves completely getting the better of the British side.

In Jenkins's case his poor showing in the singles could perhaps be traced to the morning's work where the Americans had a clean sweep of all four matches played. He was partnered by Gordon Simpson

Great Britain Team v USA 1921

THE CLUB BECOMES A CHAMPIONSHIP VENUE

USA Team v Great Britain 1921

against the experienced Chick Evans and the new comet in the sky, Bobby Jones. Even at that early stage in his career there was a large crowd to follow him in perfect weather and straightaway the Americans went for the jugular. Jones opened proceedings with his usual lack of fuss. He stepped on to the tee and before the cheers had died away or the movie cameras began to work he had driven off and was on his way down the fairway.

He and the menacing Chick Evans opened with three fours and a two and established a supremacy which they never lost. At the turn Simpson and Jenkins were five down and beyond redemption. The visitors coasted home by 5 and 3 and in the process established a profound psychological advantage over the native product. As the writer shrewdly pointed out, in the course of one afternoon we had gone from a good-natured disregard of overseas players to an excessive veneration of them. It is worth mentioning that not one of the American side reached the semi-final of the Amateur Championship which was played the following week.

In that British side were several players who would make their mark, although Cyril Tolley and Roger Wethered were still somewhat short of the finished article. There was a future Open Championship winner in the side, the Scotsman Tommy Armour who in 1931 would become Open Champion at Carnoustie.

James Jenkins had the misfortune to experience a bad day on a big day and any thoughts of renewed international experience at top level were quashed. It remains a tribute to him that this sub-standard performance is largely worthy of mention precisely because it was so a-typical.

Suddenly, in 1922, there was the shock news that Troon would be invited to stage the Open Championship of 1923. It should by rights have gone to Muirfield but that course was undergoing extensive remodelling and would not be ready. The Troon Club would have just one year to put things in readiness for their first Open, a first Open which would be their last if they could not meet that event's exacting standards. The West of Scotland golfing public was delighted to get an unexpected chance to see the two Americans who were transforming the game in the United States and whose names were Walter Hagen and Gene Sarazen.

Club Match Prestwick v Troon at Troon, 1920

The Open Championship of 1923

GIVEN that the Championship was a much less complicated affair than today – one press tent, for example, could happily cater for all press requirements – it was still certain that very large crowds would foregather and would have to be marshalled efficiently. Americans were beginning to come in numbers. Walter Hagen would be defending his title won at Sandwich and the young Gene Sarazen gave promise of being even more accomplished. Already British wins were becoming very rare birds indeed and few people thought that the two outstanding Americans could be stopped.

It was a wonderful opportunity for Troon to overtake Prestwick in terms of public recognition and esteem. Hitherto many had thought that Troon was rather the junior partner. In the *Illustrated Sporting and Dramatic News* of February 3rd 1923, Henry Leach advanced this theory:

"Troon has been overshadowed by Prestwick so near to it and the possessor not only of championships but with most impressive associations and as fine a collection of legends with cardinals, monks and all sorts of interesting people mixed up in them .... Troon is somewhat lacking in such stuff or, if it possesses it, only local use is made of it. For the most part its chief supporters come from Glasgow. They are hard-headed business men and don't believe in

The 7th green (Tel-el-Kebir) during the 1923 Open Championship

"speerits" as is done at some of the more hallowed golfing places".

Leach goes on to make an interesting point about the naming of golf holes. He mentions that such names as Tel-el-Kebir and Spion Kop still abound but hazards a guess, erroneously as it turned out, that such names would disappear, being overtaken by those of the Great War. The First World War proved too terrible to be commemorated in the manner Leach suggested.

In the field for the Championship, in addition to the two Americans already mentioned there was the alarmingly talented Joe Kirkwood from Australia. He could do anything with a ball except win major championships. He had an astonishing variety of trick shots which he would later turn into a flourishing variety act. Watching him drive arrow-straight and 200 yards at that while kneeling on the ground or doing the same thing from a waist-high tee it was easy to treat him as a diverting "turn" and forget his natural ability. He should have won at Troon in 1923.

The great elder statesmen, Braid, Vardon and Taylor were in attendance but they would add *gravitas* rather than present a serious threat. In an even more ceremonial role was the home professional, Willie Fernie, who had won the Open fully forty years before and whose last major public appearance this would be.

Fernie and Braid had been involved from an early stage in "toughening up the course for great golfers who would soon tackle it." Not all golf writers approved of this. An anonymous writer in *The Field* declared that: *"the powers that be have had an idea that playing through the green has not been sufficiently severe for a professional of fervid imagination. James Braid has been sent for to lay out new bunkers, the number of which now runs into scores. That will not prevent Walter Hagen from holing putts nor George Duncan from probably establishing yet another record for a championship green."*

The Club was learning to live in the spotlight. There was a highly-critical article in *The Daily Record* regarding the decision to relocate to Troon. Members not unreasonably felt that this was a bit hard given that the competition was yet to start. An additional burden for the Club to carry was the death of the Captain, James G. Clark Millar, only a few months before the Championship. For those who think that bad behaviour at major golf events is something which began in the 1990s, it is instructive to be told that notices would be put up requesting spectators to behave as sportsmen. Another press release stated that United States professionals would be treated exactly the same as British professionals, something that most temperate men had imagined would happen in any event.

Things very nearly came adrift before the Open had properly got started. Some competitors, almost all of them American, had punched and deep-grooved their iron clubs in an attempt to get them to

Willie Fernie with sons Edward and Tom

impart back-spin. The R&A were frequently accused of banning anything new almost as a reflex action. They now declared these clubs to be illegal but not until the day before the tournament was to start. There was a running and scurrying as messengers were sent to neighbouring machine shops and commercial enterprises for files and rasps. All through the night Willie Fernie's son, Edward, spent hours smoothing club faces. He cheerfully gave up his own opportunity to play and so impressed the American entrants that they made a special presentation to him of a gold pencil and a silver cigarette case.

MAP OF THE TROON CHAMPIONSHIP COURSE IN 1923

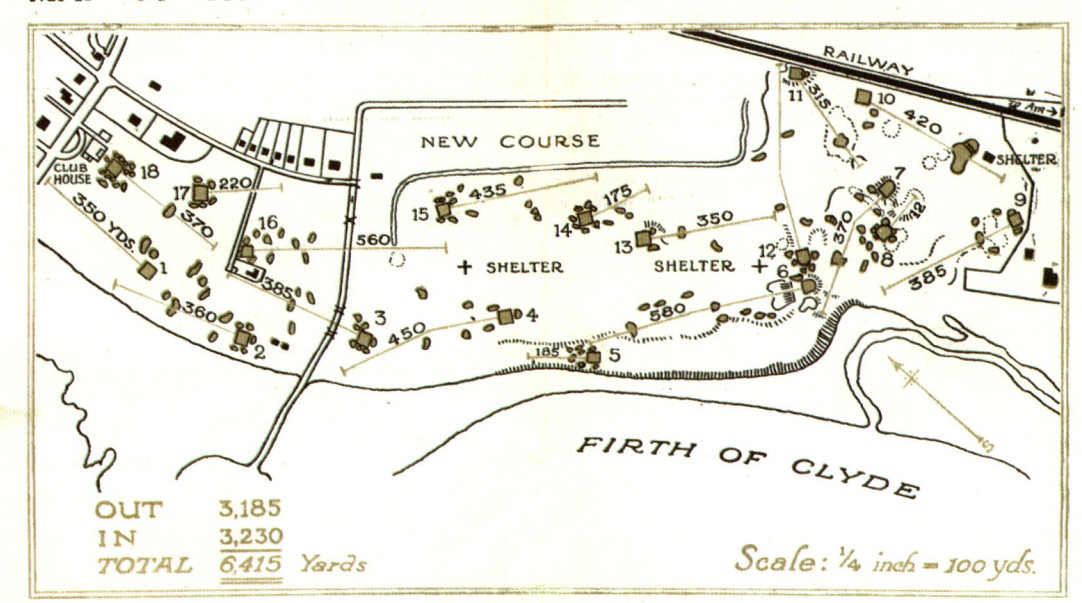

THE BLUE DUNLOP 'MAXFLI'— Best on all courses.

Who would win? The man who knew the links better than anyone else, Willie Fernie, published his thoughts on the course and how to play it in a little booklet.

The Troon Championship Course 1923

BY WILLIAM FERNIE

Open Champion 1883 and five times runner-up

O' a' the links where I hae golfed frae Ayr to Aberdeen,
On Prestwick or Carnoustie and mony mair I ween,
What tho' the bents are rough and bunkers yawn aroun',
I dearly lo'e the breezy links, the breezy links o' Troon.
                                            GILMOUR.

The word Troon comes from the Gaelic word "Strone," which means a nose or hill, and a glance at the situation of the town will show how aptly this describes the general appearance of the promontory, which stretches fully a mile into the sea.

The Troon Golf Club was formed in 1878 with a nucleus of less than twenty members. The original course was only six holes, afterwards enlarged to twelve holes, and subsequently to the full round of eighteen. When I first came to Troon, as professional in 1887, there were only some half-dozen courses in the whole of Ayrshire, now there are five eighteen hole courses in Troon alone, and nineteen within a radius of seven miles.

This part of the Ayrshire coast is world famous for its many fine courses, and Troon as a centre of golfing activity may be aptly described as the "St. Andrews of the West Coast." Golf has certainly made Troon the prosperous resort it has become, and one lives here in an atmosphere of golf. As a nursery for golfers the town has produced many fine players, some of whom were the first professionals to emigrate to America. I doubt if such enthusiasm and love for the game is shown at any other golfing resort.

The Old Course, which is to house the Championship, has been the scene of many notable matches. Here it was that Willie Park and Andrew Kirkaldy played part of their great match in August, 1890. Andrew came to Troon with a lead of one hole on the match, and after playing two rounds he increased his lead to three holes, finishing brilliantly with 22 for the last six holes.

It was at Troon that the second half of my big match with Willie Park took place. Park won the match at the "Turnberry" hole, where during the afternoon round he holed a full brassie shot.

In 1905 an International Foursome match was played over the course, Braid and Herd represented Scotland, Taylor and Vardon winning the day for England. Five years later the same match was played, and this time Braid and Herd had their revenge and triumphed for Scotland.

In 1914 the Old Course was used as one of the qualifying courses for the Championship, at Prestwick. The best returns on that occasion were cards of 73 by Harry Vardon and Fred Collins. Although the weather conditions were favourable, only 30 players succeeded in compiling scores of 78 or less, out of a total of 194 entries.

Since then the course has been made considerably more difficult, by the addition of 67 new bunkers, and new back tees, which have been planned by James Braid. The course now provides a searching test of the best golf, and calls for extremely accurate play rather than long hitting.

My friend James Braid has been very cunning in placing the new bunkers. At nearly every hole one has to hug either the right or the left side of the fairway in order to get into the most favourable position for the approach, and Braid has seen to it, that to reach that position, the player will have to take certain risks from tee. On the outward journey the course rather favours the man who can hold his drives up from left to right, and coming home the man who plays for a pull.

A great deal has been written about the start and finish of Troon being rather tame. That this is not the case many aspirants for championship honours will probably find to their cost. The start and finish of the course provide a searching test of golf, and the middle portion of the course is situated on golfing country unsurpassed anywhere.

Opinions vary as to which is the most difficult hole on the course, but certainly the most famous is the short eighth "Ailsa," 120 yards long. This hole has frequently been described as the "Postage Stamp," the "Pocket Handkerchief," and many other names quite unprintable! From the tee, which is at a considerably higher level than the green, all the difficulties and horrors of the hole are apparent. The green looks about the size of its nickname, the Postage Stamp. It is guarded, in front, and on the right, by bunkers, and immediately on the left by a high hill. The favourite way of playing this hole by local players was to try and land the ball on the face of the hill, and break down on to the green. Braid has put a stop to this practice by planning a big bunker in the face of the hill, and another round the foot. There is now only one course open to the player, to pitch his ball on the green, and make it stay there, no easy feat with even a little wind. I imagine the player who passes this hole with a three on his card will breathe a sigh of relief. There is no doubt it will be done many times in two, but will probably be done as often in six. As an instance of this, in one competition the lowest figure was one, and the highest twelve.

In my opinion the most testing hole, and in fact one of the finest three shot holes in the country, is the sixth, "Turnberry," 580 yards long. The tee is away on the right among the rough. The fairway will break the ball to the left, and undoubtedly the man who can hold up his drive from left to right will be at an advantage. The second shot, by the addition of new bunkers, has been made extremely difficult, as the player must keep a very straight line in order to be in a position to reach the green

Gene Sarazen with Willie Fernie, 1923

Walter Hagen playing in the 1923 Open Championship

with his third. The green is long and narrow, and lies diagonally from left to right.

It is guarded in front by a deep and rather rough grassy gully. Until recently this was a terrible sand bunker with a sleeper face. On the right of the green is a deep pit, and on the left is a formidable bunker. Even to the person who has hit his first shot well, and placed his second shot in the right position, the approach is difficult, but woe betide the man who requires more than a mashie for his third shot.

The tenth hole, called "Sandhills," is a grand hole. Braid has placed a new back tee which makes the carry over the famous Sandhills bunker a very formidable one. Once over the bunker the fairway lies slightly from right to left, and the player who can bring off a slight pull will have an advantage here. This fairway has many undulations. From the back tee and with no wind, the hole will be almost two full shots, even for the long hitter. It is a hole that could quite easily put "finis" to a good score. Andrew Kirkaldy will remember how long ago in his match with Willie Park he put his tee shot into the Sandhills bunker and gave up the hole.

The eleventh, "The Railway," is also a dangerous hole, the chief difficulty being the tee shot which has to be picked up fairly quickly to avoid a very nasty high sand face. Beyond this face there is a long carry over extremely rough country. The fairway on both sides is guarded by whins. The slightest mistake with the tee shot at this hole may have the most serious consequences.

The new fifth hole, "Greenan," 185 yards, has been designed by Braid among the bents close to the shore. The ground all the way from tee to green is very rough, and covered with little bumps like molehills. This hole reminds me of the new eleventh at Prestwick. Bold tactics will pay best here, because the back of the green is the only part that has not been bunkered.

THE CLUB BECOMES A CHAMPIONSHIP VENUE

The Postage Stamp during the 1923 Open Championship

Towards the 10th green, 1923 Open Championship

Cyril Tolley putting on the 18th green, 1923 Open Championship

THE CLUB BECOMES A CHAMPIONSHIP VENUE

Arthur Havers driving from the 7th tee, 1923 Open Championship

The seventh hole, "Tel-el-Kebir," has been altered lately by lowering the bank in front of the green, and making an addition to the green by cutting away the hill at the back. The new portion of the green is on a higher level than the old. The best play here is to hug the righthand side of the fairway, though the severe bunkering on the right makes this proceeding not without risk. The left looks easier, but involves a most difficult approach shot.

There is an excellent water supply laid on to each putting green now, and even though we have a repetition of the drought of 1921, the greens are certain to be in excellent condition. On the whole, the greens are rather on the flat side, and during the summer months are firm, keen and very true. The man who strikes his putting streak will put in some very useful work.

The majority of the fairways are covered with tiny undulations, so that the player will find himself with a variety of lies and stances, to surmount which difficulties brings out the finer points of the game.

The prevailing winds at Troon in the summer are westerly to south-westerly.

This is a very meagre description of a grand course; the stage for the 1923 Championship is worthily set.

Fernie was of the opinion that four rounds of 75 would be good enough to take the title. He also thought that great accuracy would overcome long hitting.

It would be some time yet before the British could stop sneering at the Americans as coarse-grained creatures who had had the bad taste to win the Revolutionary War of 1775. The leading American golfers did tend to be more flamboyant in their style of dress, particularly in their huge caps which could have done duty as helipads. The staid *Glasgow Herald* could not resist an ill-bred snigger on June 2nd 1923:

"The golfing garb of the American contingent has lately provoked some remark".

It was that contingent which provided the first shock of the 1923 Open when Gene Sarazen, tipped by many to win the event, dramatically failed to qualify. He was an outstanding writer as well as being a consummate golfer and he describes his increasingly-despairing trudging up and down the Troon streets when the low scores started to come in as the weather improved:

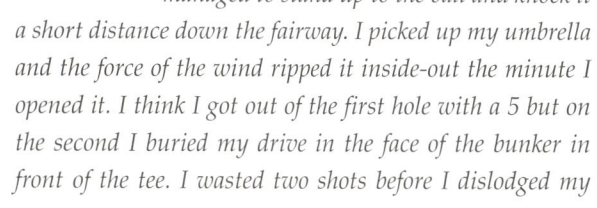

Arthur Gladstone Havers

"My first 18 was a 75, a comfortable score. I wasn't trying to break any records. I had drawn the first starting time of the day for the second qualifying round. On that morning a cold, driving storm was sweeping off the ocean with such fury that the fishermen in the town were not allowed to go out and the waves were hurdling the sea-wall and washing up to the edge of the championship course. On the first tee I warmed my hands in my pockets and after being blown off my stance once or twice, managed to stand up to the ball and knock it a short distance down the fairway. I picked up my umbrella and the force of the wind ripped it inside-out the minute I opened it. I think I got out of the first hole with a 5 but on the second I buried my drive in the face of the bunker in front of the tee. I wasted two shots before I dislodged my

41

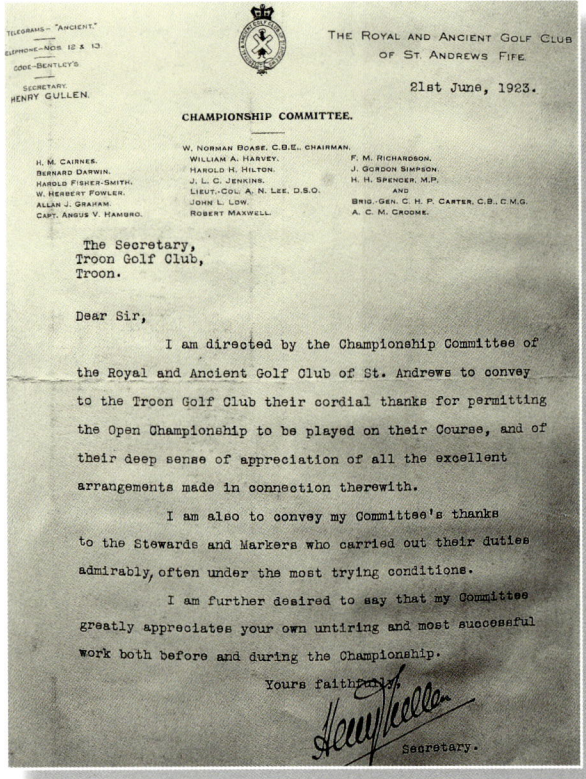

Letter from R&A, 1923

ball and wallowed away nine strokes in all on that hole.

I knew I was in trouble. By the fifth hole I had got a grip on myself and, considering the ferocity of the elements, was not playing too badly. At the rate I was going I thought I would finish in the middle eighties but I thought the other players would have just as bad a time in the storm as I had experienced. I posted my 85 and was not too uneasy about my chances of qualifying until the wind began to die down at noon and the sun came out. Then I really began to worry. The later starters, playing under relatively ideal conditions began to bring in scores in the 70's and I learned in the evening that I had failed to qualify by a stroke. That was the most crushing blow my self-esteem had ever received. I felt ashamed to face anyone and decided not to stay around and watch the Championship as a humiliated 'also-failed-to-qualify'. I returned to London."

Sarazen would win the Open Championship and exactly half a century on would have two great days at Troon but all that was in the future. He had packed and gone but his great rival Walter Hagen would ensure that the 1923 Open would go right down to the wire. He was one of four who could have won it over the last few holes. The mercurial Joe Kirkwood had shot a third round 69 as had the American Scot, Macdonald Smith, but Kirkwood collapsed dramatically at the end being six over par for the last five holes. The *Glasgow Herald* probably got it about right when it judged: *"The brilliant Australian probably handicapped himself by his knowledge of so many shots".*

In the midst of all this a tall schoolmasterly Englishman, Arthur Havers, had led almost from the start. He had attracted little attention, sooner or later he would collapse, that was what British golfers did. But Havers kept going and Hagen came to the home hole having to get a 3 to force a playoff. He drove well enough but was bunkered off his second and narrowly failed to hole his recovery shot.

Havers was a popular winner and even his expressed delight in "having kept this historic trophy in England" drew little more than the odd dry groan and admonitory whistle. The celebrated golf writer Bernard Darwin ventured to predict that *"we are now producing golfers who can withstand the best that the United States could bring against us".*

Rarely has a man made a more inaccurate forecast. The next 10 Opens were won by Americans, Bobby Jones and Walter Hagen having much to do with that. Such indeed was the American domination that the Open ceased to have the same attraction for American golfers and in the middle and late 1930's there was a notable drop in the calibre of Transatlantic entrants.

There were a few barbed criticisms of the arrangements for the running of the Open but in general it was felt that the Club had done well in its staging of one of the very top events. Certain things had to be ironed out and balances had to be struck. To be asked to hold the Open was a real honour but also to be kept in mind was the fact that Troon, like the other Open courses, was an amateur club run for the enjoyment of its members and so dislocation for them had to be kept to a minimum.

Not everyone in golfing circles necessarily wanted a spectator-orientated game. The great J. H. Taylor did not want any spectators at all: *"Many of them are idle pleasure-seekers after a little excitement who complain if they are not satisfied".* He found support in the *Glasgow Herald* which pontificated: *"The aim of the Open Championship is not to provide a spectacle for the crowd but to find the best golfer of the year".*

Local interest was strong. An accusation in the local press that the Troon landladies had greatly inflated their bed and breakfast charges was indignantly denied by the Burgh's Provost.

More serious perhaps were the stories circulating in the Press that American golfers were happy/unhappy with their reception by the Club itself. Happy/unhappy because it appeared to be that Hagen and one or two others were tailoring their articles to whichever side of the Atlantic they were writing them for. In the British press, Hagen appeared to express himself as satisfied. The previous year at Sandwich the professionals had been denied access to the Clubhouse at all. At Troon they had the use of

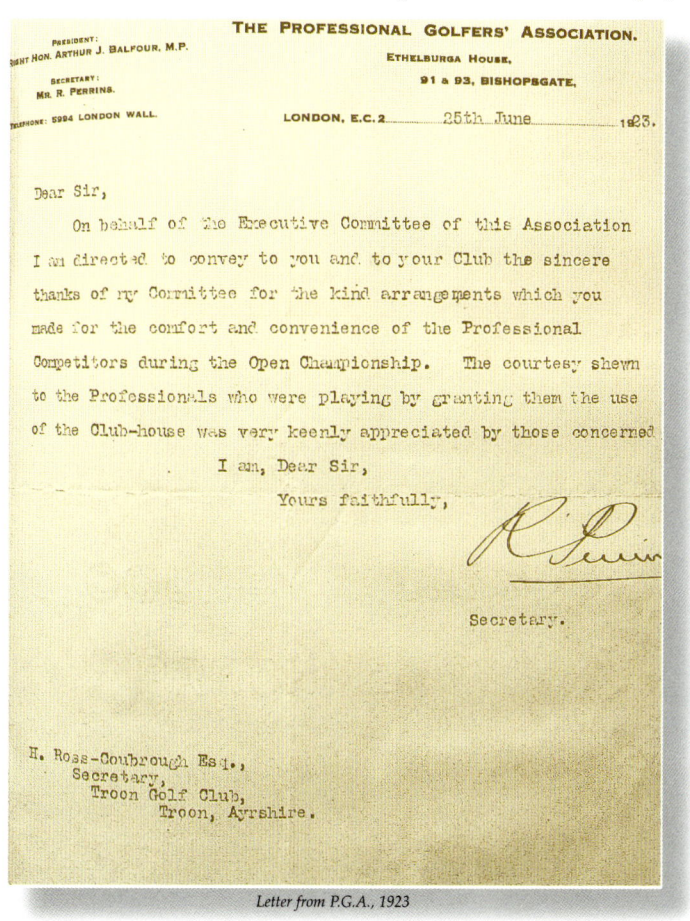

Open Championship 1923
Final Leaderboard

A.G. Havers (England)	73 73 73 76 = 295
W. Hagen (U.S.A.)	76 71 74 75 = 296
MacDonald Smith (U.S.A.)	80 73 69 75 = 297
J. Kirkwood (Australia)	72 79 69 78 = 298
T.R. Fernie (Scotland)	73 78 74 75 = 300
G. Duncan (Scotland)	79 75 74 74 = 302
C.A. Whitcombe (England)	70 76 74 82 = 302

locker rooms. With a large field it is difficult to see that more could be done but such as Hagen, used to the more free American way, chafed at any restrictions no matter how well-intended.

There is little doubt that Hagen enjoyed stirring up those British that he perceived as stuffy. In doing this, fairness sometimes got elbowed aside. He was full of praise for Western Gailes where he and Sarazen played a match for £150 against Abe Mitchell and George Duncan. The players were entertained by the Western Gailes Club to lunch and dinner. Hagen was rightly loud in his praise of the host club but a moment's reflection would have shown him that this was easier to do for four people than for almost 100 on a daily basis.

Hagen might have been the man the *Glasgow Herald* had chiefly in mind when referring to matters sartorial. He was reported as having brought nineteen suits over with him but not, among them, a dinner jacket. This led to a strange incident in which he was invited to dinner by the acting Troon Captain, Sir Alexander Walker. On presenting himself at the house, the golfer presumably in a decent lounge suit, the door was opened by his prospective host who took one look at Hagen, and said "My guests for dinner wear black tie" and shut the door on the discomfited American. The irony was that Sir Alexander Walker had extended the invitation to his magnificent home, Piersland, in an attempt to ameliorate what the

Letter from P.G.A., 1923

Letter from Arthur Havers, July 14th, 1923

American golfers regarded as a chilly reception. The whisky magnate, connected of course with the famous Kilmarnock brand, Johnnie Walker, had genuinely meant well.

Taking the 1923 Championship all in all there was far more for the club that was positive rather than negative. Crowd behaviour had been good and the event had provided a British win. Yet some of the criticism stung a bit, especially where perceived as unfair and the then secretary, Ross Coubrough, wrote to the secretary of the R&A asking for his advice on how to respond to hostile criticism. His answer was laconic, elegant and above all sensible:

"Don't".

Old Willie Fernie had not been too far out with his estimate of 300 strokes as a championship-winning total. His son, Tom, himself a noted golfer, came up with exactly that aggregate and it enabled him to finish in fifth place, five strokes behind the winner, Arthur Havers of Coombe Hill.

Arthur Havers

Arthur Havers was not greatly regarded as a national champion and much of the neglect was unjust. He was not a stylist and he had a most idiosyncratic grip which showed four knuckles on a ferociously tightly gripping left hand. He was, rather unusually in a top golfer, given to fits of shanking.

Yet his underlying method had to be sound enough. Not only did he win the Open Championship of 1923 but he had previously qualified for it at the age of sixteen and just before World War One had come fourth in the Open, so the signs were there for anyone who could read them. He was far from being the one-title wonder which was the category under which several golf writers would have liked to file him.

His post-1923 career was not spectacular – it is as well to point out that no other British golf professional won the Open for 11 years after Havers' success – but there were some isolated high points. On the back of his Troon success he went to the United States and got the better of both Bobby Jones and Gene Sarazen in challenge matches, not official

THE CLUB BECOMES A CHAMPIONSHIP VENUE

The 'Field' Challenge Cup, Long Driving Competition

matches, granted, but neither Jones nor Sarazen ever took kindly to defeat. As late as 1932 he had the lowest round of the Championship – a sparkling 68 – which that year was won by his old adversary, Gene Sarazen, over Prince's at Sandwich.

Before the Open Championship became the highly sophisticated event that it is today, there was time for some minor but enjoyable diversions. Chief of these was the Long Driving Competition, a feature of the Championship in the Twenties.

The event was held on the first hole of the New Course, as the Portland was then generally called. It is described as follows in the programme for the Hoylake Open Championship of 1924.

The Long Driving Competition of 1923

"At Troon on June 13th, 1923, the strength of the wind at the first tee on the New Course (close to the Club House at the corner of the Crosbie and Fullarton Roads) was about 20 miles an hour, but came from behind the driver's left shoulder instead of across the course (as at Sandwich) from the right, being from the north-west on a line of play which was a point or two to the north of east. Fifty-nine started out of an entry of sixty-eight, and thirty-three sent in their cards. Each competitor drove four balls. The Cup was given for the best aggregate of three drives, and was won by Mr. Roger Wethered, amateur champion for the year, with 276yds. 0ft. 8in., 264yds. 1ft. 5in. and 268yds. 1ft., total 809yds. 1in. Arthur Havers, from Coombe Hill, who won the Open Championship two days later, secured the second prize with an aggregate of over 788 yds., his best drive being 270yds. 10ins. The next best aggregates were made by W. G. Oke (785yds.), Bert Seymour (782yds.) and Walter Hagen (773yds.). The prize of £15 for the longest individual drive of the day was won by D. A. Curtis, of Queen's Park, Bournemouth, whose ball pitched on a slight slope and got more run than any other, finishing 278yds. 2ft. 6in. from the tee, an improvement of nearly two yards on Easterbrook's effort in 1922. The longest carry at Troon was Mr. Wethered's 262yds., with Abe Mitchell's 260yds. close behind. Ted Ray probably carried further than either, but did not finish on the course. Mr. Cyril Tolley's best ball was within a few inches of 264 yds. and Aubrey Boomer was less than a yard behind him. The average of the first 24 competitors worked out at just

Walter Hagen in Long Driving Competition, 1923 Open Championship

over 262 yards, which is over six yards better than that of the first 12 men at Sandwich. The wind made the width of fifty yards rather narrower than it looked at Troon, but the conditions laid down for the competition proved to be an ideal test, and probably will not be altered."

The Long Driving Competition returned to Troon in 1925 when the Troon course was used as a qualifying course for the Open Championship, held that year at Prestwick. Once again the first hole on the New Course was pressed into service and this time the event was won by the prominent English amateur Cyril Tolley with a drive a few inches short of 300 yards. Since the event was discontinued after the Open Championship of 1926 Troon had hosted two of the comparatively few occasions on which this competition was held. It is interesting to compare the driving distances then and now, given the comparatively rudimentary equipment of the 1920s.

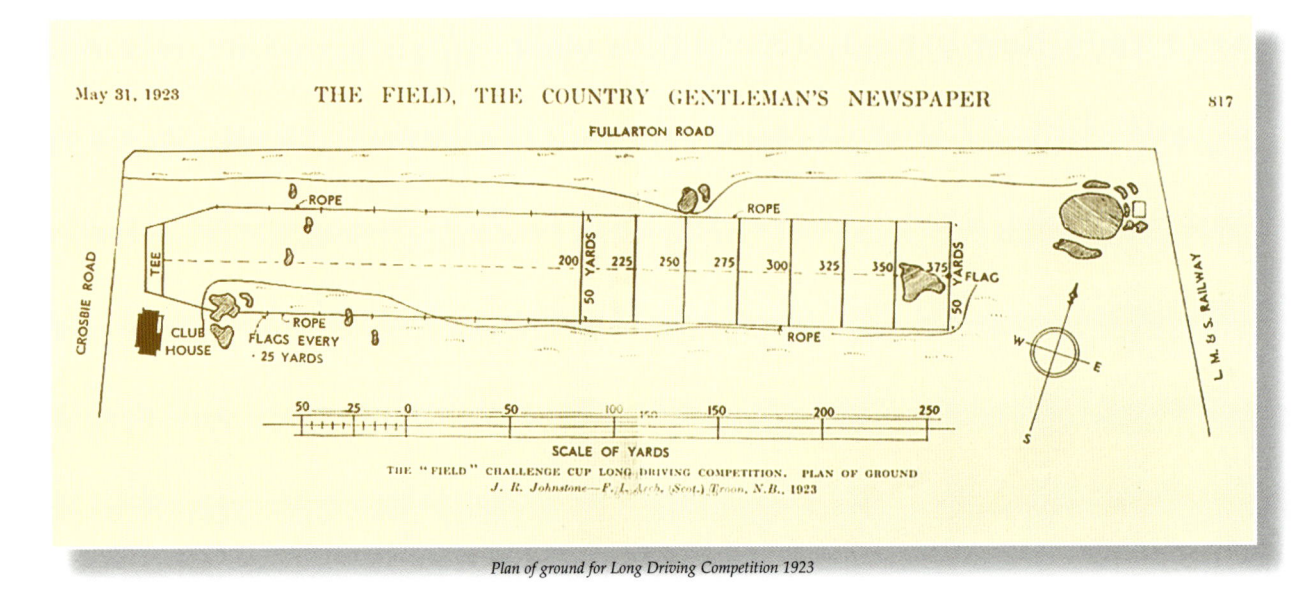

Plan of ground for Long Driving Competition 1923

The Amateur Championships of the Twenties

The 1923 Scottish Amateur Championship

THE rather abrupt awarding of the 1923 Open Championship to Troon meant that the course would host two major championships in the same year since the commitment to hold the Scottish predated that for the Open. It was to be expected that James Jenkins would be, on his own course, the hottest of favourites, the more so since at that moment he held the amateur records for Troon and Prestwick.

He did not disappoint his adherents and he reached the semi-finals before going out. The members were not deprived of a Troon win however since the less flamboyant T. M. Burrell defeated Dr A. R. McCallum by one hole. Tom Burrell was entered from Troon but he lived for much of the time in Perthshire and played some golf there as well.

He would have described himself as essentially a weekend golfer and perhaps drew strength in the Scottish from his own notion that he would not get very far but that he would most certainly enjoy the journey, long or short. This would seem to be an endearing attitude but Burrell was roundly rebuked for "playing for fun". Writing in the *Scots Pictorial*, G. C. Manford had this to say:

"Up to a point I suppose we all do this but if we enter for a tournament or match then we play to try and win, leaving the fun for afterwards. Putting fun first makes for a very empty victory and possibly we would prefer not to see people with this idea playing in competitive events."

A surprising outburst given that Burrell had won the major event but Manford's voice was happily drowned out in the torrent of congratulations that washed over the head of the winner.

Between the Wars

Social customs had been permanently changed by World War One and inevitably the question of Sunday golf soon arose. Contrary to popular belief there had been instances of the game being played on the Sabbath before the war, especially in East Lothian where the Prime Minister, Arthur Balfour, was both a frequent visitor and a lover of the game.

By 1924 there was a strong move within the membership at Troon that Sunday golf should be permitted and in August of that year a plebiscite was held. The *Troon Times* was filled with foreboding:

"If golf courses are to be open every day of the week then assuredly it is only a short step to the institution of football matches and sports and pastimes of every conceivable

Tom Burrell, Scottish Amateur Champion of 1923

character. Once that has come to pass then it is goodbye to the sanctity of the Sabbath and to all that it means to God-fearing people in every community."

The Field was rather more sympathetic to the notion in a rather oblique way: *"Hitherto such doings have been discounted in Scotland sternly. Famous players have been seen walking aimlessly about in trousers on Sundays, making up for not playing by telling each other the most appalling stories of their exploits at this hole or that from the day before."*

Despite strong resistance the tidal impetus was with the reformers. The big railway companies with famous golfing hotels such as Turnberry and Gleneagles were particularly anxious that their guests should be able to have a full weekend's golf.

In the event the yes votes had it by a comfortable 344 votes to 213. In an essentially Calvinistic compromise however, it was decided that only the Portland Course would be used at Troon. It would take another war to bring the Old Course into line. The *Troon Times* voiced its displeasure: *"Such a decision shows a sad falling-away from grace and it's highly probable that the institution of Sunday golf at Troon will, in the long run, lower the prestige of the Club"*.

The Canadian humorist Stephen Leacock lent his weight to the pros from across the Atlantic:

"Golf may be played on Sundays, not being a game within the view of the law but a form of moral effort".

The decision was taken and, no doubt to the surprise of some, on the following morning the sun was observed in the east as usual.

The Inter-War Professionals

The end of the 1923 Open to all intents and purposes meant farewell to Willie Fernie who had been at Troon for almost 40 years and who had taught two generations of members. He had retired in late 1923 and had been awarded a pension of £2 per week but he was not long spared to draw it. With his death went one of the links with the early game and the particular proud bearing which characterised the old Scottish golfer who reflected that his superiority as a golfer more than offset any social superiority that his nominal masters might possess.

In his place came Duncan McCulloch who won the Scottish Professional Championship more than once and played in the international matches against England from 1932-7 inclusive and against Ireland also from 1932-5. He was a very good player who at the outset of his career had been assistant at Hanger Hill to the great George Duncan. He had also been professional to the Troon Municipal Course and often captained Ayrshire in professional matches against Glasgow and other counties. J. H. Taylor admired his play and wrote that it was a great pity that the Scots professional, remaining at home, was so limited in the opposition available to him. Duncan McCulloch was, like his predecessor, long-serving and his spell as professional would last until 1954.

Duncan McCulloch playing in the Ayrshire Professional Championship at Irvine Bogside

THE CLUB BECOMES A CHAMPIONSHIP VENUE

He played with distinction in Ryder Cup trials in the 1930's, winning more matches than he lost. He was also an outstanding teacher, particularly of ladies and in his heyday he taught from dawn to dusk. His great maxim for improving the quality of iron play was to practice on the shore where playing off sand required a perfect strike.

The Ladies' Championship of 1925

The big event of 1925 was the return of the Ladies' Championship which produced a cliff-hanger of a final between Joyce Wethered and the rather more experienced Cecil (often rendered Cecile) Leitch, which went to the 37th before Miss Wethered won through. No Ladies' final had gone so far and when eventually one went further, to the 38th, it was at Troon again in 1952 when Moira Patterson beat Frances Stephens.

Bobby Jones had identified Joyce Wethered as having the finest golf swing he had ever seen and she also had a nice line in laconic humour. She was noted for her imperviousness to "noises off" and in the match against Glenna Collett she struck at the 11th with *The Times* describing it thus:

"Miss Wethered holed a long curly putt for a three characteristically enough with an engine snorting on the line behind her".

She herself admiringly said *"I was too well acquainted with the ways of a Scotch engine driver not to know that he was determined to see the hole played to a finish before he continued with his goods to Ayr".*

Joyce Wethered

The first two Ladies' Championships at Troon almost provided an incredible double. Lottie Dod had only entered the Ladies' Championship because she was

The Ladies Championship at Troon 1925. Finalists and Semi-finalists. Mrs T. Dobbell, Miss B. Brown, Miss C. Leitch and Miss J. Wethered (clockwise from top left)

tired of winning Wimbledon. In 1925 it was confidently reported that Joyce Wethered was giving up golf with the intention of devoting herself to Lawn Tennis, in which she had hopes of appearing in the Championship the following year. The magazine *Golfing* was moved to a poetic frenzy:

> Miss Wethered we all deplore
> Will play in tournaments no more.
> She seems, as far's I understand her
> To find at last, like Alexander
> That in the game of green and bunker
> She's left with no more worlds to conquer!
> When you and I and other dubs
> Give up the game and smash our clubs
> To start again next morn, of course
> With blistered tongue and throat grown hoarse
> 'Tis in a mood of black despair,
> Because we never can "get there"

49

The Ladies Championship at Troon 1925.
The winner Joyce Wethered receives the Trophy from Troon Captain, W. P. Stewart

Because 'tis all in vain we try
To break an eighty ere we die.
That's bad enough. It must be Hell
To stop because you play too well.

Miss Wethered seems to have had second thoughts and so the prospect of a Wethered v Wills-Moody final at Wimbledon disappeared into the distance. One can only marvel at the sportsmanlike qualities with which these early women golfers were invested. In her matches against the American, Glenna Collett – the plural is used because the two were destined to meet four years on in a St. Andrews final which Joyce Wethered won by 3 and 1 – the Englishwoman made the following point:

"It has often been attributed to me that I entered for this event in a purely patriotic spirit, with the expressed intention of preventing any of the American invaders from winning our Championship. I must really protest against this rather pretentious statement. The fact that Glenna Collett and I actually met in the final lent some colour to the rumour but I feel I should never be justified in entering for the sole purpose of hoping to prevent some other particular player from winning. A championship in my opinion is an event instituted solely for private enterprise and for the best player to win and it seems to me a pity that it need necessarily be converted into an International match on a larger scale."

The final between Joyce Wethered and Cecil Leitch had attracted a crowd which some newspapers had placed at 10,000 and inevitably there was a certain amount of congestion and stampeding over the last few holes. This appears to have upset the newspapers more than the players. Writing in the *Golf Journal*, Cecil Leitch said that, far from discommoding her, the large numbers assembled had inspired her to give of her very best and that she would remember the memorable day for ever.

No matter what stirring deeds took place on land the sea continued to erode the early holes on the Old Course slowly but remorselessly. Chespale fences had to be erected on good mattresses of brushwood and this entailed the expenditure of over £500. At the same time the groynes were to be removed from the Pow Burn.

Not a glamorous expenditure, perhaps, but to leave things as they were was not an option. We will return to this later and at more length.

The Club was developing international links. In 1926 the Old Course was made available for a party which had come to Scotland from the U.S.A. in an Anchor liner. Not long afterwards a letter arrived from the Japanese Embassy requesting that the Japanese Prince and Princess Ri should be allowed to play over Troon. This was not quite as exclusively exotic as might appear. Between the two wars the Glasgow Golf Club almost every year afforded temporary membership to Japanese naval officers who were supervising the building of warships on the Clyde.

The Scottish Championship of 1929

In 1929 at the mid point between the wars a Troon member, Teddy Dawson, came very close to taking the Scottish Championship

Probably no Troon golfer exemplifies the spirit of the Twenties more than J. E. 'Teddy' Dawson. From picture after picture he gazes, hair immaculately parted, wearing an elegant pullover and stylish plus fours with shoes burnished to a Drill Sergeant's satisfaction. Before turning our attention to the final of 1929 we should mention his surpassing feat of the following summer, in which he won the three major amateur stroke play competitions in the West of Scotland, perhaps in all Scotland.

These trophies were the Tennant Cup and the Edward Trophy, both under the ordinance of the Glasgow Golf Club and Troon's own Hillhouse Cup. To win any one of these on a single occasion would have crowned any Scottish amateur's career and what this triple success meant was that in this particular year, Dawson was unbeatable with card and pencil in hand. All three tournaments were of the highest order, the Tennant Cup remains to this day the oldest open amateur stroke play competition in the world. But that was 1930 and our immediate concern is with the preceding year.

The championship that year was at Balgownie in Aberdeen more formally known as Royal Aberdeen. The regal accolade was conferred on the Club by a letter dated 10 August 1903 from Lord Balfour of Burleigh, intimating that His Majesty King Edward VII had been pleased to signify that in the future the Club was to be known as "Royal Aberdeen Golf Club".

Dawson was well-fancied. *Golfing* had described him as "a stylist who swung the club gracefully and with great freedom". He and the other finalist J. F. Bookless arrived in an Aberdeen which had baked for days under a hot sun. Both men had connections with the sea, Dawson being a marine insurer and Bookless with a rather more direct link since he was a trawler owner and fish exporter.

Both men moved to the finals comparatively untroubled although Dawson had a close call in the sixth round when he had to go to the 20th to defeat J. N. Smith of Earlsferry Thistle Golf Club and he had to shoot an eagle 3 to do so. Dawson was not tall but he was long off the tee and in the hard, running conditions he drove the fifteenth green at 330 yards. When in the semi-final Dawson beat the infinitely promising student called Sam McKinlay, then playing out of the Alexandra Club, hopes were high for ultimate success.

Photographs of the two men setting off on the final rounds afford a piquant contrast. Dawson as ever was a golfing fashion plate, Bookless in a long black coat and slouch hat bore a disconcerting resemblance to Wyatt Earp. Victory alas went to the long gun and in all honesty Bookless was never extended in winning 5 and 4.

On either side of this final Teddy Dawson gave proof of his high order of ability. He reached the final

Teddy Dawson

Dawson and Brookless in the Final of the 1929 Scottish Amateur Championship at Royal Aberdeen

16 in the Amateur of 1927 played over Hoylake. He had a 69 over Old Troon to his credit, one under the amateur record which had been set by Charlie Gibb. When the match against England grew with the introduction of Ireland and Wales to the Home Countries International matches he played four times against Ireland and twice against England between 1927 and 1931 and he was now among those who took part in the first Quadrilateral series in these championships.

There was another fine Troon player at this time, scarce overshadowed by Dawson. This was James Brock who proved difficult to beat whether at club or international level. He was selected for his country against Ireland in 1927 and again, after quite a gap, in 1932. He also had the distinction of holding the captaincy of Prestwick St. Nicholas. J. B. Stevenson made up the triumvirate from the town.

The Secretary, H. Ross Coubrough was by 1929 winding down into retirement. The post of Secretary was one of the most keenly coveted in Britain by this time and no fewer than 203 applications were received, the bulk of them from England. The daunting task of succeeding Ross Coubrough was allotted to W. H. Johnson who served jointly with him in 1929 for six months and then discharged the duties single-handedly in the frenetic days which ran from that year to the middle of the war in 1942. His latter years were devoted simply to holding the club together, but before that he had been much involved in the Club's biggest event for some 15 years, the holding of the Amateur Championship of 1938.

In 1932 the Home Internationals were played for the first time with all four countries competing and Messrs. Dawson, Brock and Stevenson did very well over their local venue, Troon. As the merest shadow of things to come Paramount made application to film the matches but there is no record of the success or failure of that application.

There were rumbles of discontent from Troon Portland over that club's inability to increase its membership without the sanction of the parent club. The whole question of membership was exercising the Troon Committee. There was a widespread feeling that the Old Course was overplayed and it could be very difficult to get a game, especially at weekends. It was not the best time for the suggestion from the Committee that membership should be increased to 600 from 550 but that members should pay five shillings a round if they played on Saturdays and Public Holidays. It is fair to say that no proposal in the Club's history till then ever got shorter shrift.

W. H. Johnson, Secretary 1929-1942

The 1932 Scottish Team: From left to right (standing) R. B. Denholm, E. McRuvie, J. N. Smith, S. L. McKinlay, J. B. Stevenson, D. McBride, J. Wilson and W. Campbell; (secretary) (seated) J. E. Dawson, A. Jamieson, W. Tulloch, J. McLean and J. Brock.

Something of this hostility spilled over to the A.G.M of 1937 when a proposed increase of three guineas in the subscription was too much for the membership. The Committee was forced to come back with the agreeable proposal that everyone, Members and Extraordinary Members alike should pay six guineas.

1932 Home International Matches at Troon

Scotland 9 Wales 6
Scotland 11 Ireland 4
Scotland 8 England 7

J. B. Stevenson, James Brock and J. E. Dawson all played for Scotland in the series: Against Wales J. B. won his singles 5&4 and foursomes 6&4. Interestingly, he played foursomes in this series with Andrew Jamieson of Pollok who beat Bobby Jones in the British Amateur at Muirfield in 1926.

Against Ireland, Dawson won his singles 3&1 and foursomes 4&2.

Against England, Dawson won his foursomes 4&3 and singles 4&2 while J.B. halved his foursomes but lost his singles 5&4.

James Brock also had a good Home International baptism. He lost his singles against England but, partnered by the redoubtable Jack McLean, he got a half point in the foursomes. Against Ireland and Wales he was on the winning side in both forms of the game.

The Troon trio therefore contributed greatly to the Scottish wins.

The 1938 Amateur Championship

IN 1938 the Club had an enormously attractive week in prospect. It was a Walker Cup year and the Amateur Championship would be held at Troon with a strong American presence guaranteed. Ayrshire golf had never been stronger. Might there be, not only a British winner but a local winner? Such was the demoralised state of British golf where anything to do with the United States was concerned that it had become almost axiomatic that an American would win the Amateur Championship whenever the Walker Cup match was held in Britain. It had certainly been so in recent years, Jesse Sweetser winning in 1926, Bobby Jones in 1930 and Lawson Little in 1934 by a landslide margin (14 and 13) over the unfortunate Jim Wallace from Troon Portland. The star of the American Walker Cup side of 1938 was Charles Richardson Yates, a fellow Atlantan of Bobby Jones although a bit younger. Yates, the most amiable of men, nevertheless had a fierce ambition to take the Amateur title and thus emulate his guide and mentor.

In those early days Walker Cup matches and Amateur Championships held in Scotland attracted greater newspaper interest and larger crowds than when the event was held down south. A Scots venue naturally meant a more numerous Scottish entry and hopes were high for a native-heath Scot to be victorious. There were good judges, Sam McKinlay among them, who thought that Troon's own J. B. Stevenson might do very well when the championship got under way. McKinlay found himself in the unusual position of being both a noted competitor and covering the matches in his capacity as a golfing correspondent.

He was to take another celebrated Scots golfer, Hector Thomson, to the twentieth before conceding defeat. He regretted this because he felt it had weakened Thomson's chances in a later match against Yates. Even then Thomson would give Yates a semi-final to remember. It has to be remembered that two rounds per day was the norm and McKinlay as we have seen had pushed Thomson all the way. So too did his next opponent, L. G. Crawley – an equally good cricketer – and once again Thomson got through after a gruelling test and prepared to meet Charlie Yates in the semi-final.

Most people felt the schedule to be too demanding for Thomson and there were knowing nods when he went three down after eight holes. The gallery was fairly placid, they liked Yates' pleasant manner and if Thomson put up a respectable show they were happy enough. Then suddenly Thomson found a new source of strength and fought back

Amateur Championship at Troon, 1938
Wm. Howie, R. J. Shanks, F. Caldwell Kerr, D. White, Wm. Fergusson, J. W. G. Wylie, A. M. Holm, W. H. Johnson, W. Lindsay Carlow, J. L. C. Jenkins, F. D. B. Black, D. McCulloch.

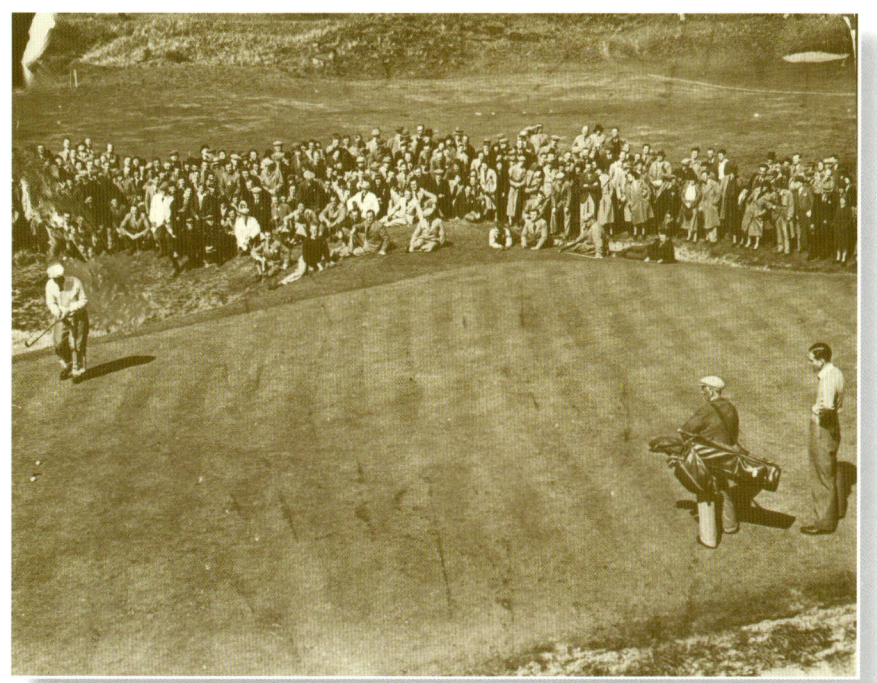

Thomson and Yates on the Postage Stamp green during their semi-final match, 1938 Amateur Championship

fiercely. The crowd rallied to his side as three down became two, became one, became all square, became dormie one in his favour. At that stage a par at the home hole was almost certainly enough. The Scot unfortunately pushed his shot to the eighteenth and Yates grabbed his chance.

The momentum was back with Yates although the crowd was still anxious that the Scot should win. He was however, now overdrawn at the Extra Hole Bank. He got a brave par at the first extra hole but Yates with the killer instinct birdied for hole and match.

His opponent in the final was formidable enough in all conscience. Cecil Ewing, "the Sligo dentist", had learned his golf in the West of Ireland and, like any good Connaught man, regarded what passed for winds on *"the breezy links o' Troon"* as mere gentle zephyrs. For many years to come he would be a stalwart player in the Irish international side and was both playing and non-playing captain. At Troon in 1938 he had the additional incentive that a win would mean a first-ever triumph for an Irishman in the Amateur.

He might almost have done it. In the first 18 holes he missed five putts of ten feet or less. As the wind rose until it was good Sligo standard, it was necessary to move forward the tees at the 10th, the 16th, and the 18th.

Chances there had to be taken and in the afternoon, Yates was always in command. The final margin was 3 and 2 and Cecil Ewing, who had been a semi-finalist two years before, had this time fallen at the final hurdle. The war almost certainly ruined any chance he might have had of going that one tantalising step further.

Charlie Yates was modest and humorous in victory and that summer he managed something far more difficult – to be humorous and modest in defeat. It was his misfortune to play for the American side in its first ever Walker Cup defeat at the hands of Great Britain, the match being played over the Old Course at St. Andrews. The British side won by seven matches to four with one halved but the rock of the American side had done his share. In the foursomes partnered by Ray Billows he defeated Alec Kyle and Charlie Stowe by 3 and 2 (there was a small irony here in that Kyle would succeed Yates in 1939 as Amateur Champion). In the singles his performance was even better since in the top of the list match he had a 2 and 1 victory over the Irish Wunderkind, James Bruen. Yates could fairly be said to have led by example.

It was not enough however. The Cup came here and Charlie Yates is rendered immortal by the graciousness of his bearing in defeat. To be beaten in representative games always hurts Americans deeply, perhaps because it is a comparatively rare occurrence.

The Cup had been presented, the speeches were being made, it was the turn of the Americans and

Yates stood up to say: "We're enjoying ourselves too much for any more speeches." He had noticed that an anaesthetised caddy was good-humouredly conducting a crowd some distance off using the broken shaft of a club as his baton. Yates seized his moment and called out to Gordon Peters, his great friend on the British team, "Let's give them our song Gordon." The song in question was "A Wee Deoch and Doruis" and from then on it was to be the Atlantan's trademark.

It was to be the beginning of a long and continuing link with Troon Golf Club.

In 1978 he was made an Honorary Member of a Club which could now prefix its title with the word Royal. Typical of the man, he bestowed one of his most prized possessions on his new Club, the telegram which Bobby Jones had sent him before the Amateur Final of 1938. It hangs in the Clubhouse to this day. In failing health, Yates was unable to travel to Troon for the Millennium Dinner but through the medium of video he delivered a message to his fellow members. His affection for the Club and for all things Scottish was patent and he found time in a busy life to put two or three thoughts together about his golfing experiences in Scotland.

The Road to Royal Troon

BY CHARLES R. YATES

My hopes and dreams in golf were achieved in 1938 when I won the Amateur Championship at Troon. This is the story of how my dream came true, going back to when I was eight years old and trailing Bob Jones around the East Lake Golf Course.

Bob was eleven years older than I and was unbelievably kind to allow me to follow along behind him. He personified that well known adage, "A man never stands so tall as when he stoops to help a boy." I followed his amazing career which climaxed in 1930 when at the age of 28 he won all four major championships in one year. Those were the Amateur and Open in Great Britain and the United States Amateur and Open on our side of the water.

I remember so well in 1926 when I was thirteen years old that I spoke to him after he had lost the U.S. Open by one stroke. That was in large part because he called a penalty on himself for his ball rotating as he prepared to shoot from the rough with no one looking on. I said to him a few days later at the East Lake Club, "I am sorry you lost." Bob's reply was, "Don't worry about it, son. You never know who your friends are until you lose."

In those pre-teen years, I was quite small but fortunately I put on some height and flesh by the time I was seventeen. That was the year that I won my first tournament of importance, the Georgia State Amateur. By this time, Bob had completed his competitive career.

He continued his love of the game but the pressure of tournament golf caused him to retire and, thereafter, he played mainly with his friends. Happily, Bob asked me to play with him from time to time and I had many enjoyable rounds with him. Thank goodness, our matches were usually four ball. I was smart enough to know that was the mode I should be in when playing with him. He did not try to coach me but let me play my own game. There was one exception to this on the par 3, 8th hole on the No. 2 Course

Bobby Jones and Charlie Yates at East Lake Country Club

at East Lake. It was a hole of 165 yards and I hit it ten feet from the hole with a right to left hook with a hooded seven iron. Bob reached in his bag, pulled out a five iron and wound up six feet from the hole. He said to me, "Charlie, what club was that you used?" I proudly said, "A seven iron." He said, "Don't you have anything but seven irons in your bag?" That taught me a great lesson about playing within myself.

Back in those early days of the Masters it was not hard to get an invitation to participate and it was my good fortune to play in the first eleven of these tournaments which, interestingly, is the same number that Bob participated in. He still was a beautiful striker of the ball but having been away from competition for four years, his putting suffered tremendously during the Masters. For example, one day in 1940 he shot a 64 on East Lake.

I had no expectation that I would win many championships. I didn't think I had the game to do so. Besides, I had worked hard in school and wanted to remain an amateur. My great hope was to make the United States Walker Cup Team which first came my way in 1936 at Pine Valley. At that time the matches were played over 36 holes and I was fortunate enough to win my singles match and my foursome match turned out to be a tie. Imagine my delight in 1938 when I was chosen for our team to play the match on the Old Course. I talked with Bob about some of the more critical things that I needed to do in order to prepare myself. He said we had the choice of playing with the British ball which at that time was 1.62 diameter or the American ball which was 1.68. He preferred that I consider the small ball as it was not as affected by the wind as would be the larger one. He was kind enough to get me a dozen small balls out of Canada and I worked hard trying to learn to play this ball. One day, I hit a particularly good drive on No. 16 and he asked, "Did you hit that one pretty good." I proudly said, "Yes." He promptly proceeded to pull out his big American ball and knocked it about fifteen yards further than mine. At the same time, he gave me his sly grin which I remember so well. He also advised me to work on pitch and run around the greens and play punch shots with my irons.

That year we sailed aboard the German liner, Bremen, and for several days after going ashore I still felt the rocking motions of the ship. I couldn't make a putt three feet long in my practice rounds at Troon and I so well remember that after hitting a fine second shot on No. 7 to within three feet, I did not even hit the hole with my putt.

I said to myself, you can't do any good taking your time so just walk up to the ball as quickly as you can and try that. It was a miraculous turn around and, thanks to my new method, I putted extremely well all week. I realized that it was mainly this fortunate putting experience that caused me to win.

My toughest match during the Amateur was in the semi-finals with Hector Thomson who had won the Amateur several years previous. The wind came from the right off the firth on the outgoing nine and I was able to fade a ball into the wind. Therefore, during the week I usually was up at the turn, but when I started playing home I kept losing an occasional hole. In playing against Hector, I found myself one down and one to go. Luckily for me, he pulled a drive into the rough on 18 and I hit a fine tee shot. My greatest memory is of the 4-iron I hit within eight feet and two putted on this last hole to square the match. We went to the 19th where I holed an eight foot putt for a birdie for the win. I won the finals, three and two against Cecil Ewing the jovial Irishman. Years later, he and I were partners in a foursome competition. He hit a beautiful second shot three feet from the pin and it was my time to putt. I did not even hit the hole. He said, "You certainly did not miss any putts like that at Troon."

After the final match was concluded I remember many spectators in the gallery coming up and congratulating me so warmly that I felt like I had never left home. I did not have a jacket with me for the trophy presentation on that Saturday night so I borrowed one from my great friend on the British Team, Gordon Peters. The Cup was presented by Troon Captain Lindsay Carlow.

Gordon had taught me some of the Scottish songs when we were at the Pine Valley matches two years previous. I remember that one song we made up was to the tune of Joyce Kilmer's Trees. It went like this:

"I think that I shall never see
a course as tough as Pine Vallee,
with trees and sand traps everywhere

*and divots flying through the air,
a course laid out by fools like me
but only God can make a three."*

At the end of the competition at Troon we headed to St. Andrews for the Walker Cup. I was deeply touched and honoured that Captain Francis Ouimet put me in the top

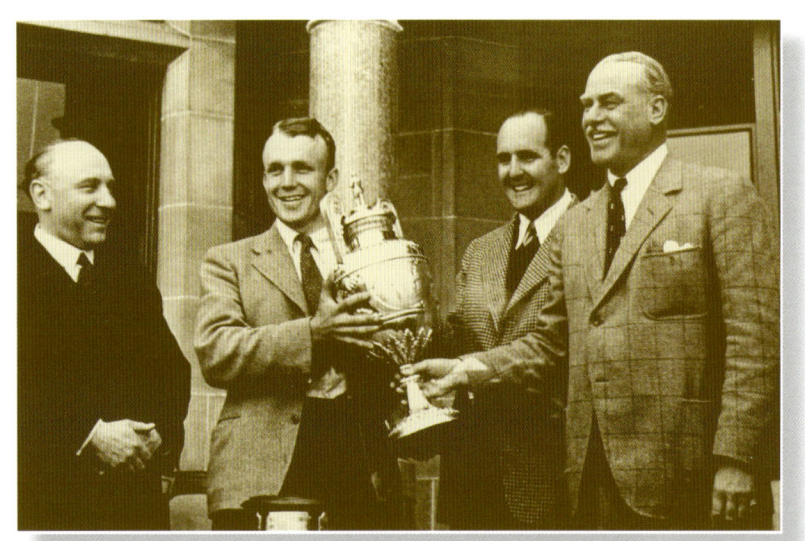

Charlie Yates receives Amateur Trophy from the Captain W. L. Carlow, 1938 Amateur Championship. Also pictured is losing finalist C. Ewing and H. Gullen, Secretary of The Royal and Ancient Golf Club

match where my opponent was a great teenager, Jimmy Bruen, who we promptly nicknamed "Bruen, The Bear." Jimmy's heart was so set on winning the Walker Cup that he decided not to play the previous week in the championship. We had quite a battle and I won on the 35th hole. I considered myself very lucky because you could easily foretell what a great career he would have in golf thereafter.

That was the year that the British side won the Walker Cup for the first time and there was such a degree of excitement that one cannot readily imagine. They called on some of us to say a few words to the crowd which was lined up all the way out to the Swilken Burn.

Behind the 18th green a bagpipe band was playing to beat all hell and it was being led by a caddy using a broken golf shaft for a baton. He was obviously as drunk as a hoot owl.

I had not expected to be called upon but when I walked up to the microphone I got the feel of the crowd and how joyful they were. As I walked up I saw Gordon Peters seated in a chair at the aisle nearest me. He had taught me that great Scottish song, A Wee Deoch and Doruis.

I said, "Brother Peters, come up here and help me sing this song because this crowd is too happy to hear any more speeches." Gordon had won his match nine up and eight to play and he obviously had been enjoying himself in the clubhouse while the rest of us were out struggling on the course. He came up and we did this song which since then I have repeated many times in various locales. Some years later, the President of the United States Golf Association said to me, "Charlie, you have gotten more mileage singing A Wee Deoch and Doruis than Bing Crosby has singing 'White Christmas'."

One of my fondest memories goes back to 1938 when our team came ashore at Southampton. There we were interviewed by the British working press. Now I feel so comfortable with the many gifted British writers. It has been my privilege to serve for many years as Chairman of the Press Committee at the Masters. Many in the media have come to be great friends and I am honored that I am an Honorary Vice President of the British Golf Writers Association.

In 1978, I was thrilled to receive an invitation to come to the Centenary celebration of the founding of Troon. That was the year that this wonderful Club was honored by being called Royal. In the chair as Captain was Bill Boucher-Myers whose son Bryan has this honor today.

Also this was the 40th anniversary of my great good luck at the Amateur and I was made an Honorary Member of Royal Troon. I thought it might be appropriate to make a gift to the Club on this historic occasion and accordingly had framed the original telegram I received from Bob Jones in 1938. I am proud that his cable is now hanging on the wall at the Club.

I want my fellow members of Royal Troon to understand there are many things I admire about golf in Scotland as compared to how the game is played here in

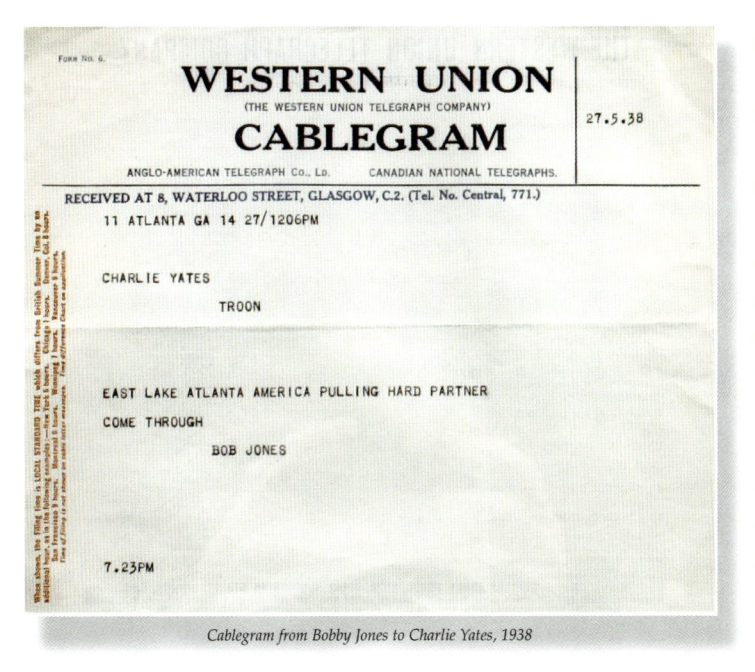

Cablegram from Bobby Jones to Charlie Yates, 1938

America. An indifferent shot that happens to wind up on the green receives no applause. Also, your handicap system is so much better than ours. This is because your handicaps are established only in competitive medal rounds. There is more good fellowship the way you play the game and, happily, a more friendly atmosphere. Also the dress code is much more traditional.

I wish to conclude this paper by relating a touching incident involving Bob Jones. You might think his office would have many photographs of important persons that he had met and played with but actually there were only two things related to golf on his walls. One was a line drawing of the Old Course at St. Andrews and a drawing in the attic of an old golf bag with wooden shaft Clubs and a golf cap over the driver. Alongside was this beautiful poem written by our famous journalist, Grantland Rice. It reads:

"When the one great scorer comes
to write against your name
he writes not that you won or lost
but how you played the game."

Memories of 1938

There had been high hopes that J.B. Stevenson would make the Walker Cup team and that he would be drawn against Charlie Yates in the Championship proper. Neither was to come to pass. The Troon player had been at odds with his putter from day one, although he achieved a temporary improvement by borrowing that of his sister for his second match round against Dennis Kyle. There was a place open in the Walker Cup side because of injury and there were three candidates for it, Cyril Tolley, Cecil Ewing and J. B. Stevenson and of these the Scotsman was widely held to be favourite.

His sister's magic wore off when he was called upon to face Cecil Ewing in the quarter-final and, in losing, he tamely missed three putts of a yard or under. This was a thousand pities because in the high winds of the first two days most of the American side had been dispatched. With great foresight *The Bulger*, as the *Evening Times* golfing correspondent, William Wilson, styled himself, pointed at the probable winner:

"The United States team, Charles Yates apart, have not the ability to play sterling golf when the elements are against them. He (Yates) has a pleasing briskness of approach to his short game. A rapid glance, a wide stance and away rolls the ball."

Over the piece *The Bulger* was pleased with the deportment of the crowd at the championship: *"There was a deal of stampeding but no untoward incidents occurred".*

In the championship Yates had got better as the tournament progressed, his outward 33 against Cyril Tolley was a magnificent exhibition of golf. On the eve of the final he received the tremendous boost of a telegram from his illustrious neighbour and friend Bob Jones, as Yates habitually called him. The wire read: *"Pulling hard partner. Come through."*

He survived a Ewing comeback in the afternoon and won the title comfortably enough.

At St. Andrews he did his best to rally his minimum squad of eight. Things were level looking after the first round of the foursomes, Great Britain well ahead in two and well behind in two. It looked like a division of the spoils, but from somewhere H. G. Bentley and Jimmy Bruen conjured up a half. Then John Beck, the British Captain, took the bold decision to leave out the heroic Bentley and go with Alex Kyle and Charles Stowe whose performances in the foursomes had been abysmal. Each responded by winning his singles on the Saturday.

There were crowds charging around with great velocity all over The Old Course and as things worked up to a climax, the noted Scottish amateur, Donald Cameron of Kirkintilloch, was given the task of acting as a 'minder' to Charlie Yates. On the eighteenth green the American showed more concern for his putter than for his own well-being and passed it to Cameron for safe keeping. The latter took it, looked at it and was astonished to behold a rusty-headed club with a shaft that was tied up in several places.

Eventually it was over and done with. Yates was Amateur Champion and he had taken points in both his Walker Cup matches. The Walker Cup itself however, would stay in Britain for the first time in 17 years for the Americans had lost possession of it. It was time for a song. *The Bulger*, scarce knowing whether to cheer or disapprove, summed up the general reaction well.

"Never before had such a thing been known but the grave R&A heads gradually lifted to reveal smiling faces and to forgive this display of American democracy".

The amateur/professional distinction was enforced in no sport with greater rigidity than in golf. Just before the Championship there had been a general admonition from the R&A to all amateur golfers that prizes won in competition could not be used for the purchase of wearing apparel or consumable goods. This may account for the superfluity of clocks and barometers in the homes of the top amateur golfers of the time. Increasingly top amateurs were arriving at the course in motor cars and the 1938 Amateur Championship was the first occasion on which it was necessary for Troon Golf Club to issue parking regulations.

It was scarcely 20 years since the war to end all wars had ended, and indeed many of the membership at Troon would be actively involved in both conflicts. There were ominous signs. Now the Territorial Officers were allowed to play over the course without charge as were the officers of the Fleet Air Arm, flying out from what was then known as Monkton Aerodrome. In a sad little postscript to the peace time years six Argentinian professionals were, in May 1939, granted permission to play Old Troon although not to use the Clubhouse. They were on a tour of Britain and Europe which had to be cut short as the international situation worsened. Once again the administrators of the Club would be faced with problems of war, although these would be very different from the difficulties of 1914.

The Second World War

THE problems of 1939 were not to be those of 1914. True, conscription was introduced immediately but it was a phased process. War was now more technical and there was no point in the mass rush to the colours that had happened first time round. Everyone of military age, however, would be eligible for call-up sooner rather than later. The revenue outlook was therefore bleak, assuming, as eventually happened, that members on active service would be excused in the matter of subscriptions and that the course would be opened gratis to visiting officers of the Services and those stationed close by.

Very unlike 1914, civilians would at once be involved, for war now meant the probability of aerial bombardment. An immediate blackout was imposed and that was bound to affect the desirability of the Clubhouse on a winter's night. Moreover there was food rationing from the onset and although Clubmaster and Clubmistress over the years performed miracles of improvisation, catering became steadily more difficult and by the early 1940s virtually impossible.

Economies would have to be made from the outset and in the very first month of the war there were swingeing cuts in staff. A clerical assistant, an assistant Club Mistress, a Kitchen Maid and a Table Maid found that they were no longer required. The green-keeping staff was almost halved, eight men replacing the original fifteen. All competitions were suspended for the time being and when they limped back into a rarified existence the proceeds tended to be for the Red Cross or the military charity Jock's Box, rather than for any individual winner.

It took about a year for the war really to get underway. Before that, there had been two false dawns and a promise of a return to normality. The Caddies' Treat went ahead as usual in January 1940 when they were bussed to Ayr, taken for high tea, given five shillings each and a packet of cigarettes or chocolates as their tastes dictated. The evening was rounded off with a visit to the Gaiety Theatre to see the well-known comedian, Jack Anthony, after which the buses were waiting to return them to Troon.

In May of that year, an attractive Exhibition Match was played in aid of the Red Cross Fund. The foursome was distinguished, the participants being Henry Cotton former and future Open Champion, Richard (Dick) Burton, then currently Open Champion, Alec Kyle, then Amateur Champion and finally, Jimmy Adams, the Troon born professional. The match was very well attended and the Red Cross was the better off by £520.

By May 1941 the Club was only serving meat dishes on Saturday, such was the extent of food rationing even at that early stage. A timely placement for an order of fifty cases of whisky and fifty cases of gin, not unconnected with the foresight of Sir Alexander Walker, postponed for a while the possibility that drinks would likewise have to be rationed.

The year 1942 was ushered in with the sad news that J. Harling Turner, the Duke's agent, had died. He had been an Honorary Member almost since the inception of the Club and had proved himself an influential and constant friend. It was another reminder that the 'originals' were slipping away.

There was little time to mourn his passing for, less than a month later, news came that the Admiralty intended to requisition the Clubhouse until the termination of hostilities. This seemed a fatal blow. If necessary one could play golf without food or drink but scarcely without a Clubhouse. What followed was a marvellous example of wartime co-operation.

The Troon club moved into accommodation in the Ladies' Clubhouse and the Portland. The occasional member who complained about the cramped facilities was tersely reminded that it was just as cramped for the receiving clubs and that a little gratitude would not go amiss. The Troon Clubhouse presented a grim sight, swathed as it was in barbed wire that started in the middle of the home green. Jock Brown, a well-known Troon Portland player and later member of Troon Golf Club – to say nothing of his having been a Scottish Cup – winning and Scottish international goalkeeper with Clyde – recalls that on the approach to the eighteenth on the Old Course, if down and the game gone, it was customary to be deliberately long with the pitch so that the ball would run through the barbed wire. This would mean that the ball would be eventually returned by one of the Wrens (Womens Royal Naval Service) – a good-looking bunch by all accounts – who worked in the Clubhouse and this would brighten an otherwise dull day.

W. H. Johnson retired as secretary in 1942 his successor being Alastair G. Brander, who had been Manager of the Union Bank of Scotland, in Troon and a member of the Club since 1935. He took up his new appointment in November 1942 and came as an experienced official for he had already discharged that post at Old Ranfurly. He came to a spartan situation for with the commandeering of the Clubhouse by the Royal Navy he did not even have an office of his own and perforce had to operate from a small office in the Ladies' Clubhouse.

In his favour was the fact that many peacetime duties were now superfluous, for the moment at least. The Old Course if playable was only just so, the fairways narrow beyond belief. When at length the war ended there was the protracted business of arranging compensation payments owed to the Club by the government for the latter's occupancy during the war.

Having endured privation for five years or so, it is pleasant to record that A. G. Brander stayed on in office to see better and easier days. He had the distinction of having a local landmark named after him, as a large section of casual water which was a permanent feature of the fifteenth fairway was affectionately know as Loch Brander. He retired in 1966.

Long before Alastair Brander's retiral the almost unthinkable had happened, Troon had a Lady Secretary, to be more precise an Assistant Lady Secretary. Miss Ethel Dawson discharged this post with great efficiency from 1942-70 and for the whole of that period was also Secretary of the Ladies' Club. She was unexcelled in her ability to recognise Members and occasionally non-members.

The number of green-keepers fell to three, the irreducible minimum one would have thought and surely the call-up could not now bite any harder. In another place, Norman Fergusson will describe what it was like trying to keep the course playable while landing craft simulated attacks, tanks drove up and down the fairways – and the greens too if not checked – and the occasional aircraft crash-landed on the course. There was little or no fuel for the tractor and in those pre-custom-built waterproof days it was a case of huddling against the weather in a surplus service greatcoat.

A. G. Brander, Secretary 1942-1966

Oddly enough, the Club was doing rather well financially, not so much because of incoming revenue as because of timely economies. The wage bill was down of course and perhaps the fact that the average age of the membership was rather higher than with most clubs meant there were never quite as many away on active service as had been feared.

As far as playing went things were very quiet and

*His Grace William Arthur Henry,
7th Duke of Portland, K. G.*

it was really a case of staggering on from month to month. In 1942 it was not found possible even to hold the Autumn Meeting and a Red Cross competition attracted a miserable eight entrants. Things grew tighter and tighter. The professional, Duncan McCulloch, was called to the Forces and his shop was requisitioned. There were persistent rumours that the Ministry of Aircraft Production intended to take over the Portland Clubhouse and that really would have been that. Strangely there were still eight regular caddies on the staff, including the famous "Kilwinning" Norman Fergusson will tell us about.

In the dreary depths of the Second World War, in the April of 1943, the Club sustained a heavy blow with the death of its Honorary President, the 6th Duke of Portland.

William John Arthur Cavendish-Bentinck had succeeded to the title the year after the Club had been formed and his association with it stretched over sixty years. Indeed if we add the 7th Duke's tenure of office then these two peers were the Club's patrons for 98 of the first hundred years. The 6th Duke was in every sense a well-wisher and no golfers ever had a better landlord. Time and again he demonstrated his interest and he readily made ground available for the Relief Course and the first Ladies Course.

Following the death of his father, the 7th Duke of Portland, William Arthur Henry Cavendish-Bentinck, was appointed Honorary President of the Club.

The first death of a member on active service to be noted in the Minutes occurs as late as November 1943 but before the conflict ended 19 members had given their lives – heavy enough in all conscience. J. L. C. Jenkins had, by this time, been elected Captain and he oversaw the return to a peacetime operation. This would be long and weary. People had begun to come to the course by car by the 1930's but petrol rationing would long survive 1945 and indeed the nation would live on short commons almost to the Coronation of 1953.

Combined Operations Golf Trophy

In May 1945, the Club received a letter from the Commanding Officer, Dundonald Camp inviting them to attend a meeting to discuss the offer of a golf trophy. A similar letter was received by Prestwick, Western Gailes and Barassie Golf Clubs and, in Troon's case the Captain J. A. McAra agreed to attend. The meeting held on Saturday 9th June ended with the Clubs agreeing to accept the offer of the new Trophy, which would be played for as documented in the Club's General Committee minute of 21st June 1945:

i) The Trophy to be competed for annually on a Saturday in September on courses of the four Clubs concerned in the following order: – Western Gailes, Barassie, Prestwick, and Troon.

ii) Foursome play by teams of six, handicaps of each foursome to aggregate NOT LESS than 12; Knock out competition, winners of the first round to play-off in the afternoon. Squared matches to be decided by playing extra holes, first hole won to decide.

Smoke Room War Memorial, 1939-1945

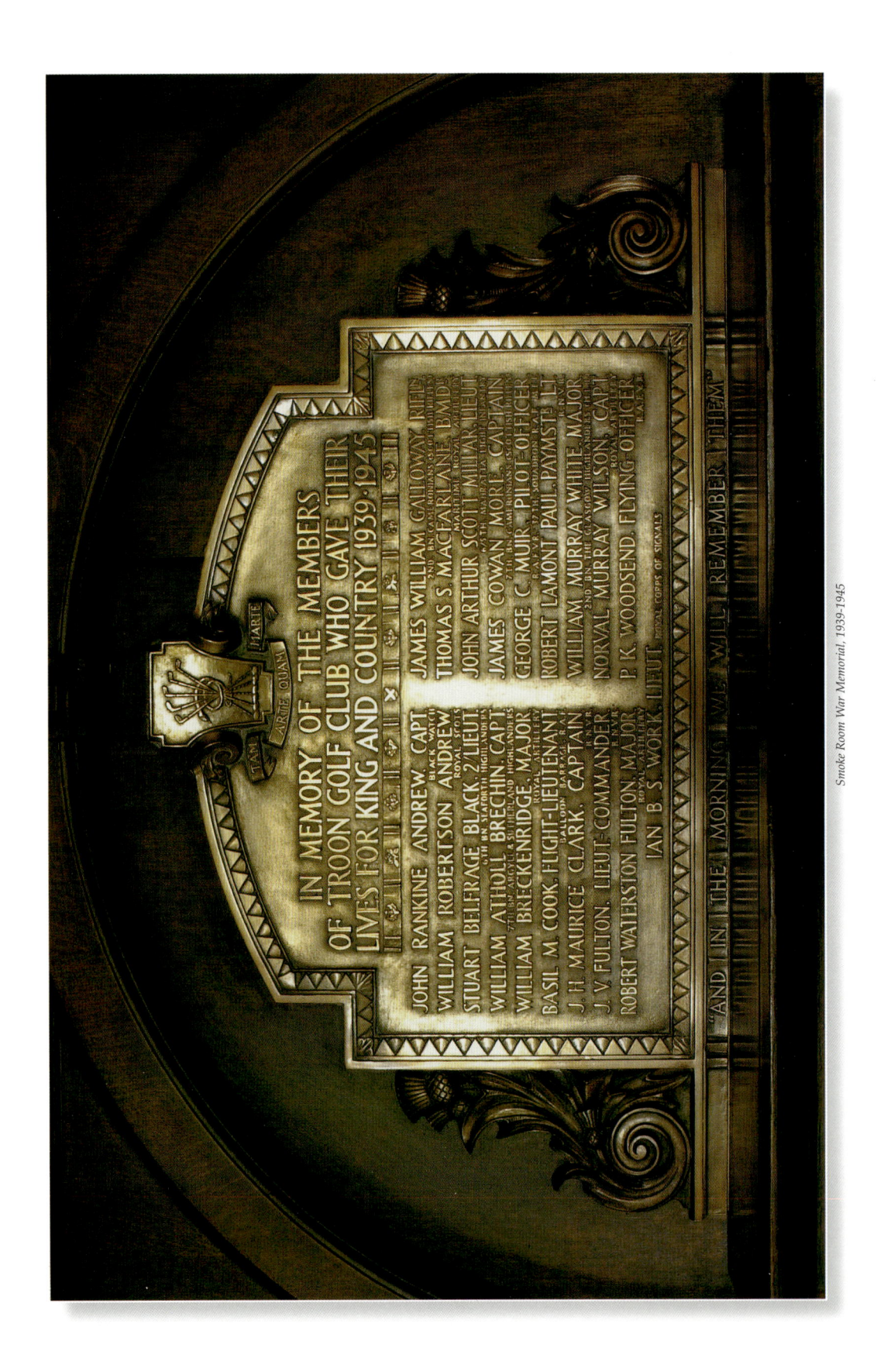

The first competition for the Combined Operations Golf Trophy was played on Saturday 15th September 1945 at Western Gailes and has continued annually. The trophy is rather unique in golfing circles being a scale model of a Commando landing craft.

Wartime Reminiscences of Dr. W. T. Sommerville

From 1939-45 the Clubhouse was occupied by the Royal Navy who used it as an Operations H.Q. At that time the Clubhouse was known as H.M.S. Gannet with a predominance of W.R.N.S among the naval personnel. It seemed to me at the time that my older brother must have courted most of them!

In like manner the Marine Hotel was commandeered and renamed H.M.S Dinosaur, occupied by a large number of high-ranking senior Naval Officers who when they could escape from their arduous duties were given the courtesy of the courses.

Meantime those members of Old Troon who were left had the courtesy of changing facilities and the use of the Bar in the Portland Clubhouse and due to the scarcity of golf balls played most of their golf over that course which had well-kept fairways and excellent greens.

I cannot remember that the Old Course was ever officially closed but the rough was horrendous, encroaching on fairways till they were more like rifle ranges while the greens got smaller and would be cut at most once or twice a week in summer. It was only near-scratch members such as Jimmy Jenkins or old Bob Garson who would venture there. Even one visit to the rough was "Good-bye golf ball!"

This was best exemplified by the case of the two Berts, Bert Bryson, a 6'2" ex World War One R.F.C. pilot who almost invariably played with one of the smallest members, "wee Bertie Wilson". One nice calm day they ventured on to the Old Course for "six out, six in" though neither had the requisite skill. They were back in the clubhouse in just over an hour when Big Bert told the assembled company in the bar that, while looking for his ball on the right of the fourth, he lost his clubs for five minutes and at the next hole where wee Bertie had a violent hook he himself was lost for five minutes. They walked in from there without a golf ball between them.

Another reason that the Old Course was hardly ever played was that the army practised landing tanks from landing craft. They would come zooming up over the dunes, which seemed much higher then to a 13-year-old boy, churning up the rough from the fourth to the sixth holes. As I recall, they were fairly respectful of our hallowed turf, avoiding fairways and greens wherever possible.

Another vivid memory is of a test pilot suffering engine failure as he attempted to land a Mustang. He calmly put the plane down on its belly on the fourth fairway, which was then 100 yards shorter. He ploughed a gully three feet deep diagonally from the right side of the fairway towards the green for some 200 yards. Fortunately he pulled up just short of the green.

My father told me that Archie Fraser, who lived in Blackrock House and was himself a pilot – indeed in 1939 he gave his Gipsy Moth to the R.A.F. to be used as a trainer – was first on the scene where he found the uninjured pilot sitting calmly on the wing, finishing a cigarette and retaining sufficient coolness and discrimination to accept a proffered Perfecto Fino.

The clubhouse was in a dilapidated state when the Club resumed possession of the by now bare-floored building. Two members deserve to be remembered in particular for their generosity to Troon. Robert Morton was the owner of Blackwood and Morton's carpet factory in Kilmarnock, later to be known as B.M.K. He donated new carpets for the Smoke Room, Dining Room, Hallway and Dirty Bar, which was then a cosy little room adjacent to the back door behind the 18th green. One entered, dirty wet shoes and all, straight off the course and in those pre-breathalyser days nobody ever passed through to the changing rooms without a dram or a G&T.

The other generous member was Robert Auld who ran a large lace mill up the valley, I think in Darvel. He donated lace curtains and heavy drapes for the rooms Bob Morton carpeted.

As far as I know subscriptions paid for the new post-war furniture though there may have been other wealthy benefactors such as Archie Fraser himself or Sir Alexander Walker who lived in Piersland Lodge and as the owner of Johnny Walker Whisky would have been able to help the club. Sir Alexander was an exceedingly keen though not over-talented golfer who would play literally in all weather. My father recalled sitting in the Dirty Bar one pouring wet windy day having thought better of going out when in walked Sir Alex in dry waterproofs to enquire "is there anyone here as daft as I am?" The reply was in the negative but he went out anyway.

Arnold Palmer receives Open Championship Trophy

CHAPTER THREE

Back to Normality

The Post War Years

THE first thing was to put the Club back on a sound financial footing. There was a mountain of work to be tackled. It could hardly have been otherwise as the course had been on a purely 'care and maintenance' basis for the last six years. There were debts owed to the other two clubs (Troon Portland and the Ladies') which needed to be paid. There was new staff to be recruited. The membership knew this well and although the increase in subscription proposed was 50% (six to nine guineas) there was little or no opposition.

Two major items of news occupied the headlines in 1949. It was announced that Troon would once again stage 'a British Open Championship' – an odd misuse of the phrase but it was so described. After a 27 year gap, the Open was coming back to Troon and again the notice of exactly one year was certainly not over-long.

At the Annual General Meeting of 1949 it was agreed that golf could henceforth be played on the Old Course on Sundays. It had of course been possible to play Sunday golf on the Portland since 1924 and on the face of it the time lag seems surprising, although the outbreak of the Second World War delayed matters. Having said that, the margin in favour of opening up the Old Course for Sunday play could hardly be described as a landslide at 48-42. There are several claimants for the honour of having hit the first Sabbath ball on the Old Course and claims and counter-claims of having waited in the Marine Hotel until midnight finished chiming and then going out to hit a ball by the light of car headlamps.

Minutes of Annual General Meeting, held In the Clubhouse on Saturday 30th July, 1949, at 2p.m.

Notice: The Notice calling the Meeting was taken as read.

Present: Mr. J. W. G. Wyllie, Captain, in the Chair, and eighty-seven Members present.

Apology: An apology was intimated from, D. M. Martin.

Minutes: The Minutes of the Annual Meeting, held on 31st July 1948, were read, approved and signed.

Finance: The Captain referred to the Audited Abstract of Accounts for the year ended 30th April 1949, and moved their adoption. This was seconded by Mr. Charles Carlow and agreed to.

Sunday Golf: Due intimation of a Motion by Mr. W. C. H. Gray having been given, this was seconded by Mr. R. D. R. Walker and put to the Meeting, "That, in view of the fact that there is no legal objection the Old Course should be opened for Sunday golf with immediate effect." Mr. A. W. Harvie moved, seconded by Mr. Stanley Dickson that the Old Course should not be opened for Sunday golf. On a vote being taken, the amendment was defeated by 6 votes. 48 for the motion, 42 against.

The Open Championship of 1950

THE Open Championship of 1950 at Troon marks the beginning of the lowest period of that competition's fortune. With isolated exceptions, such as that sense of history which impelled Ben Hogan to come and win at Carnoustie in 1953, American participation dwindled almost to vanishing point. Indeed there were years when the most likely American winner was not a professional golfer at all but the talented amateur, Frank Stranahan. The Open running was made by Commonwealth players such as Bobby Locke and Gary Player of South Africa and Peter Thomson of Australia. Even against such diminished opposition there were few British successes. Peter Alliss was promising but unfulfilled and later Neil Coles had great ability but his dislike of air travel meant that he could never cut a figure on the world golf stage.

If the golfing outlook was bleak it was matched by what was happening in the wider world. Britain was still firmly locked into the age of Austerity. Food was still rationed as was petrol and, more damaging in the estimation of some members, whisky was still on a quota allocation. Housewives had been cheered up by the recent bonus of an extra pound of sugar. Life was utilitarian and something of the wartime grimness lingered. There could scarcely have been a starker contrast to the cloche-hatted flappers of the 1923 Troon Championship and the optimistic jazz music.

Prior to the 1950 Open Championship one major change had been made to the Old Course. This involved the resiting of the 10th green from its position adjacent to the railway to its current position.

In that splendid summer of 1950 – which followed an equally splendid summer of 1949 – there was concern among the members of Troon that the course would not prove tough enough even against what was not exactly a vintage field. Still, Bobby Locke was a first class player and he would be defending the title which he had won at Sandwich. He himself perceived hay fever as his likeliest obstacle if the weather stayed fine. It is said, he persuaded the green staff to water the greens, having first of all won over the Captain, James Wyllie. This drove the mercurial Welshman, Dai Rees, into an incandescent rage when he found out. He declared that even at this early stage the Championship had been handed to Locke on a plate. Locke seems to have thought so too as he bestowed a set of woods on the Captain, not long after the presentation of prizes. The long-headed little Australian, Norman von Nida, obeyed the classic maxim of not getting mad but getting even by investing heavily on the chance of a Locke win. John Panton seemed the best home hope. He had the game if he could overcome a certain diffidence.

There would be 100 qualifiers of whom a maximum of 40 would play on the last day when the players would go out twice. By this time a lobby was building to support the notion that qualifying scores should be quite separate from the tournament itself. It took many years for this to happen. Indeed in the very early years of the tournament there was no mechanism for a cut and, in theory, all last day players had to go the distance. As this not infrequently meant running out of daylight, the expedient was adopted of sending officials out on the course. There they ascertained which players were 15 or more strokes behind the leader and these golfers were offered 5 shillings to stop playing. Most of them, being golf professionals and nothing if not pragmatic, were quite happy to sign off early in a situation where there was no money for a completed round.

Meanwhile the qualifying rounds came immediately before the main event and a young man, playing out of Troon St. Meddans because his handicap was lower there than at Troon. had a memorable day at the beginning of the 1950 Championship. He was Jimmy Armour later to be Professor Sir James.

There were eleven players from Troon Clubs who took part in the qualifying for the Championship, nine amateurs and two professionals. The amateurs were Brodie Lennox, J. B. Stevenson, and W. C. H. Gray from Troon Golf Club, J. Armour and G. S. Henderson from Troon St. Meddans, A. McKinnon and J. B. Brown from Troon Portland and J. T. Shaw from Troon Burgh. The professionals were Duncan McCulloch, Troon Golf Club's Professional and James Murdoch from Troon Municipal.

It was pleasing to do well in the qualifying rounds but there was always the danger of "leaving all the good stuff in New Haven" as they used to say in the American musical theatre. The outstanding round was a sparkling 65 by the Belgian, Flory van Donck, over the Old Course while Bobby Locke had a rock-solid 68 over Lochgreen. Every entrant of course had to qualify at that time so patriotic Scots were quite pleased with the performances of Eric Brown and John Panton who were on 71 and 74 respectively.

The Postage Stamp figured prominently, as it usually did. A German amateur, Hermann Tissies was going well enough until a prolonged acquaintance with sand at the eighth saw him run up a ghastly 15 and removed him from public life. Some played the hole well, some badly, some played it boldly, some timidly but the most intelligent playing of it in the whole week was by the Argentinian, Roberto de Vicenzo, a future winner. At the Postage Stamp he put his tee shot into a bunker. In reviewing the situation he remembered that there was an experimental rule in being by which in such situations shots deemed unplayable were only penalised distance. De Vicenzo went back to the tee and from it got down in two more. He thus saved his par and in doing so perhaps convinced the R&A that the temporary dispensation was a bad thing and should be terminated forthwith.

The de Vicenzo incident bore the highest profile, obviously, but the current Rules Secretary of the R&A, David Rickman, has stated that there were a number of incidents in 1951 and 1952 which indicated that the 'distance only' penalty was too lenient. This represented a change of heart for opinions had previously been canvassed. There was a majority in favour of lenity among the R&A membership and governing bodies at home and abroad had initially declared for 'distance only'.

The distressed state of British golf can be seen from the fact that of the top ten qualifiers for the tournament proper two were Australians, two were Americans, one was South African and one South American. In fairness things would look rather better after the four rounds had been played.

There had been certain difficulties with crowd

J. B. Stevenson and Jimmy Armour, an early photograph

Bobby Locke, 1950 Open Championship

control over the Old Course during the qualifying rounds. The pairing of Max Faulkner, a kenspeckle figure who would win the following year in Ireland and Dai Rees had attracted a gallery of almost 1000 who, almost to a man, ignored the ropes at the first and the eighteenth holes.

Programmes went well – 3000 were sold but there were no scores posted on the huge scoreboard. Those spectators who complained at this had their protests met with "There's no space for the qualifying scores and anyone who wants to know them can read them in the newspapers."

When all the qualifying scores were in there were one or two disappointments for the host course. Jimmy Armour's marvellous opening 71 followed by a 76 enabled him to qualify but then shooting 77 and 74 he missed the last two rounds by three strokes. Also out was the enormously gifted J.B. Stevenson from whom great things had been expected. On day one the British golfers, who had not shone in the qualifying rounds, began to hit back. Two inter-war stalwarts – Arthur Lees and Ernie Whitcombe – were round in 68 and 69 respectively. This was remarkably good golf but even although they were out early they must have been surprised to play right round to the home hole without a single spectator. To save their blushes they were joined at the home hole ... by a single spectator!

General opinion was that neither of these fine golfers was the likely winner and general opinion proved correct. Conditions on the second day were marginally trickier, although still good and there were only four rounds below 70. Dai Rees with a fine 68 did his best to falsify his own prophecy about Bobby Locke and led on 139 with Bill Branch a stroke behind and Locke a stroke behind Branch. This was exactly where Locke was at his most dangerous, tucked in behind the leaders' shoulders and graciously allowing them to take the spotlight ... and the attendant pressure.

There was a good finish in prospect. There would be 35 golfers contesting it and among them were five home Scots. These were the three professionals, Hector Thomson, Eric Brown and John Panton and the two amateurs, D. A. Blair and J. C. Wilson. Blair had already acquired youthful distinction by becoming the first player to win the Scottish Boys Championship which he did in 1935.

Open Championship 1950
Final Leaderboard

A.D. Locke (South Africa)	69 72 70 68 = 279
R. de Vicenzo (Argentina)	72 71 68 70 = 281
F. Daly (Ireland)	75 72 69 66 = 282
D.J. Rees (Wales)	71 68 72 71 = 282
E. Moore (South Africa)	74 68 73 68 = 283
M. Faulkner (England)	72 70 70 71 = 283
F. Bullock (England)	71 71 71 71 = 284
A. Lees (England)	68 76 68 72 = 284

Bobby Locke

On the third and last day Bobby Locke completed a record-breaking aggregate of 279, holding off his South American rival Roberto de Vicenzo. The contrast between the men was stark. De Vicenzo was intense, athletic, a little lucky perhaps, he was described as 'erratic' but escaped punishment. Locke went on his sedate way, giving the impression that he was auditioning for the part of Jeeves. There was almost no overt display of emotion, everything was in control and he had set his own slow rhythm. He was praised for his 'monumental calm', his 'unvarying precision'. Certainly his routine over putts never varied. He took ages over the three and four footers but any incipient irritation in the gallery was quelled by the undoubted fact that he holed nineteen out of twenty.

At the end of the day he had a two-stroke margin in hand over de Vicenzo. He had become only the fourth man in the twentieth century to defend his title successfully, following the trail of James Braid and the two Americans Bobby Jones and Walter Hagen. If the British were looking for hopeful signs they were there although it was something of a false dawn. Still, Rees and Daly had finished joint third and Fred Daly had had a wonderful last day with rounds of 69 and 66. The American amateur, Frank Stranahan also returned a 66 to prove that he was much more than the fortunate son of an extremely wealthy father. Fifty-one years later this remains the lowest round by an amateur golfer in the Open Championship although Stranahan has been joined on the 66 mark by Tiger Woods at Lytham in 1996 and by Justin Rose at Birkdale in 1998.

As usual when the captains and the kings departed the briefing was mixed. General opinion was that the event had been splendidly managed. The *Glasgow Herald* stated that on the last day the biggest crowd in the history of the championship had attended and that the spectators had behaved admirably despite earlier fears. But Henry Cotton had not been satisfied and stated that the Open championship must not be played again at Troon.

This roused the *Glasgow Herald* which retorted with a ferocious riposte though the article was attributed only to 'our golf correspondent'.

"Why does he (Cotton) say so? Surely not because at Troon his own record figure – shared by others – was well and truly beaten by a golfer (Locke) who has twice thrown down the gauntlet to him to my knowledge and still awaits a visit from the seconds.

The fact of the matter is that Troon, short by championship standards as it undoubtedly is, was just a little too good for the 200-odd players who were quite convinced that they could put it in its place once and for all."

So Troon had a second Open Champion and the almost deferential Locke, whose fingers seemed ever to be touching his cap in acknowledgement of a holed putt, joined Arthur Havers who had won in 1923. Havers had been correctly identified by Bernard Darwin as belonging to "that class of men who having achieved greatness once, find that their ambition has been satisfied".

Probably the Second World War had much to do with the fact that Locke was 32 before he won his first

Bobby Locke practising for 1950 Open Championship

Open Championship. In its review of the 1950 Open Championship, the *Playfair Golf Annual of 1951* made an interesting observation about the putting of the South African;

"He has always been a great putter on every type of green and unlike other great putters before him, he has no favourite distance. For instance, Bobby Jones was a wonderful approach putter but was not by comparison, a great holer-out. Sarazen was devastatingly good from the middle distance and they say that Vardon was a bad holer-out. Locke, on the other hand looks comfortable whenever his putter is in his hand and while he can be perfectly human sometimes, day in and day out he is probably the best all-round putter in the world today."

Locke was in certain ways a golfer well ahead of his time. His conservative demeanour and conventional dress disguised a very sharp and forward thinking mind. He was well aware that in the post World War Two world, the United States would make the running in world golf and he decided in 1947 that he would concentrate his efforts there.

In the short term the plan was brilliantly successful and that year he won six events. But golf, like so much else in the States, was and is severely protectionist and Locke found the atmosphere increasingly chilly, rather like the man who walks away from the casino with full pockets. He would not be alone in detecting a certain animosity towards him. Gary Player would have the same experience some ten years later.

Locke therefore decided to concentrate on the easier pickings of Great Britain and of his native South Africa. In the pre-Palmer years, American interest in the Open Championship was negligible and Locke was able to pick up three Opens in four years until another Commonwealth player, Peter Thomson of Australia, assumed control of things in the fifties.

An interesting footnote is to record the purchase by Royal Troon of Locke's Championship Golf Medal in 1993 when his family auctioned all of his trophies. It is now displayed in the Smoke Room.

Bobby Locke receives Trophy from the Captain, J. W. G. Wyllie, 1950 Open Championship

Open Championship Medal A. D. Locke, 1950

Back with the Club

THE successful ending of the second Open Championship to be held at Troon almost, but not quite, marked the end of the long years of austerity. Whisky was still delivered on a quota basis and housewives were expected to be grateful for an increase in the sugar ration six years after the guns had stopped firing. But there was a feeling that the worst was over and that people had begun to stop looking back.

In September 1951 the Club honoured the great American golfer Francis Ouimet by making him an Honorary Member and in so doing honoured itself. Ouimet had been the first American to break the anaconda-like grip of the great trio, Vardon, Taylor and Braid to win the US Open of 1913. He was now on his way to take up the captaincy of the R&A, an event brilliantly chronicled by Sam McKinlay in one of the greatest golf articles ever written – "Francis

Francis Ouimet playing-in as Captain of the Royal and Ancient Golf Club of St. Andrews, 1951

plays himself in" – in the *Glasgow Herald* of September 20th 1951.

It is worth noting about this pleasant ordeal that Ouimet drove the ball 250 yards straight as a die and that the retrieving caddie received, not the customary gold sovereign, but a specially minted gold five dollar piece. Worth noting too is the fact that at the pertaining exchange rate five dollars was worth almost exactly one pound. In this year too, *de facto* became *de jure* when the Ailsa hole officially became what everybody had long since been calling it – the Postage Stamp.

January 1954 saw the arrival of a new professional W. J. Henderson. He was a native of the far North, hailing from Brora in Sutherland and almost before his golfing career got started, he had been briefly at the local course. He then underwent four years' imprisonment in a Prisoner of War Camp. From there his path took him south to the Southcliff course at Scarborough thence back to Scotland with spells at Nairn and Buchanan Castle before he ended up at Troon.

He was a steady player, performing well in the Open a couple of times and a popular figure when the Northern Open was played a good deal nearer his native Sutherland. He also performed well in a number of professional tournaments, but was pre-eminently a teacher, regarded as quite excellent. His spell of sixteen years with the Club saw him earn the respect and affection of the membership.

Bill Henderson,
Club Professional 1954-1970

There was another change in 1953 caused by the sudden death of the Head Greenkeeper, Willie Fergusson. His successor was to hand, in the person of William's son Norman, who would be chiefly responsible for the state of the course throughout four Open Championships and whose views on the course were both penetrating and whimsical. When the military and naval presence was at its height during World War Two he somehow contrived to remain unperturbed and brought to bear his family's three generations of greenkeeping expertise.

William Fergusson, Head Greenkeeper 1923-1953

The Amateur Championships of 1956

CHAMPIONSHIPS and Troon were like the proverbial London buses. You waited ages for one and suddenly two came along together. In 1956 it was the Amateur and the Scottish.

The various championships which have been held at Troon have produced some noteworthy outcomes. Jack Cannon, for instance, was the oldest player ever to have won the Scottish and Cecil Leitch and Joyce Wethered in going to the 37th in the Ladies' Championship final in 1925 had set a new record for durability and a protracted finish. Even this marathon duel would be out-topped in 1952 when Moira Paterson was taken to the 39th hole by Frances Stephens.

Similarly, the Amateur Championship of 1956 produced the youngest winner ever with John Beharrell being crowned champion at the unbelievably young age of eighteen years and one month. Very few things are unique in golf and almost half a century later another Infant Phenomenon as the Americans would say, would emerge in the shape of Tiger Woods. John Beharrell's feat was nevertheless truly remarkable, not least in the cool command and mental stamina that he exhibited over the course of the week at Troon.

The championship of 1956 was a remarkable one for other reasons. There were no fewer than eight past or future Captains of the R&A in the field and tucked modestly away among the entrants was an American, Doug Saunders who would come within four feet of winning the Open 14 years later. J. B. Stevenson lost in the third round to Peter Grant, an eccentric American who was known as "Whisky Grant". This bibulous golfer struck a psychological blow on the 1st tee by having offered J. B. Stevenson a whisky. Grant indulged throughout the round and, on the brink of a one hole victory rather superfluously ordered his caddie to "Open the bar, Joe".

Beharrell's opponent in the final was Leslie G. Taylor of Ranfurly Castle who came into the championship in good form since, in the previous year, he had won both the Edward Trophy and the Tennant Cup. These trophies either had been or would be later won by such luminaries as Hector

Reid Jack putting on the on the 18th green against Joe Conrad

Thomson, Reid Jack, Bernard Gallacher and Charlie Green. Taylor would therefore be a formidable opponent although at the start of the Amateur there was no great reason to think of him as more than a golfer with a very good local reputation. Age would tend to favour him although Beharrell had the advantage that one of Britain's best professionals at the time – Charlie Ward of Little Aston – had long kept a beneficent eye on him.

There were approximately 4000 spectators when the final began. Taylor had got stronger as the week progressed and, although given a good examination by Ian Harris, a current Royal Troon member, in the 5th round, he won his quarter-final and semi-final by large margins – 4 and 3 and 6 and 5 respectively. It should be noted that 1956 was one of the two years in which the quarter- and semi-finals were played, on an experimental basis, over 36 holes. One of the quarter-finalists who had to work overtime in 1956 was Troon's own Herbert Thomson who had a fine championship although he actually competed in the Amateur flying the Newtonmore banner as his handicap there ensured that his entry would be accepted.

Beharrell, on the face of it, had had much the harder passage and already had the scalps of C. D. Lawrie, Frank Deighton, Reid Jack and Jimmy Bruen.

It had been a windy, dry week and on the final day the greens were lightning fast. The gallery was divided in its loyalties. There was a natural sympathy for the young Englishman but, equally naturally, there was also the desire to see the native Scot prosper. For a long while it looked as if the occasion had got to Leslie Taylor. John Beharrell, whose regimen was reputed to have included a 10pm bedtime, was off to a flier and was four up after eight holes, a strong position which he improved to the extent of being six up with eleven to play.

Charlie Yates and John Beharrell, Captain of the Royal and Ancient Golf Club, during the Centennial Celebrations of the Atlantic Athletic Club 1998

It appeared all over but Taylor rallied splendidly and took four holes in a row. Quite suddenly the match was open again. The surge was with Taylor and so, increasingly, were the sympathies of the crowd. Beharrell calmly asked the match referee how the state of play stood – and then pulled away at the next two holes to win by a comfortable five and four.

By way of a footnote, Leslie Taylor would return to Troon for the Amateur of 1978 and he would still be good enough to record a three and two victory over the young South African, Wayne Player, son of the illustrious Gary.

As for the winner, time was closing in on John Beharrell as it does on so many amateurs. He had been given a couple of years right at the beginning of his working life in which he could play golf but now the family business called. Henceforth he would almost exclusively play for enjoyment and contribute to the game as a selector for the England side and as an administrator. He proved as adept in this department as he had been as a player and he would attain the captaincy of the R&A. His most abiding golf memory would be of the day when, only a year out of school, he battled through strong crosswinds to become the most precocious golfer ever to win the Amateur Championship. More than forty years on he recollected that memorable week.

The Amateur Championship of 1956

BY JOHN C. BEHARRELL

When it was suggested that I write about my 1956 win of The Amateur Championship at Troon some forty-four years ago I sat down with a degree of bewilderment.

Many of my trips to Scotland have brought fond and lasting memories mostly devoted to golf and fishing. I remember our family holiday to Machrihanish in 1951 when I was thirteen. It was a big adventure and a long journey in a pre-war car and I can remember holing a seven foot putt on the last green to beat eighty for the first time.

In 1955 The Boys Championship was at Barassie when I experienced the genuine keenness and support for golf. It was a memorable week and Brian Aitken from Glasgow beat me in the semi-final and in turn he lost to the local star Stewart Wilson. There were four of us who carried Stewart back to the clubhouse from the scene of the final hole.

Recently, Stewart and I were able to recount some of the fun we had that week both being a little fatter and what hair we have somewhat greyer!

It was during that week that it was suggested I should perhaps consider entering for the Amateur at Troon in the following June. Under normal circumstances I would still have been at school. However, when aged sixteen I contacted a virus illness which prevented me from playing in The Boys Championship in 1954. The outcome was that the medics of the day suggested I should spend plenty of time outside playing golf for the next eighteen months but then I had to get involved with the real world of work and study.

I received encouragement from my parents to play golf and I am sure they wondered where it would lead. Having three children and now seven grand children I can see how doubts must have been in their minds. I was lucky enough to have a good coach in Jack Cawsey and was determined to make the most of this golfing sabbatical. At my home club, Little Aston, I was able to play with international golfers and especially Charlie Ward who was a magical golfer and a top Ryder Cup player from whom I learnt a lot and against whom I could measure my performance.

In 1955-6 I was able to play in a number of top professional and amateur events but the quality and standard of the entrants was very different then.

In 1955 for the Boys Championship I stayed at The Sun Court Hotel overlooking the 16th fairway at Troon followed by the beauty of the Clyde and Arran in the distance. That year I never set foot on Troon but I got the feeling it was something special and it set me a target for the Amateur in 1956.

I played in the English Amateur Championship in April 1956 at Royal Lytham St. Annes where I had the good fortune of beating that charming man Alan Thirlwell by a convincing margin. Alan had won the English Championship in 1954 and 1955 and that gave me added confidence for when I arrived at Troon a few weeks later. The Amateur was the big one and meeting the star players was a thrill. There were players such as Joe Carr, David Blair, Guy Wolstenholme, Gerald Micklem, Tony Duncan, Reid Jack, Max McCready and many others. I think it was only J. B. Stevenson who played from the home club that week. I had four practice rounds two of which were with Michael Bonallack.

On the Sunday before the Championship started the course was closed and most of the players devoted their time to practising and hitting shots up The Portland Course. At the time I felt reasonably confident with my long game so found a small corner on the Junior course where I spent six hours just practicing run-up shots realizing the course was running fast and the greens were small. It was my confidence in that shot that carried me through.

In the Fifties the amateur game received much publicity which sadly is not the case today. Television had not touched the sports arena at all but the press certainly went to town. It can be said with certainty that all the players were playing for the fun of amateur golf with perhaps one exception and that was Doug Sanders – from America – who very shortly after being beaten in the first round turned professional. Players in those days saved their pennies and used their precious holiday allocation to play in championships.

Golf was just beginning to get back on the road after the Second World War so there was much interest at Troon where the keenness throughout the West of Scotland was *second to none. I know that Charlie Yates who won in 1938 felt the strength and following of golf at Troon was very special.*

It's always good to get away in the first round of a championship after all the waiting and my first opponent said that if I could control some of my emotions I might get through a few rounds – I took heed. Dr Bill Tweddell and his wife Dods from The Midlands took their annual pilgrimage to The Amateur. He won in 1927 and was runner up in 1935 and was full of support for me and gave me much useful advice during the week. Their son Michael remains a good friend and strangely we first met on the cricket pitch. The crowds showed immense appreciation for good shots and in spite of natural eagerness for a Scottish winner, I received much encouragement. In the Fifties there were few players in their teens so I was the exception, which is very different from today.

The course has undergone changes since the Fifties with the main alterations being at the sixth where there used to be a large valley in front of the green which I seem to remember made for a blind third shot. The other major change was at the eleventh which was a short sharp dogleg to the right and now of course there is the new long eleventh resulting in the new twelfth.

I felt quite calm as the week of the championship progressed and enjoyed more and more the atmosphere of Troon and the championship. I managed to get a few notable scalps early on and then in the sixth round I came up against Gene Andrews who in 1954 and 1955 won The Public Links Championship of The United States. It was my seven-iron run up shots that came to my rescue and I had my closest match of the week and won by 2/1. I was recently told that it was Gene Andrews who taught Jack Nicklaus the art of measuring distances on a hole about which Jack was so particular. This in turn has had a considerable influence on the modern game of today.

At the 1956 championship the quarter-final, semi-final and final were all 36 hole matches and in spite of my earlier illness I felt there was no one better prepared than myself having spent much time in running and getting fit and strong. In the quarter-final against Dr Frank Deighton I played my best golf of the week and this allowed me to play Reid Jack in the semi-final. He was quite rightly regarded

John Beharrell playing his second shot to the 7th hole in afternoon round in the final, 1956 Amateur Championship

as the best player in the latter stages. We had a tough match and like many close encounters there was one turning hole. This was at the famous Postage Stamp in the morning. For the first time in the week I was one down. Reid played to the green first and just cleared the front bunker with his ball staying above ground – I followed and pitched within inches of Reid's ball and the ball fell back into the bunker. From there I holed out and won the hole and went all square instead of two down which can be typical of match play.

In the final on Saturday I played Leslie Taylor from Ranfurly Castle who had a strong list of achievements in Scottish golf. When I arrived at the clubhouse I was handed a pile of telegrams from well wishers. The day was grey and windy with a big crowd that kept growing and gradually I saw faces of friends from home who had travelled up overnight which in those days was a long journey. My doctor even came to give support. By the sixth hole in the afternoon I was five up and then at the seventh I had the good fortune of holing my pitch which made me six up. All was not over because then I lost the next four holes. The wind had risen to force eight and the crowd was still growing with dust flying. We waited on the twelfth tee for twenty minutes allowing the crowd to clear. During that interval I said to the referee, Neil Selway, Chairman of The Championship Committee – "Excuse me sir, can you tell me the score?" The press made quite a meal out of that including Leonard Crawley the golf correspondent for The Daily Telegraph. I then managed to hole a slippery down hill putt on the twelfth and won the thirteenth and fourteenth for victory.

Every match that week was played in the true spirit of the game and all my opponents were gracious in defeat which could not have been easy when I was a lad of just eighteen. By the end of the week I had played eleven highly competitive rounds.

John Beharrell receives Amateur Trophy from the Club Captain, F. D. B. Black, 1956

I can still remember being escorted from the fourteenth green back to the clubhouse by two large policemen and then of course there was the prize giving. This took place just outside the main front entrance with the car park full of spectators. It's an experience that will remain with me for the kindness of the members and the support of the crowd. Even now that I have more time to enjoy golf I keep coming across people who say they remember watching me at Troon etc etc,

People now ask if it would have been better to have had more experience and was it just a flash in the pan? I believe if you have a chance it must be taken and during a week the winner has to come away with a few breaks. During the rest of 1956 I played reasonably well and played in The Dunlop Masters at Prestwick and in the Home Internationals at Muirfield. There were added pressures without doubt and I did have to keep my part of the bargain with work and study. My grandfathers, father and uncles were engaged in industry and commerce and it was expected that I would go in the same direction. My week at Troon did present a time of decisions but all I can say is that I am here to tell the tale some forty four years later and in spite of golf's many frustrations I still love playing. I played in five more Amateur Championships and reached the latter stages in two of them. With a young family and a job it was inevitable that golf tended to drift into the background. I played at Royal Troon in the Amateur in 1978. My preparation that year was to hit a few practice shots on the playing fields of my sons' school in Yorkshire at seven in the morning because half term clashed with the championship.

I played in the Sean Connery Pro Am at Royal Troon and had a memorable two days playing with Brian Huggett and Cliff Michelmore. Brian had of course finished third to Arnold Palmer at Troon in The Open of 1962.

In order to compile these few words I have borrowed from my mother the scrap books which she still keeps and it becomes frightening how one can remember events so far back compared with happenings of a few weeks ago!

It was a great thrill to return to Royal Troon as Captain of The Royal and Ancient Golf Club in 1999 when I was made to feel so welcome. Then to be made an Honorary Member was the greatest honour which I accepted with very considerable pride and gratitude.

There are certain clubs which as one approaches one feels special excitement mounting and Royal Troon is one of those clubs. With the membership, course, clubhouse and *general ambiance it all goes the whole way in allowing Royal Troon to make such a major contribution to the traditions and standing of golf.*

John Beharrell
2 June 2000
(Forty four years to the day of my win.)

The Scottish Amateur Championship of 1956

The Scottish Amateur Championship of 1956 was chiefly notable for three things. It followed custom in providing a worthy champion in Dr. F. W. G. Deighton, there were fine performances from Troon members J. B. Stevenson and Herbert Thomson and there were rainstorms of Old Testament proportions.

For J. B. Stevenson, starting on his quarter-final against Deighton there was the knowledge that he was forty-four and this might be his last realistic shot at the Championship. He had been around for a long time and had indeed been a semi-finalist as far back as 1931.

He made a deceptively bright start against the tall doctor, winning two of the first three holes but gradually Deighton hauled him back. One up going to the eleventh, the Glasgow man then played the shot of the championship. He was 25 yards through the green with J.B. sitting nicely at the green's edge. An exquisite approach over the twelfth tee saw the ball draw up a foot from the hole. Stevenson was visibly shaken and the predictable three putts left him two down where he might have been all square. Deighton was never close-hauled again and when he rounded off a 4 and 3 victory he was two under fours.

It is not always the biggest names that prove dangerous and in the whole of the tournament nobody gave Deighton a harder run than A. D. Gray of East Renfrewshire where there was only one hole in it.

It was though a good week for Troon golf. There was a sporting chance that Troon would provide another finalist in the shape of Herbert Thomson who had reached the quarter-finals in the Amateur Championship and was currently West of Scotland Champion. He survived until the sixth round when another member of the Thomson clan, Sandy who played football for Rangers and golf at Falkirk Tryst had a very convincing win thanks to a disastrous loss of six consecutive holes by Herbert.

As so often happens, after so many cliff-hangers the final itself was something of a procession. Deighton in tremendous form, established a comfortable lead thanks to a first round of 69. There was no letting up in the afternoon and his margin of victory over Alec Macgregor of Largs was a conclusive 8 and 7.

Frank Deighton with Scottish Amateur Championship Trophy, 1956

Ayrshire Golfers 1930-60

IT would have been difficult in this period to have found a more exacting area than Ayrshire in which to play top class amateur golf. Fife would have some claim to equality, perhaps from time to time the Lothians and Renfrewshire, but year after year the Ayrshire coast produced golfers of the top flight. Partly this was because an abundance of courses made it possible for youngsters to take up the game fairly easily whereas it was much more difficult to get launched in Glasgow. In the 1930's, the heyday of the Saturday morning golfing trains from Glasgow, it sometimes seemed that there could hardly be a man left in the city, so dense were the throngs that alighted at Gailes, Barassie, Troon and Prestwick.

The brightest star in the Troon firmament was, by common consent, J. B. Stevenson who was described by those who played with him as a "supreme stylist". He was widely held to be a better stroke-play player than a match-play one and it is true, however surprisingly, that he won neither Scottish nor Amateur Championship, both of which were reckoned to be well within his capabilities. He was doubly unlucky in the time he lost from the game. There was of course little or no competitive golf during the Second World War but that affected everyone. What made Stevenson's case so angering was that when war broke out he was just coming off a four year break from the game due to an R&A ruling that his job as the representative of a golf ball firm rendered him ineligible for amateur competitions.

There were times when it seemed as if the object of the authorities was to stop as many golfers playing as could be done. Two other prominent Scots golfers would be debarred from professional tournaments (the Open Championship excepted) in the five years following 1945. These were Jack McLean and Hector Thomson although this exclusion was the doing of the P.G.A. and nothing to do with the rule-making authority.

They started young in Ayrshire and James Armour had won the British Boys Championship at 17 years of age. His victory at Hoylake in 1947 put him on the same roll of honour as Laddie Lucas and Jimmy Bruen and in years to come he would be joined by Michael Bonallack, the ill-fated Finlay Morris, killed in a car crash at the outset of his professional career, and Jose-Maria Olazabal. In 1955 Stewart Wilson emulated James Armour's feat when he won

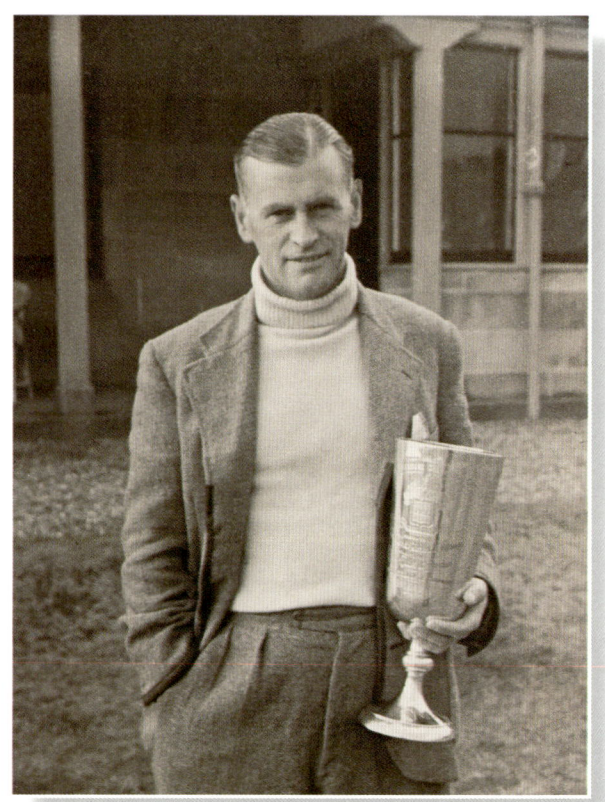

J. B. Stevenson with Hillhouse Cup, 1954

the Boys' Amateur Championship while playing out of Troon St. Meddans. Stewart Wilson had only to go along the road to Kilmarnock Barassie but in another sense he travelled far, for no final had gone to such lengths as his. Thirty nine holes had been played before he squeezed through against the tenacious B. J. K. Aitken of Glasgow Academy. John Wilson in 1957 almost became Troon's third Boys' Amateur Champion but had to give best to David Ball at Carnoustie, 3 and 2 the margin. Three years after his win, James Armour did something rather more remarkable.

In 1950, Locke's year at Troon, he qualified for the Championship proper. He would also win the County Championship in 1952, his club mate H. C. MacLaine (Colin) having done likewise the year before. To win this championship meant almost certainly that a couple of internationalists would have to be bested en route to the championship and the prospect of having to overcome a Walker Cup player was quite realistic.

It should perhaps have been even more realistic since Ayrshire golf abounded with players who appeared to have established their credentials beyond any doubt but who did not catch the eye of the selectors. Most judges thought J. B. Stevenson good enough and although the fact that 4 countries made up the British Isles side meant that some horse-trading was inevitable, the continued omission of Hamilton McInally of Irvine raised hackles and not only in Ayrshire. "Hammy" had won three national championships but could not force his way into a side which could muster but a single point in the United States.

This omission would be put right by proxy, as it were, for his cousin, Jimmy Walker, in 1961 was both finalist in the Amateur and a member of that year's Walker Cup squad. Further up the coast was the mighty Jock Morrison of West Kilbride, now a Troon member. He was then a phenomenally long hitter who literally hit balls out of shape and the manufacturers had an agreement whereby he would return such balls to their laboratories for further testing. Also starting at West Kilbride was Sandy Sinclair, a semi-finalist in the Scottish in 1947 and a future captain of the R&A, although by then he had long played his golf at Drumpellier. He will emerge again in these pages to play a very prominent role at the time of the Troon Centenary in 1978.

Playing out of Prestwick and a Troon Member of many years standing was another talented amateur golfer W. Crawford H. Gray. Crawford reached the final of the Scottish Amateur Championship in 1954, at Nairn, losing to J. W. Draper. He was first reserve for the Scottish Team in 1954, but never achieved a full cap.

The Prestwick St. Nicholas Club also produced many fine players in this area notably W. C. (Cammy) Gibson who won the Scottish in 1950 at Prestwick and the redoubtable J. R. McKay who lost the 1953 final at Western Gailes. Both men had the same opponent in their respective finals, Major David A. Blair. Both players would also represent their country in the Home Internationals.

Of the several golfers who are members of Troon and who won the West of Scotland Championship

Herbert Thomson with son during Evening Times *Tournament of 1954*

during this period, special mention must be made of H. V. S. (Herbert) Thomson who took the title in 1956 and became a revered senior member. He alone won when entered as a Troon member whereas Sandy Sinclair, Jim Hastings and Gordon Cosh ... the latter a multiple winner ... were Troon members but all entered from other clubs.

Frequent opponents were the top players of Troon Portland. Possibly their best player between the wars was James Wallace who reached the Amateur Final at Prestwick in 1934 only to find the American, Lawson Little, in devastating form and himself on the wrong end of a 14 and 13 margin. Other notable Portland golfers were the Clyde and Scotland goalkeeper, Jock Brown, Alastair McKinnon and A. C. Miller, another golfer footballer. "Minty" Miller, as he was generally known, was adept at both games. He was on the verge of Rangers' first team and in 1955 he reached the final of the Scottish Amateur Championship before giving best to Reid Jack. Thereafter medicine claimed him and he was lost to both sports.

And finally, W. D. "Dick" Smith's club affiliations were numerous. Ayrshire born, he played his golf at Prestwick and latterly at Troon but in his heyday as a golfer he carried the banner of Selkirk. This was in the Open Championship of 1957 when he finished a highly-creditable fifth and thus took the Silver Medal awarded to the leading amateur. The medal was later presented to Royal Troon. The next year he won the Scottish Amateur and the year after that his reward for making the Walker Cup team at Muirfield was to be drawn against Jack Nicklaus in the singles. He acquitted himself well, his first 18 holes were achieved in level fours but, Nicklaus being Nicklaus, Dick Smith was a blameless five holes down and five and four was the margin. It was appropriate that he should win his Silver Medal in a

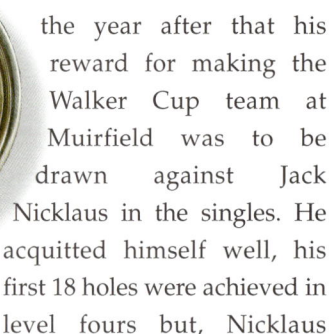

Silver Medal.
W. D. Smith
Open Championship 1957

year that Locke won the Open. Both men were highly efficient, both achieved considerable success with an almost total absence of flamboyance.

Observations from H.V.S.

Herbert Thomson (H.V.S.) was a very senior member of Royal Troon and one of the dwindling number who could still recollect golf in its pre-1939 days. On a cold winter afternoon he reminisced as he looked out of the clubhouse windows:

H.V.S.: J. B. Stevenson was the best player I have seen in my time here. For a while he was an automatic pick for the Scottish team, playing 1 or 2, but he said to his national Captain, Bertie Brand, "Captain, I'm not playing well, I think you should drop me down." He meant, of course, to 6 or 7 but Bertie dropped him right out of the team and he never played again.

R.A.C.: *How good was he in Scottish terms?*

H.V.S.: One of the very best. He was an artist. Particularly, he was red-hot with a three wood from the rough. I felt that of all the amateurs round here, he never got full credit.

R.A.C.: *It was widely felt in Scotland that there was a bias against Scottish players when it came to Walker Cup selection. Do you agree?*

H.V.S.: It never affected me! But perhaps it did wee Eddie (Hamilton). His record was astonishing – two championships and two semi-finals in the Scottish Amateur Championship in four consecutive years. He just didn't seem to fit. I can say the same thing for Hammy McInally.

R.A.C.: *Which professional made the greatest impact on you?*

H.V.S.: Arnold Palmer was by far the most charismatic.

R.A.C.: *What makes the difference between the very good amateur and the professional?*

H.V.S.: The real professional is more in control of his functions, above all he has the ability to repeat.

R.A.C.: *Have you always played in Ayrshire?*

H.V.S.: Not at all. I started at Newtonmore where I acquired my shinty swing. Then I played at Arbroath for a while before coming down here post-war.

R.A.C.: *Did you play much golf during the war?*

H.V.S.: Practically none. Equipment was very short, you know. In 1946 I had heard the Scottish was to be played at Carnoustie. I managed to get two golf balls from the N.A.A.F.I. (Navy, Army and Airforce Institute) and another one from a shop at the top of Buchanan Street in Glasgow and with my three balls set off for the championship.

R.A.C.: *How did you fare?*

H.V.S.: Pretty well. I qualified from the stroke-play with just the three balls and when I qualified for the match-play I got some more from the Carnoustie professional. I got to the last 16 and went out to J. C. Wilson of Cawder.

R.A.C.: *Which of the Troon professionals did you know best?*

H.V.S.: Bill Henderson was a great chap. He was very well read, not very formally educated but very well read. He was a good player and was twice fifth in the Open Championship, once when it was held at Portrush.

R.A.C.: *You won the West of Scotland Amateur Championship?*

H.V.S.: Yes, at Prestwick in 1956. I beat J. R. Cater one up.

R.A.C.: *You led off the Open, so to speak, in 1962 – were you petrified?*

H.V.S.: Not at all. It was a lovely morning and a neighbour of mine, Archie Holmes, came down in his carpet slippers to see me started. Then he went home. On looking at the starting board the day before Peter Thomson had thought that my time was his.

R.A.C.: *Did you see much of him?*

H.V.S.: He and I played a bounce match against another couple and we lost 2 and 1!

R.A.C.: *How do you assess him?*

H.V.S.: He was the most natural player. He used his eyes and in those days you used your eyes not charts.

R.A.C.: *Have you any bad memories?*

H.V.S.: I once, as it happened, beat a very promising young golfer 10 and 8 in a big match and I did not enjoy that.

R.A.C.: *What changes have you seen in your time at the Club?*

H.V.S.: In general, Ayrshire golf was much more competitive than where I started in the North-East. But back in the 1950's Troon was not a bustling club. Very few people for example played in the evenings. It is now a thriving club and very much healthier than, say, 30-40 years ago.

Herbert Thomson and Bill Henderson

The Open Championship of 1962

THERE was not nearly so long to wait for another Open Championship this time around. The first had been in 1923, the second not until 1950 but the wait for the third was a comparatively modest 12 years and there were good grounds for believing that this would be the most important yet as a young man from Latrobe, Pennsylvania had almost single-handedly rescued the event.

It would scarcely be an exaggeration to say that the Open Championship was preserved as a major golfing event by the exertions of one man and that man was Arnold Palmer. In terms of international prestige the Open Championship had never stood lower. In the middle and late 1950s it had almost disappeared from the schedules of the top American professionals. Ben Hogan, with a stronger sense of golfing history than most of his compatriots, had come over and won at Carnoustie in 1953 but he did not feel particularly obliged to defend his championship. There were years when a severe judge would have said that there were only three players of world class in the field, those three being Gary Player, Bobby Locke and Peter Thomson.

Arnold Palmer came to Troon in 1962 as defending champion but he had won at Birkdale from a less than stellar field. However, it is fair to say that Dai Rees – only a stroke adrift- came near to pulling off an unexpected British win. But in the year since Birkdale Palmer had been doing his recruiting sergeant and the result was a much more representative American entry. The still young Jack Nicklaus would be there, so too Phil Rodgers and Sam Snead, although the latter was moving swiftly towards the veteran stage.

The focus of attention however was Palmer who from the start of his professional career had shown a marvellous faculty of attracting a faithful coterie of supporters, "Arnie's Army". Perhaps more than any other golfer of his time he brought people to watch major golf events who hitherto had taken no interest in the sport. In the short term this was not necessarily advantageous on a course as long and narrow as Troon.

Members of courses on the Open Championship roster tend to be splitminded once the championship begins. They enjoy the kudos which comes with the record-breaking round but they do not want their course to appear to be an easy touch. Sam McKinlay of the *Glasgow Herald* had no fears for Troon on this score:

"The course will be rigorous enough. The week's winner will have to think well and play well before he can master the New Troon"

Arnold Palmer and Kel Nagle on 18th green during Open Championship of 1962

The major Course alterations prior to the 1962 Open Championship were the creation of the new eleventh green and the re-routing of the twelfth hole. The change to the eleventh required the clearance of a large area of whin bushes as the green was moved a hundred and fifty yards in a northerly direction, to today's location. This was the first occasion that Troon's greenstaff had the assistance of mechanisation, when a bulldozer was brought in to clear the whins for the new fairway and to create the green. After the area was cleared, many trailer-loads of topsoil were transported in to create the fairway following which it was seeded. On the twelfth hole a new tee was created and the routing of the hole changed. This did not involve the same amount of work as a tractor path already existed on the line of the new fairway. However, it did involve the construction of a new tee for the fourteenth hole on the Portland Course, the tee of the day located on today's twelfth fairway on the Old Course.

At this stage in the history of the Championship there was increasing dissatisfaction with the qualifying arrangements which involved every entrant. These were disliked on two counts – they were a deterrent to the top overseas golfers and entrants had a widely held feeling that all their "good stuff" was being left behind on the qualifying courses. Cyril Horne, writing in the *Glasgow Herald,* called for the abolition of qualifying rounds from the championship proper, saying that they should be over and done with long before the Open week itself.

The 1962 Troon Open got off to a good start with a Scot, Eric Brown, leading the qualifiers with rounds of 70 and 69. A stroke behind came Joe Carr and Bruce Devlin of Australia who may both have thought that they had peaked too soon. Sam Snead perhaps had a point to prove in being the only man, apart from Eric Brown, to break 70 on the Old Course in the qualifying rounds. Financial rewards at this time were still very modest and for leading the qualifying field Eric Brown received a meagre £50.

There were seven players from Troon who took part in the qualifying rounds Gordon Roberts, the Club's Assistant Professional, H. V. S. Thomson from Troon Golf Club, and the Club Professional Bill Henderson. The other players were J. B. Brown from Portland and a trio from St. Meddans A. G. Gordon, J. T. Lambie and S. C. Wilson all of whom became members of Troon Golf Club. From the seven players only Herbert Thomson and Stewart Wilson progressed from the qualifying stages.

One of the fascinations of the Open was the emergence after one round of a virtually unknown leader who was not going to be a serious contender in the long haul but who earned his day of newspaper headlines. K. McDonald, partnered with Arnold Palmer, was the only player to break 70, his 69 leaving him two shots ahead of a handily tucked-in Palmer. Even this early there were signs that the Open title would be destined for an overseas player as nine of the first 21 golfers fell into that category.

There were some early prominent fatalities. Eric Brown effectively put himself out of contention by finishing 5535 although the *Herald* commented acidly:

"Both Brown and Paul Runyan lost strokes through the behaviour of spectators who almost certainly were on a golf course for the first time".

The hole which was wreaking havoc this time was not the Postage Stamp but the eleventh, the Railway Hole which inflicted an 11 on a past open Champion, Max Faulkner and a 10 on a future one, Jack Nicklaus.

The cut at the end of two rounds provided a more than usually dramatic interlude. The putt that Charlie Green holed on the last green removed Gary Player and Gene Littler from further participation as well as a handful of Green's amateur colleagues, Sandy Sinclair, Joe Carr, Sandy Saddler and Jack Cannon being among them.

In the second round Palmer had returned a 69, thanks to a magnificent inward half of 32, and in the process had equalled the Course record. He had moved to the front and had a two stroke lead from Kel Nagle, the fine Australian golfer. From here in the race was to become a procession.

With a 67 in the third round, Palmer scattered the

field. He increased his lead over Nagle to five strokes and at one time on the last day he led by ten strokes. His capacity to generate excitement and attract personal adherents caused problems in the last stages of the championship when the *Scotsman* estimated that:

"not one in 20 of the massed crowds, which I put at 15,000, saw the final putts of the Championship".

Tom Scott writing in *Golf Illustrated* was graceful in his acknowledgement of the role played by Palmer in restoring the prestige of the Open:

"I believe that once again the British Open Championship (sic, and an odd slip by Scott) is taking on a new stature. It has been forsaken by the Americans for a long time but now they regard it as one of the musts."

The Troon members had every right to regard the 1962 Open as a worthwhile exercise. They had seen a great golfer win with a record low aggregate and the weather had been fine. Improbably, Palmer would not win the Open again, indeed he would not even come particularly close. He had done something however, which was more important, he had convinced his fellow top-ranking American professionals that this was a worthwhile tournament and one to be cherished. In 1960 Palmer himself had been the only American of note at St. Andrews. By the time the Open came back to Troon in 1973 four of the first five in the Championship were Americans and at Turnberry four years later there was a total eclipse with the first eight championship places going to golfers from the U.S.A.

British golf would eventually improve and Palmer's own recollections are both thorough and generous. Shining through his account are his unfeigned love of Scotland and the Scottish galleries, together with a deep appreciation of his Honorary Membership of Royal Troon Golf Club. Here follows Palmer's account.

My Memories of 1962 at Troon
BY ARNOLD PALMER

I may have been caught up just a trifle in the euphoria of the moment, but, reflecting on my comments nearly 40 years later, I stand by what I said after I won the 1962 Open Championship at Troon Golf Club: 'I've never, I mean never, played better golf.' Time and again over the years, I have pointed to my performance that week in Scotland as one of the finest all-round efforts of my career.

In only one other of my seven victories in professional majors did I win as decisively – I landed my fourth Masters two years later by the same six-stroke margin – but I must say that I faced considerably more difficult course conditions at Troon that July than I did at Augusta National two years later. Furthermore, the 276 score I posted that week in Scotland was the Open Championship record (tied by Tom Weiskopf at Troon in 1973) until 1977 when Tom Watson shot 268 at Turnberry.

My mood was not particularly good when I arrived at Troon that year. It was just a few weeks after I had lost the U.S. Open to Jack Nicklaus at Oakmont in my own backyard in Western Pennsylvania and I hadn't really shaken that off yet. First things first, I had to go through the 36-hole qualifier at another course that was required of everybody, including the defending champion (me, in this case) until some lobbying by several of us players brought about a modification, after the 1964 Open. I managed that all right, but the weather and my first practice rounds did nothing to improve my mindset for the main event.

The famous Open winds were up and the temperatures were down, the chill cutting through us. And I found Troon to be all that it was reputed to be – a long, tough course with tiny greens and extremely penal rough, some very narrow fairways, dangerous sod bunkers and deep burns. These challenges had been magnified by a long drought in

Open Championship 1962
Final Leaderboard

A.D. Palmer (U.S.A.)	71 69 67 69 = 276
K.G. Nagle (Australia)	71 71 70 70 = 282
P. Rodgers (U.S.A.)	75 71 74 69 = 289
B. Hugget (Wales)	75 70 72 72 = 289
B. Charles (New Zealand)	75 70 70 75 = 290
P.W. Thomson (Australia)	70 77 75 70 = 292
S. Snead (U.S.A.)	76 73 72 71 = 292

Scotland that had baked the fairways dry, making every tee shot an adventure. With all of the course's ridges and humps, who could predict where any shot would wind up?

I made up my mind after the first practice round that I would not let the few bad bounces that I would surely have in the championship get me down. Everybody else would have to contend with the same thing. I decided that I would aim for the centre of the fairways and let the chips fall where they may. But, my back was aching, I was hitting my drives off line to the right and my putting was woeful. In a word, I described my game on the eve of the tournament as "terrible."

Still, I got off to a pretty decent start in the tournament proper. With long johns on under my regular cold-weather gear and my ailing back bathed in liniment, I got around in 71 and wound up in third place, even though my putting had left a lot to be desired. I remember that Troon took a heavy toll of several of the other top contenders. Jack Nicklaus shot an unbelievable 80 and was on his way out of the tournament along with Gary Player and Gene Littler, the previous year's U.S. Open Champion, who also missed the 36-hole cut.

My putting improved a bit the second day, although I really didn't get it straightened out until my wife, Winnie, offered an unsolicited observation late in the round. I shot 69 and the 140 total, gave me a two stroke lead on the field. The key to that round – and really the victory itself – was my play on the 11th hole, which was, by consensus, the hardest on the course. It was a fearsome, 485-yard par-five called the Railroad Hole, which played dead into strong winds most of the week. The tee shot was a 230-yard carry over wasteland to a 30-yard wide fairway guarded to the left by a jungle of bushes and scrub and to the right by a stone wall and the out-of-bounds railroad tracks that gave the hole its name. The little green, flanked by bunkers could only be reached with a fairway wood or long iron. I chose a one-iron off the tee in all four rounds, never missed the fairway and went for the green with my two-iron. The

Arnold Palmer receives Trophy from Captain Norman S. Smith, 1962 Open Championship

second day, my second shot at the 11th landed on the front edge of the green, rolled, within 20 feet of the cup and I made the eagle putt (I had birdied it the first three times I played it, twice in practice rounds, and followed the eagle with a par and another birdie the last day.)

Even though I had taken the lead that day my putting was still, as I said, substandard. As I came off the 17th green after missing a makeable birdie putt, Winnie approached me and said that she and Bob Drum, my old golf writer friend from Pittsburgh, who had accompanied us from the States had, concluded that my head was moving on my putts. I went to the practice green and realized immediately that they were right. As a consequence, I rattled off nine one-putt greens as I shot 67 that Friday morning and assumed a five-stroke lead over Kel Nagle. It was a cakewalk after that. Driving into every fairway and playing almost flawlessly, I mushroomed my lead to 10 strokes after 12 holes that afternoon before settling for the exhilarating, six-shot triumph. It pleased me to know then that I was the first American player to win the Open Championship in successive years since it was done 40 years earlier by Walter Hagen, the great American pro who had so kindly called from the U.S. to congratulate me when I won the year before at Royal Birkdale.

The Scottish galleries were marvellous at Troon, cheering me all the way in and virtually inundating me as I played to the clubhouse at the 18th. That evening, Winnie

Arnold Palmer and Winnie at the time of Honorary Membership, 1982

and I celebrated the victory with a leisurely dinner with friends at our hotel just off the course. The evening was capped when they brought me a huge white cake bearing the words "Worthy Champion." As I stood up to thank the waiter, the room erupted in applause. I thought it appropriate to have cake served to everybody. After all had been served, they arose in unison, holding up their plates in a touching salute. I nodded my thanks and was greeted with one final round of applause.

If the Scots fell in love with me there that week, I certainly had the same affection for them and do to this day. I am a member of more than 100 golf and country clubs around the world, but am particularly proud of the Honorary Membership tendered to me – in 1982 – by Royal Troon Golf Club.

Palmer's successful playing of the 11th, it could be argued that it won him the championship, could largely be attributed to the Club professional, Bill Henderson. Arnold Palmer had asked for advice on how to play the course and Bill Henderson had stressed that the American should never use a wood off the tee at the Railway Hole, nor did he.

Despite Palmer's generosity of spirit there could have been no clearer indication of the appalling weakness of British professional golf at this time. Tom Scott, no merciless critic but a moderate man, had this to say of the 1962 Open in *Golf Illustrated:*

"British golf sank to a low ebb. Only Brian Huggett finished in the first seven... Never, however have home players trailed so far behind the winner as this year. Palmer's victory meant that the championship has been won by overseas players for eleven consecutive years... All sorts of excuses may be put forward for this monopoly by players from overseas but the fact must be accepted that they are better players than our own ... A shake-up in British golf is long overdue".

Seeking consolation where they could, Scots found solace in the news that the popular Charlie Green had at least salvaged the silver medal which was the reward of the leading amateur. With regard to the paid ranks the British were coming – but not yet.

The new men were fast arriving. Palmer was established, Nicklaus would clearly make a name for himself, Gary Player would be a major force.

A death on Christmas Eve 1964 provided a fine example of the historical continuity of the game. A man died who predated Jones, Hagen and Sarazen, who stretched back to the days of George Duncan and Abe Mitchell in the paid section and to Roger Wethered and Cyril Tolley among the amateurs. He was J. L. C. Jenkins, probably the finest golfer who consistently played out of the Troon Club. Amateur Champion in 1914, he had also shone in the Open at Prestwick that year.

As his playing ability dwindled – and that was a long process and not to be mentioned casually in his presence – he served the Club

J. L. C. Jenkins, an impression

both as Captain and by being pivotal in the move to bring the Open to Troon in 1923. On his death his widow presented the Club with the medal which he had so gloriously won at Sandwich more than two wars before and it is proudly on show to this day.

The Scottish Amateur Championship of 1963

In the immediate wake of Palmer's epoch-making Open Championship win came a remarkable final to the national Championship with Ronnie Shade registering the first of his five consecutive Scottish championships and the venue on this occasion was Troon.

Scores can sometimes be misleading and the margin of 4 and 3 to Shade over Newton Henderson looks comfortable enough but the reality was otherwise. The first eighteen holes saw the match still level, largely due to the almost inhuman recovery work of Henderson who time and again was outplayed through the green and time and again thwarted Shade by getting down from the green edge.

The outcome was in doubt until the tide turned at the 28th. Henderson had take a breathtaking 13 single putts over this stretch and indeed had briefly gone into the lead at the 23rd. Few golfers could have resisted such brilliance on and around the green but Shade managed to keep in contention until the 29th when a good par was sufficient to let him edge in front and prompted an erratic hook by Henderson at the twelfth.

When Henderson conceded victory on the 33rd Shade was 1 under fours for the 33 holes played. *The Sunday Post* described his achievement thus: "This was great shot-making on a 7045 yard course with narrow fairways, countless bunkers and knee-high rough on both sides."

Over the next four years Shade would retain the championship at Nairn, St. Andrews, Western Gailes and Carnoustie. What will stick in the mind of those who saw his first Troon success will paradoxically be the great retrieval work of Henderson to which Shade paid eloquent tribute.

"Never once did I think I had won until I parked that No.3 iron against the stick at the fifteenth. Newton has such a great short game that you never feel you really have him until it is all over."

Ronnie Shade, with the Championship Trophy, 1963

A Time to Reflect

THE criticism directed at the course in 1962 had seldom anything to do with its fairness and certainly nothing to do with any deficiency in preparation. Generations of Fergussons would see to that. No, the charges levelled at Troon were more at its suitability as a container of very large and, in the later stages of competitions, very mobile galleries.

It was suitable enough as it was for the Scottish Amateur to be held there in 1963 when Ronnie Shade began his long monopoly of the Scottish title by beating Newton Henderson of Aberdeen by 4 and 3. Turning professional at a comparatively late age he perhaps lacked only great length to be a top paid player though Henderson did well to hold him until the last half-dozen holes.

In 1966 the Club had a new Secretary, Alastair Sweet, who had been Manager of the Bank of Scotland, in Troon and a member of the Club since 1927. His term of office saw the development of Troon Golf Club to a modern spectating course with a Clubhouse, which reflected this fact. He took up his post in 1966 and demitted office in 1972 by which time the Sean Connery Tournament of 1970 had gone a long way to convince the R&A that they need have no serious qualms about the Open Championship of 1973. So impressed were the R&A by his work at the pro-am tournament that they invited Alastair Sweet to act as local Championship Secretary.

In the 1960s television was taking its first faltering steps on the course. There was an influential body of opinion which said that the game did not lend itself to the new medium. Only the first few and the last couple of holes could be covered and, in early Walker Cup matches, there were a few embarrassing moments when ties finished way out in the boondocks, out of shot.

Ironically, televised golf took off in Great Britain because of a series of matches organised in the United States. World Championship Golf with commentaries by the former American Tour player Dutch Harrison and the former bandleader Bob Crosby – who by this means became almost as famous as his crooning brother – had a sensational impact in Britain. This was in no little measure due to the laid-back commentary of the men named.

Alastair Sweet, Secretary 1966-72

Clearly there was a massive potential public for the game and any club staging a major championship even semi-regularly would be well rewarded. But if people came in large numbers to see, could Troon cope? There were genuine doubts and they did not always emanate from ill-wishers. Wilbur Muirhead, the Chairman of the R&A Championship Committee, let it be known in January 1969 that if Troon were to continue to figure on the Championship Rota then the course must be wider. It was as a result of this that Frank Pennink made his celebrated visit to the course and confirmed that the trick would be to get the galleries to remain seated.

Course alterations would be made and these will be discussed later.

Tom Weiskopf

CHAPTER FOUR

The Years of Expansion

The Amateur Championship of 1968

A venerable sporting cliché has it that "The honours go round" – to which one can only say "Not in amateur golf in the 1960s they didn't" for Michael Bonallack dominated the game in England while at exactly the same time R. D. B. M. Shade of Scotland could well have been investigated by the Monopolies Commission. The difference between these two fine golfers was that Bonallack was also almost unbeatable at British levels, winning the Amateur Championship on five occasions of which three were consecutive – a terrifying standard of consistency. With the tendency of good young amateurs today to turn professional at the very first opportunity it is difficult to see this achievement of Bonallack being equalled, let alone surpassed.

In 1968, the first year of the trilogy so to speak, Michael Bonallack came through to meet Joe Carr of Ireland in the final over Troon. At 46, Carr was giving

Joe Carr putting on the 7th green in the final, 1968 Amateur Championship

his opponent 13 years and it was widely felt his best days were behind him. He remained however a golfer of great charisma, immensely popular with the galleries who loved his risk-taking and ability to recover from seemingly impossible lies. If ever there was a Cavalier golfer it was Joe Carr and through the week there had been a sizeable Irish contingent to which Carr had responded by appearing in a different shade of green every day.

Bonallack was widely regarded as unbeatable at this time, certainly in a British context although his Walker Cup performances were nothing like as productive. In the final, the proverbial two-horse race, he was quoted at 9-1 on and these proved to be realistic odds. For Joe Carr, in the words of the Gershwin song "It all began so well but what an end" The first three holes were each won with a birdie and Carr had two of them. Bonallack then applied pressure to which Carr had no answer. Worse, he missed two chances to keep the deficit in the first round to manageable proportions. On the last two holes before lunch he missed two putts of just under a yard and Bonallack lunched in the impregnable comfort of a six hole lead.

Throughout the Championship, Bonallack's putting had been awesome. A journalist who had followed him all during the competition was adamant that he had missed nothing under ten feet. The afternoon session of the final did not detain him very long and with a seven and six margin he won his third Amateur Championship and in doing so equalled Carr's own record.

When Bonallack was on song there was little that anyone could do about it, except perhaps admire. In an earlier round in this championship he had beaten Leslie McClue of Sunningdale five and four which sounds very conclusive and was, but it has to be said that at that stage McClue had parred every hole!

There was a very good Troon result registered when a local man, Matt Lygate, eliminated Peter Oosterhuis who in 1982 at the same venue would finish only a stroke adrift of Tom Watson in the Open. There had once again been great hopes of a Scottish success with 10 Scots in the last 16 but R. D. B. M. Shade, on whom many hopes were fixed, went out to an excellent if little known golfer – Reg Glading of Addington Palace. The latter made no claim to be anything but a weekend golfer and had been condemned for his agricultural swing but it had taken him to within two games of the title.

Michael Bonallack would win the next two Amateur Championships. In each instance, curiously enough, his opponent was the same – the American Bill Hyndman. His later career would be inextricably bound up with St. Andrews, first as secretary of the R&A and, that finished, as Captain of that club. Across the years he recalls his impression of the 1968 Championship at Troon

The Amateur Championship of 1968
By Michael Bonallack

Unfortunately, I am not a golfer who is able to recall every round of golf he has played nor the results of matches played in the Amateur Championship. However, overall impressions of events have stayed with me and thanks to my wife, Angela, keeping a book of press cuttings I am able to remind myself of some of my better moments, as well as some I would rather forget.

The Amateur Championship 1968 at Troon (as it was then) certainly comes high in the first category.

During the previous winter I had decided to re-model my swing with the help and tuition of Leslie King, who taught in a converted squash court in Lowndes Square, behind Harvey Nicholls in London. Although some people said they noticed very little difference, I myself felt I was, as a result of these lessons, hitting the ball far more consistently and solidly and this led to a very considerable increase in my confidence. This combination enabled me to make a very successful start to the new season, winning the Royal St. George's Champion Grand Challenge Cup, The Golf Illustrated Golf Vase and the English Stroke Play Championship. Thus when I came to Troon I could not possibly have felt better about my game or my chances of winning.

M. F. Bonallack defeats W. D. Smith in 1968 Amateur Championship

It so happens that my first Amateur Championship was also at Troon in 1956, when I lost in the second round to an American J. B. Golden. However, in spite of losing I was enormously impressed with the magnificent course and remembered it as being testing but fair. Twelve years later I felt that with my "new" swing and improved striking, it was exactly the right course for me to win the Championship for the third time. Unusually for me, my practice rounds went very well, which only increased my confidence, and although in the first round I was drawn against Leslie McClue, a Scot from Sunningdale and who I knew would be difficult to beat, I managed a fast start and won by 5/4 having completed the holes played in five under par, having had six birdies.

In the second round, in spite of apparently missing three short putts, (thanks to a press cutting reminding me) I beat Peter Flaherty, an Irish International, by 3/2. From then on my putting improved and wins of 3/2 and 4/3 against Rodney Gorton and Nigel Paul saw me through to the fifth round where I found myself up against W. D. (Dick) Smith, a player for whom I had a great deal of respect. Luckily my game stayed with me and after a close match I eventually won by 2/1 which meant I now had to play Charlie Green in the last eight.

Once again I got off to a good start and played as well as I could for the fifteen holes of the match which I covered in five under par, winning by 4/3. The semi-final against Geoffrey Marks was another good match which I won by 3/2 to set up a Final with my old rival and good friend Joe Carr.

My first Amateur semi-final had been ten years previously at St. Andrews where I also played Joe. At that time, before my swing change, I had great difficulty in driving in a left to right wind, something which Joe recognised and reminded me of in his usual jocular fashion. I had actually played the first nine holes in three under par to be 2 up but when we stood on the twelfth tee, having turned for home, the wind was now left to right, whereupon Joe in an aside to his caddie, which he made sure I could hear, said "we've got him now, Andy, he can't play in a left to right wind". Of course, he was right and I lost the 36 hole match by 4/3.

For some reason, when we arrived on the first tee for the 1968 Final, the referee decided we should toss for the honour, although Joe having been in the top quarter of the draw with myself in the bottom quarter, should have driven first. I won the toss which gave me the opportunity to declare the make and number of the ball I was playing, whereupon Joe said "You can't play that, that's the make and number I use" and added for good measure, "and I have been playing a lot longer than you". Anyway, I suggested Joe would change and teed up my ball and addressed it, only to hear Joe's parting shot "I hope you lose the bloody thing". At which, the referee looked distraught, until both Joe and myself started laughing, at which he realised I was pulling Joe's leg and did change my ball to another number.

Joe birdied the first hole, which put me one down for the first time during the week, but I myself birdied the second to square the match only to lose the third to another birdie, before myself squaring again with a birdie at the fourth. In spite of taking 6 at the sixth hole, two birdies at the 8th and 9th saw me out in 33 and 2 up. Now we turned for home, and standing on the 10th tee, we both felt there was a strong breeze blowing from left to right.

Now, however, unlike 1958, I was able to handle a wind such as this, whereas Joe now found it very difficult and remembering his remark ten years ago, I made a point of holding up a handkerchief and noting to my caddie, Willie Aitcheson, that the wind was now over our left shoulder. Joe grinned and called me a 'b —— d' and then aimed his drive another 20 yards left. Unfortunately he pulled it and finished next to a sky lark's nest from which he got a free drop. Sadly for him however, he lost the hole and three others so that I lunched six up.

I remember two other funny incidents in that last nine. At the thirteenth hole, Joe hit a soft slice off the tee which hit the President of the English Golf Union, full toss in the middle of his back. Joe was incensed when he went to apologise to be told "Not to worry, it did not hurt at all, as it was not hit hard enough".

On the fifteenth hole, we were looking for another of his drives when we were approached by someone with a tin making a collection for the blind. The tin was put in front of Joe who said "I haven't any money and I haven't any sense, or I wouldn't be out here looking for this ruddy ball". Although we halved the first hole of the afternoon round in birdie threes, Joe who was thirteen years older than myself began to tire with the result that I eventually won the match 7/6.

This win gave me enormous pleasure, for Joe was a player who I had admired and respected more than anyone else from the time I had first seen him. Not only was he a tremendous shot maker and magnificent golfer but he also played the game with such a wonderful attitude and in a truly sporting manner and looked as if he was enjoying every minute. Certainly, those who watched him and the many people he beat, including myself, felt privileged to have watched such a great player and sportsman.

The Amateur at Troon, remains one of my most enjoyable golfing experiences, not only because I played well and won, but also because the course was playing as a true links course in perfect condition, and in addition has members who made everyone so welcome and who were, and still are, so supportive of Amateur Golf.

Michael Bonallack receives Amateur Trophy from the Club Captain, J. E. Dawson, 1968 Amateur Championship

An Outside View

GOLFERS of surpassing skill have come to Troon from all over the world to win titles but perhaps the most remarkable of those who have successfully pursued a national title comes from just up the road. Jack Cannon was born in a little mining hamlet near Irvine called Bartonholm. This microscopic settlement, originally a couple of miners' rows, has produced no fewer than three Scottish champions, the other two being Hamilton McInally and his cousin, Jimmy Walker.

Even in the era of Tiger Woods the achievements of Jack Cannon are worth noting. He was the oldest man ever to win the Scottish Amateur Championship, which he did in 1969 when he was almost 53 years of age. He tied for the Scottish Amateurs Seniors in 1978 and two years later he won the British Seniors. His career is the more remarkable in that he lost almost all of his twenties to the Second World War at a time when the county selectors were already noticing him as a coming man.

He believes passionately that the way to get fit for golf is by playing golf and regards with an amused tolerance the regime of calisthenics that some of the up and coming young players put themselves through.

His connection with Troon is lifelong. He was blessed not only with a vitality which resisted age to the extent that in his late 60's he was playing three competitive rounds in a day, but his golfing longevity was likewise remarkable. He remained a scratch golfer for 45 years, reaching the mark when he was 19 and retaining the status until the age of 64. Consider the implications of this. He retained his length and he retained the sharpness of eyesight which enabled him to read the baffling variations of the Ayrshire greens.

He was and is a competitor to his fingertips. He had a brief membership of Lochwinnoch Golf Club which lasted just the one year but that was enough for him to become club champion. At 67 years of age he was good enough to win the Ayrshire Championship for the fourth time twenty years after he had first lifted it. He wryly admits that one of the few benefits of advancing age is that it becomes marginally easier to shoot less than your present span. In the Millennium year, he proved his point by going round at the age of 83 in 75 strokes.

He is one of the fast-dwindling number who can accurately remember golf before the Second World

Jack Cannon on his way to winning the 1969 Scottish Amateur Championship

War. He remembers his Championship success of 6 and 4 against A.H. Hall as being rather less stressful than he anticipated although he also remembers the relaxed and easy courtesy of his opponent. The final against his Kirkudbright opponent was played in wet conditions and Cannon was a master in the wet. He was three up going to lunch but Hall got it back to one by the 23rd. He then succumbed to an attack of hooking and Cannon had a comfortable 6 and 4 win. He does not admit ever to have felt nervous when playing for his own hand, only when playing late in his career for his country.

Of the great amateurs of his early days he remembers Jack McLean and the coin he used to keep "in his oxter" to make sure that his hands did not come away from his side. Sam McKinlay he recalls as a fine golfer if a little aloof, a real classicist.

With regard to Troon golfers he missed out on James Jenkins in his hey day but knew Teddy Dawson by repute and had a high opinion of him. He follows the conventional rankings by placing J.B. Stevenson at the head of the golfers of his long overview. His liking for Stevenson does not, however, prevent the balanced judgement. "A vastly gifted golfer, but not a vastly gifted putter and perhaps a better medal player than a match one". Jack Cannon is inclined to think that this may have caused J.B. Stevenson to lose the chance of a Walker Cup place at St. Andrews in Charlie Yates' year of 1938.

Jack Cannon on several occasions fell just short of qualifying for the final stages of the Open Championship itself. The nearest he came was when Charlie Green holed a putt on the last hole at Troon which cut a swathe through an expectant knot of Scottish amateurs. The Irvine man knows that he was fortunate to have the idyllic kind of upbringing that led him from first club in hand in a field to the municipal course, Irvine Ravenspark, and thence to Bogside. He worries that youngsters do not seem to be coming into the game in large numbers, especially those whose fathers are not themselves players.

He has no plans to retire and his opponents and partners alike will hope that his no-nonsense swing and calm putting will adorn the Ayrshire courses for a "wheen" of years. Should he make 100 then his next round will be extremely interesting. Meanwhile he has made his own history. Almost at the exact moment he won the Scottish, John Cook of Calcot Park was taking the English title. His wait had not been as long as Jack Cannon's, 34 years shorter in fact since Cook at 19 was the youngest-ever English champion.

The Seventies

TROON'S cause was greatly helped by a charitable venture, virtue bringing not only its own but other reward. In May 1970, the Sean Connery Tournament came to Ayrshire, organised and supported by the Saints and Sinners. There were various innovations that, although now commonplace, had the charm of novelty then. Thus, each hole was subsidised by a different sponsor at £1000 per time. In beautiful weather the course showed to its best advantage and not only to a domestic audience because the golf was being transmitted by Telstar to the United States. In a decade where Bond mania was at its most heightened, the combination of some eighty top golfers and entertainment celebrities was indeed a heady mix.

Stars taking part were Roger Hunt, Jim Baxter, Colin Stein and Jimmy Hill from football, Ken Scotland from rugby and Ken Barrington from cricket. From broadcasting came Cliff Michelmore and Arthur Montford and from the world of comedy Bruce Forsyth, Harry Secombe, Eric Sykes and Jimmy Tarbuck. Representing the cinema were Stanley Baker, Christopher Lee, Albert Finney and of course Sean Connery. From tennis came Rod Laver and from the wider world Douglas Bader, Ian Collins and Sir Ian Stewart were among the players.

The tournament was staged on behalf of charities sponsored by the Saints and Sinners Club. Unusually it was a 36 hole event with one professional partnered by the same two amateurs on each day. Some of the personalities were fine golfers in their own right. Stevie Chalmers and Ronnie Simpson both of Celtic were probably the best of the footballing golfers, both being single figure players as was Colin Stein of Rangers.

Each of the holes was individually sponsored with prizes given for outstanding performances at that particular hole. Primarily it was a golf tournament to be played seriously with a glittering cast of world-famous names. Of the 25 golfers who answered the starter's call there were ten past or future Open Champions and the event attracted huge and well-behaved crowds. Bobby Locke, Peter Thomson, Roberto de Vicenzo, Tony Jacklin, Kel Nagle, Max Faulkner, Bob Charles, Lee Trevino, Gary Player and Arnold Palmer were all there – a testament to the popularity of Sean Connery and the lure of the Troon course.

This was the last major event to take place while Bill Henderson was professional. He died, untimely, in August 1970. Arthur G. Dunsmuir tells a revealing story of his last days. *"Bill Henderson started building himself up after surgery for lung cancer. He started by walking and then he carried a couple of clubs*

The Sean Connery Tournament, Bruce Forsyth, Russell McCreath Tony Jacklin, and Gordon Hyslop

and he would hit a few shots. He gradually worked up doing nine holes like this. On the last occasion that he played golf he invited me to play with him over Portland. We played the second nine and Bill carried a 3 wood a 7 iron and his putter. His putter is now a major prize, competed for every year by Portland Golf Club.

Bill was a delight to golf with. At the 18th he hit three easy 3 woods to about twelve feet and rolled the putt in for a final birdie." A fitting end for a fine golfer.

To replace him came R. Brian Anderson who started, as had Willie Fernie, in Dumfries-shire, in Brian's case at Powfoot. Four years later he came to Ayrshire to the Kilmarnock Barassie Golf Club and after a comparatively short time there came on to Troon where he has been for almost thirty years. He has worn a Scotland sweater at both Boys and Amateur level and has a strong interest in the history of the game, particularly as it relates to club making and historical artifacts. He is the latest in the distinguished group of five professionals who between them have served and taught Troon members for a century and a quarter.

Bill Henderson, Club Professional

Brian Anderson at his presentation to mark 25 years as Professional to the Club, 1996

The Committee were also turning their attentions to the Clubhouse in the belief that improved facilities would be required to host future Open Championships. Following discussions in Committee, it was agreed to present the proposal for consideration by the membership. The proposed improvements comprised the building of an extension which would include a new Mixed Lounge, a ladies' powder room and toilet, a new Professional's Shop, a members' caddy-car store and the converting of the caddies shelter to a new locker room. The extension would also include a new east-facing entrance.

The estimated cost of the building works was £32,000, with a planned completion date of summer 1971. The proposals were presented to the Membership by the Club Captain Hugh McMaster at the Annual General Meeting on 25th July 1970 and were duly approved. Work commenced in December 1970 and was completed on schedule. Captain David Henderson officially opened the new facilities on 21st September 1971, when a large turnout enjoyed an informal Cocktail Party.

In his poem The Tiger, the poet Thomas Blake uses the phrase "could frame thy fearful symmetry". It is just possible that he had the Home Internationals over Troon in 1972 in mind which were nothing if not symmetrical. The result was a tie between England and Scotland who drew five matches all with five halved after both countries had beaten Wales and Ireland.

As the holders from the previous year retained the cup Scotland held on to the Raymond Trophy. It is perhaps worth remarking that although Home Internationals involving the four countries had been held since 1932 this was only the second drawn match between the two leading nations, the previous one having been recorded at Turnberry in 1960.

Troon had a special connection with the Raymond Trophy for it was presented in 1952 when the matches were also played there and Scotland was the first name to appear on it, the Scots winning all their three matches.

The internationals returned to Troon in 1984. When they did England exacted their revenge.

Alastair Sweet retired as Secretary in September 1972, but Russell McCreath had been in joint harness since May 1972 and this was invaluable in the run-up to the 1973 Open Championship. It allowed Archie Alexander some five months of seeing how things were done and gave him the advantage of Russell McCreath's profound knowledge of the Club.

Archie Alexander qualified as a Chartered Accountant in 1934, and after spending a few years in Glasgow went to work in the Far East where he spent the next twenty-seven years first in British North Borneo and then in Malaya. When he retired in 1964 he took up residence in Troon.

He flourished as he grew to the job and contributed greatly to the Club's Centenary Year. He was one of those remarkable men who survived Japanese captivity and a spell on the Thai railway during World War Two. He retired in 1980 and was made an Honorary Member of the Club.

In 1973 as Archie Alexander was taking over the reins as Secretary, Mrs. Margaret Stuart, later to become Mrs. Margaret Millar was appointed as Assistant Secretary. Mrs. Millar had been one of Troon's most popular Librarians and was a most successful Assistant Secretary. She would act as Assistant to four Club Secretaries and retired in 1989.

A. H. B. Alexander, Secretary 1972-80

Clubhouse with new Extension

The Open Championship of 1973

WHEN the Open returned to Troon in 1973 after a long gap of 11 years, one or two radical changes had been put in place. Toilet facilities had been improved beyond all recognition ... they had been castigated with justice in the aftermath of 1962 ... and the thousands who had merrily gained free admittance from the shore then were to find that this bolthole had been effectively stopped.

With the expected growth in the spectator numbers at the Open Championship, the Club had been advised that to remain on Championship rota, major course alterations were necessary to assist with spectator movement and to accommodate modern play. The Committee on the advice of the R&A asked Cotton, Pennink, Lawrie and Partners, Golf Course Architects to prepare proposals. Frank Pennink and Charles Lawrie visited the Course in February 1969, following which they made a number of recommendations. These were considered by the Committee and Members and subsequently approved.

The major changes started at the third hole with the construction of a new tee adjacent to the beach, the existing tee sited next to Blackrock House. The work on the third also involved the creation of a new fairway nearer the beach and the final removal of the old Fisherman's Huts. At the sixth hole a new green was built to the right of the old green and at the foot of the large sandhill, which is situated at the edge of the beach. At the twelfth the green was moved to the left reducing the dog-leg and enabling the construction of a new Championship tee for the thirteenth hole, some sixty yards further back, creating a challenging 465 yard par four. The resiting of the sixth and twelfth greens eliminated what was regarded as a major bottleneck for crowd control.

New Championship tees were also created at the sixteenth and eighteenth holes, the former being moved to the right of the fifteenth green, the latter twenty yards further back. All of these changes were completed well in advance of the 1973 Championship.

Arthur Havers, Gene Sarazen and Keith McKenzie, Secretary of the Royal and Ancient Golf Club, 1973 Open Championship

A further change to the Course, which had been undertaken earlier, saw the construction of a new fourth green. The location of the new green was about a hundred yards further back, extending the length of the hole.

Apart from the normal pastime of spotting a likely winner, much interest was focused on the veteran American Gene Sarazen then as now at 71 years of age the oldest player to have participated in the Open. It was fifty years since he first appeared at Troon. His reputation was already abundantly assured but in a fiction-defying outcome he was to confer further immortality on the eighth hole, the Postage Stamp.

Tom Weiskopf en route to the Title, 1973 Open Championship

When this hole was formed there were loud cries of protest from the members. There were complaints that there was no known golf shot which could catch this shortest of holes (126 yards) and remain on the putting surface. There were however powerful advocates to defend the hole. In 1910 after Vardon, Braid and Taylor had played over the reconstructed course, Braid wrote to this effect to the Secretary of the day.

"We are all unanimous that the four new holes are excellent and we especially emphasise this with regard to the eighth. This we consider to be all that a short hole should be, it is very difficult and demands that the tee shot shall be a perfect one."

Perhaps one of the best descriptions of this tormenting hole came from Aubrey Boomer, a golfer whose professional career spanned either side of the Great War and who spent much of his time establishing the game in France. This is what he had to say in his description:

"The green is garrisoned by an archipelago of bunkers and looks even smaller than it actually is as you stand trembling and uncertain on the tee. In front is a waste of rough, on the right is a deep bunker and many a poor soul has played ping-pong from hill to bunker and from bunker to hill. Formerly the custom was to play for the hill with the hope of trickling down to the green. Before the qualifying rounds for the Open of 1925 (held at Prestwick) James Braid placed two bunkers on the hillside, leaving little more than a bee's knee between them. But if you catch that dot the ball should roll down on to the green leaving a sporting chance for a birdie 2."

Not everyone was convinced by such advocacy. Peter Thomson was very dismissive:

"If I built a hole like that as a course architect I'd expect my client to ask for his money back. The club members would not like it a bit".

In those days of 1973 you would not have found Gene Sarazen complaining for incredibly he played two rounds during which he expended but three strokes on the Postage Stamp. By great good luck a television crew captured his first round ace, a perfect five iron shot and we have it for posterity. Sarazen, who all his professional life had a nice line in laconic humour, covered the hole with his cap to prevent the ball having second thoughts. Later, on receiving a videotape of the unusual eagle, he declared that he would take it with him "when I go up to see Hagen, Jones and Armour otherwise they won't believe me".

THE YEARS OF EXPANSION

Johnny Miller driving at the 2nd hole, 1973 Open Championship

They might just have believed him but if he had then told them that the following day he had a birdie two there thanks to holing a recovery shot from a bunker, they might have thought that their old rival was drawing the long bow.

In a delightful little note to the Club, Sarazen points out that second time round he played the Postage Stamp only half as well and that his putter then turned mutinous because he had not required its services at the eighth on either of the first two rounds.

Sarazen, of course, would not win the Open, he would not even qualify for the last two rounds. No matter. What he had done was more remarkable, more individual. The winner would come, the pundits thought, from Johnny Miller, Lee Trevino, Jack Nicklaus (the favourite), Arnold Palmer, or one of the young Americans. Christy O'Connor might do something if it blew an absolute gale for four days. Nobody quoted Tom Weiskopf.

The big difference between 1962 and 1973 lay in television coverage. The rest of the world could now see the Championship live as the four-day struggle developed. Before battle commenced Jack Nicklaus gave a wry interview, perhaps hoping to exorcise the demon of his 10 at the 11th in 1962. Nicklaus was asked, courageously, if he thought his previous experience of the course would help:

"It's not a course I remember much about. That's unusual for me, even although it is 11 years since I last played here. When I went to Muirfield last year I remembered every hole though I hadn't played there for years. The difference is that Muirfield was a course I wanted to remember."

Unlike Carnoustie in 1975 and Turnberry two years after that when the sun shone gloriously, the Clyde coast in 1973 was at its avenging worst.

Much of the press coverage was sour almost to the point of being jaundiced. Thus John Fairgrieve in *The Daily Mail*:

"It is the geography of the course that causes the trouble. The ninth is so far from civilisation that one expects to see the occasional St. Bernard prowling around, looking for customers."

John Rafferty in *The Scotsman* was scarcely more complimentary:

"It (Troon) is emerging as unsuitable for spectators, at least for walking spectators. The organisers have tried to compensate with an abundance of stands in the hope that

Jack Nicklaus' course record, 1973 Open Championship

105

Captain David K. Henderson with David Russell and Gene Sarazen and their presentation bottles of whisky, 1973 Open Championship

spectating habits have changed and that those attending will stay put."

The golfing authorities were well aware that the future of golf spectating lay that way but the habits of the Scottish onlooker could not be changed overnight. Enjoyable spectating for them was charging after one's favourite at a high rate of knots.

The important thing – the golf itself – started and the unregarded Weiskopf, arrow-straight all week, jumped into an instant lead which he was never to lose. He had a first round 68 which was one better than Nicklaus and Bert Yancey with Johnny Miller a further stroke behind. It seemed there would be no British challenge to speak of even at this early stage but, despite the highly indifferent weather, there were 16,000 spectators on the second day to see Weiskopf go one better. His 135 meant his lead over Miller was extended to three strokes.

He was pulled back a bit in the third round by a Johnny Miller charge but going into the last round his total of 206 saw him in the lead by a single shot. Could anyone catch this man who was the quintessence of coolness? Miller was never out of contention until the last couple of holes but the thrust, or thrusts, came from two other directions. Neil Coles, a British golfer who had every quality necessary for greatness, save perhaps sufficient self-belief, came in with a fine 66 and his four birdies in the last nine holes were enough to have Weiskopf looking quizzically at the leaderboard. Out on the course too, Nicklaus – the Golden Bear – was reeling off birdies on his way to a superb 65 but he was hung with the millstone of his third round 76. At the end Weiskopf had a nicely-paced three strokes in reserve. He would not win another major although no one ever came closer than he did with four second places in the Masters and one in the U.S. Open.

His winning total of 276 equalled the previous lowest aggregate, that of Arnold Palmer who had won at Troon in 1962. To compare these feats is not necessarily useful; perhaps one should say that Arnold had much the better of the weather though at Troon protracted sunshine does bring its own difficulties.

Two Members of Troon Golf Club, Alan Sym and Hugh Stuart, came through the final qualifying at Glasgow Gailes to take part in the Championship itself.

Open Championship 1973
Final Leaderboard

T. Weiskopf (U.S.A.)	68 67 71 70 = 276
J. Miller (U.S.A.)	70 68 69 72 = 279
N. Coles (England)	71 72 70 66 = 279
J. Nicklaus (U.S.A.)	69 70 76 65 = 280
B. Yancey (U.S.A.)	69 69 73 70 = 281
P. J. Butler (England)	71 72 74 69 = 286
L. Wadkins (U.S.A.)	71 73 70 74 = 288
C. O'Connor Snr (Ireland)	73 68 74 73 = 288
R. B. Charles (New Zealand)	73 71 73 71 = 288

Tom Weiskopf receives the Trophy from Captain, David K. Henderson, 1973 Open Championship

Alan Sym was the current Club Champion and played from the home Club, whereas Hugh Stuart's home Club was Forres where he played his golf prior to moving to area. Neither player progressed to the latter stages of the Championship, Stuart missing the thirty-six hole cut by one shot.

The dismantlers moved in and the members, with sighs of relief, prepared to resume occupancy of the course. It had been a great contest and the Sarazen moments had been unforgettable. He and a young amateur, David Russell of Blackwell (who had also holed in one at the Postage Stamp) were presented with huge bottles of whisky to commemorate their feats. Weiskopf headed for Prestwick Airport proudly bearing the Old Claret Jug. Many, probably most of us, have fantasised that walk down the 18th en route to collecting that same jug. Yet as Weiskopf came up to the last green his reflections were tinged with melancholy by his father's recent death.

In the debriefing the Club felt that some of the criticism to which it had been subjected was ill-founded and the Captain, D. K. Henderson – sadly not fated to survive the championship by very long – sprang to its defence as was his privilege and duty:

"Some of the criticisms have to be answered and the insinuations repudiated. The critics should have mentioned the litter-free state of the course, thanks to the efforts of the Marr College pupils. They might also have referred to the excellent toilet accommodation and to the very good traffic movement."

At this time there was little doubt that the future of Troon as a championship course lay, somewhat, in the balance. Pennink saw that the difficulties were caused by the fact that an essentially narrow course went straight out and straight back and wherever there was a little loop there would be trouble. There was never any support to remove Troon from the Championship rota since every argument marshalled against the Ayrshire course could have been used against the Old Course at St. Andrews and no one suggested doing without THAT.

The answer was to persuade the gallery to sit and in the meantime to fight off whatever attacks might come.

We may leave the last word on the course with a distinguished visitor to Troon in 1973... Francis Ouimet, international golfer, Walker Cup Captain, Captain of the R&A and the first American to have taken a major title. He said this:

"Golf courses in the United States are manufactured whereas great courses like St. Andrews and Troon are created by God. I prefer God's work to man's."

In his considered review of the Championship Weiskopf remembered those who had helped him and the father who was not there to share his crowning hour.

The Open Championship of 1973

By Tom Weiskopf

Even though time passes by so quickly, my memories of Royal Troon and The Open Championship of 1973 are ever present. Coming into that championship I was extremely confident and in total control of every aspect of my game. I came in a week early as usual, to prepare for the Championship. But as that week progressed, I became confused and uncertain as to how to strategically play each hole on the golf course because the course was playing extremely firm and fast. However, as luck would have it, the "golfing gods" sent rain everyday the week of the tournament, softening and lengthening the course dramatically and playing directly to my long game.

I confidently birdied the first two holes that first round and eventually took the overnight lead. I never was tied or relinquished my lead after the first round. As I recall, my third round lacked the precision of the other three, and I relied on my putter to carry the day. I do recall standing on the seventy-first hole, the long three playing into a very strong wind, and being quite anxious because I only had a two-stroke lead at that time over Johnny Miller. I really believe that the one iron that I struck, which landed on the green a mere fifteen feet from the hole, gave me the Championship because Johnny Miller missed the green and bogeyed. I was totally unaware that if I parred the final hole I would tie the great Arnold Palmer's seventy-two hole Open record. The memories of those who had helped me in my past and the loss of my father earlier that year were my only recollections as I struck my tee shot in the fairway and played my second onto the left front of the green and two putted. I do not know if I ever really remembered my feet on the ground as I covered those 400 plus yards. I am sure I was floating.

A lot of credit has to be given to my loyal caddy of many years, Albert Fyles. It was the first time in tournament golf that I really felt the presence of a gallery that supported me from start to finish. I truly believe that the fans in Scotland are the greatest. I could really sense that the Scots were pulling for me to win.

Royal Troon will always hold a special place in my heart. I believe, without a doubt that the back nine at Royal Troon is the toughest, fairest nine holes when played into the wind in any Open Championship. I wish to thank everyone at Royal Troon and the Club for granting me Honorary Membership.

Tom Weiskopf receives Honorary Membership 1995, (left to right) Past Captain Prof. Sir James Armour CBE, Captain Ian Valentine, Tom Weiskopf, Jeanne Weiskopf and Honorary President Bill McFarlane

The Advancement of Technology

Prior to the 1973 Open Championship, the Committee was anxious to improve the quality of the course and to benefit the long-term playing conditions for Members. A pop-up system around the greens and tees was completed early in 1973, thus eliminating the need for hand watering.

In 1975 concern was felt about the dry, dusty fairways and in the latter part of 1975, supported by the views of Jim Arthur, the R&A Agronomist, the Committee decided to install a fairway pop-up sprinkler system as an experiment on the first and second fairways. The work was completed in March

1976. The improvement to these fairways was so significant that in July 1976, the Committee at the Annual General Meeting proposed that a further six holes should benefit from a fairway sprinkler system. When H.V.S. Thomson, as Green Convener put the case to the Members, not only was their approval given, but also a near unanimous view that the other six Par 4 and Par 5 fairways be included in the project and worry about the extra cost later!

Thus Troon's Old Course became the first course in the U.K. to have a fully automated pop-up fairway sprinkler system, which allowed precise control and therefore, minimal irrigation levels, so advisable for links courses.

The project was completed by April 1977 at a cost of around £20,000 partly funded by a levy on Members of £20 – payable in two £10 instalments

The Captain's Badge

On his retirement from Secretary of the Club the Members presented Alastair Sweet with a gold badge as a token of their esteem. After his death in August 1975, Mrs Moira Sweet generously presented this badge to the Club expressing the wish it might be worn by the Captain. To this the Committee had much pleasure in giving its assent. The badge is unobtrusive but authorative and is now worn by the Captain of the day.

The Captain's Badge

The Scottish Amateur Championship of 1977

In 1977 Allan Brodie of Balmore took the Championship which he had so narrowly missed in 1973 when he defeated Paul McKellar of East Renfrewshire in a truly memorable final. It went to the very last hole and held a crowd of 2000 absoluty entranced.

Each man had played seven matches in five days and had then been presented with a day of driving rain and wind to surmount. It was a match of spectacular turnabouts. Brodie was three up at the turn in the morning but then encountered the wind shrieking like a dervish and his opponent playing as a man possessed. In the space of six holes, as John Campbell of the *Daily Telegraph* was to say, "McKellar went from three down to two up and he retained the lead until there were only five holes left of this Homeric contest". At the fourteenth Brodie's par 3 was for once not matched by the tall man from East Renfrewshire.

The match ended in a blaze of birdies. At the sixteenth two magnificent wood shots created the birdie which put Brodie ahead for the first time since the twelfth in the morning. A thirty foot putt at the seventeenth put McKellar on terms and all hung upon the last hole. McKellar was in the right rough but found the green and putted dead. His four was secure. Brodie was 20 feet left of the hole thanks to an exquisitely judged nine iron. The gallery was enthralled.

J. B. Stevenson delivered his opinion as Brodie lined up his potentially title-winning putt. He said to a companion "There's a borrow like a dog's hind leg on Brodie's putt. No stranger ever reads it right". His companion nodded, J.B. knew his golf and it was widely known that Brodie's weakness was his putting which indeed could be markedly erratic.

But not this time. The ball was firmly rapped into the centre of the hole and Brodie was champion. The reception from the crowd was tempered by recognition of a gallant fight in a losing cause. To the end of a distinguished amateur career Paul McKellar was not fated to win at Troon.

Allan Brodie, 1977 Scottish Amateur Champion

The Royal Troon Crest

CHAPTER FIVE

The Club becomes Royal

100 up

1978 celebrations, The Captain and friends

WHEN the 7th Duke of Portland died in 1977, it was the first of three deaths in the title within ten years. The title drifted out to remote and remoter cousins before eventually becoming extinct. The fact that these far-out kindred were not resident in the United Kingdom meant that the original ties were first weakened and eventually severed. This was inconvenient since there were ceremonial duties required of an Honorary President from time to time but the need was satisfied by appointing an Honorary President from the ranks of the Past Captains. Mr. F. D. B. Black had been appointed in 1971 to discharge these duties.

By now Troon Golf Club had long been capable of making its own way in the world. Yet it had cause to be grateful for the active and benevolent patronage of a noble family which came to prominence with the arrival of William of Orange in 1688 and had also briefly in 1807 provided the country with a Prime Minister, in the person of the 3rd Duke. This connection had brought lustre to the Club at a time when social distinctions were much more stratified than they are today.

Any sporting organisation which has achieved its 100th anniversary and survived two World Wars in so doing, is entitled to celebrate the event. Troon would do so in 1978 and preparations for this landmark began three years earlier.

There was a wish to recreate the circumstances in which the club was founded. To that end, Captain, Committee Members and some Members dressed in what would have been the height of golfing fashion in 1878 and drove to the Portland Arms Hotel in horse-drawn conveyances to re-enact the original Founding Meeting. The Minutes of that meeting served as a script and the scene was played out. Other clubs had done something similar – the Glasgow

1978 celebrations, Captain and Members at the Portland Arms

112

THE CLUB BECOMES ROYAL

Centenary flag with Bob Doig, Caddie Master and Fraser Rowan, Club Steward, 1978

Club had marked its bi-centenary by playing on that piece of Glasgow Green where the Glasgow Club had begun and by playing moreover with clubs of the 18th century and the taxing 'featheries'.

Various items of memorabilia were made available such as a limited number of gold cufflinks together with centenary glasses and a special centenary tie which, on a plain background, would have one club crest plus the centenary dates. This was also to be the pattern for the new club flag.

There would be a Centenary Dinner which would be rather more elaborate than normal. To mark the anniversary the club had been awarded the Amateur Championship and it was agreed to invite the three previous Amateur champions over Troon – Charlie Yates, John Beharrell and Michael Bonallack – to attend. The Royal and Ancient Golf Club also suggested that similar invitations be extended to the three winners of the Open at Troon – Tom Weiskopf, Arnold Palmer and Bobby Locke.

The course would be marked for the competition with special course flags – a cautionary note said that these should be taken in at close of play to deter souvenir hunters. This practice was to provide a scary moment in the 1989 Open when, following normal usage, each flag was taken in as the hole was played. Suddenly there was a four-hole play-off required and a mad dash round holes 1, 2, 17 & 18 to reinstate the flags and allow play to proceed!

At the Annual Dinner in March 1978 there were 150 members plus guests among whom was Sandy Sinclair, the President of the Scottish Golf Union and the prime mover in the awarding of Royal status to the Troon Golf Club.

At the Centenary Dinner in June 1978 there were presentations from various other Royal and local clubs. As noted, Charlie Yates presented Royal Troon with a superb piece of golfing memorabilia – the cable which he had received from Bobby Jones to mark his appearance in the Amateur Championship at Troon back in 1938. The cable is displayed today in the Clubhouse as is the new Club Crest which was submitted to the Lord Lyon and approved by him. It was the happy lot of the Captain, Bill Boucher-Myers, to make the announcement of the Club's elevation in rank with the awarding of the Royal title. A memorable evening closed with the conferral of Honorary Life Membership on Sandy Sinclair in recognition of his efforts to win Royal status for the Club.

Major B. W. S. Boucher-Myers, DSO Captain 1977-79

Top table guests and Members Centenary Dinner 1978

The Club becomes Royal

A CLUB CENTENARY is a notable event in all conscience but when it is accorded Royal status then the centenary becomes doubly momentous as happened in the case of Troon Golf Club. It had been decided that the Club should make application for, Royal status.

Such an application would have to be well grounded and well presented. The title of Royal is not conveyed in a scatter-gun manner and certainly not without proper justification. It is a rare honour, so rare in fact that it has never been conferred before or after the case of Troon in the reign of the present sovereign.

The application was made by letter and the proposer was Sandy Sinclair, then President of the Scottish Golf Union and he put a compelling case.

The burden of the argument was that there was no Royal Golf Club in the West of Scotland, even though that area was one of the hotbeds of the game. It was felt that, by now, Troon had firmly established itself as one of the regular courses on the Open rota and that the conferral of Royal status would be peculiarly appropriate in the Club's Centenary Year.

One might have expected the letter of approval to be inscribed on vellum but the authorising document is considerably more restrained than that.

The modest form of approval did not of course in the least diminish the honour which had been bestowed on the Club. The great news was announced at the Centenary Dinner on June 3rd 1978 and the Captain, Bill Boucher-Myers was given a standing ovation as he informed the diners. His joy must have been tempered with relief that the strain of keeping the news from all but a couple of people need no longer be undergone. There had been some close calls on the secrecy aspect, notably when the Secretary wondered why the Club was stalling for so long on its normal purchase of headed stationery!

The Royal connection was later cemented by a visit to Troon by H.R.H. The Duke of York to play over the course on 10th July 1997 – a few days before the Open Championship. He was entertained to lunch and then, partnered by the Captain, Ian Valentine, he played against David Smyth (Vice-Captain, Chairman of the Royal Troon's Championship Committee and several times Club Champion) and Peter Greenhough (Chairman of the Championship Committee of the Royal and Ancient). Ian Valentine records modestly that the round was

Letter intimating conferral of Royal accolade

enjoyable but that success that day did not sit in the Duke's helm.

The Royal visitor had clearly enjoyed his day for he returned just over a week later to follow play on the Saturday of the Championship. In company with the Captain he attended a lunch at which were present also the Vice-Captain of Royal Troon, the Secretary and past Captains, the Royal and Ancient Captain, officials and the Lord Lieutenant.

The Duke of York showed himself to be genuinely devoted to the game and he crowned the day by accepting the invitation of Honorary Membership of Royal Troon Golf Club.

Rank hath its obligations and this is true of the band of Royal Golf Clubs. It is not a very numerous group and political developments make it very likely that the numbers will reduce in times to come rather than increase and this is especially true of Africa and Asia.

Nearer home the Royal Troon Golf Club set about establishing ties – if they did not already exist – with clubs of equivalent rank. By 1984, matches had been arranged against Royal Lytham, Royal Birkdale, Royal Aberdeen, Royal County Down and, later, Royal Dornoch and Royal Liverpool (as Hoylake had come to be known). The links with this last club were particularly long-forged since, back in 1895, both clubs had been among the handful which subscribed for the purchase of a trophy to be presented to the winner of the Amateur Championship. Hoylake as it then was had floated the idea of an Amateur Championship and invited clubs to subscribe for a trophy.

Royal matches follow a rigid if convoluted pattern. The matches are played 12 a side and are biennial so, just as cricketers have an Australian tour every four years, an away Royal match crops up at the same interval. The visiting side arrives on Friday to play the course and have an informal evening in the host club's bar. Saturday is devoted to two rounds

Left to right, Captain Ian Valentine, H.R.H. The Duke of York, Vice-Captain David Smyth and Peter Greenhough

of foursomes at the end of which a simple statement e.g. 'Royal Troon/Royal Lytham wins' is made. That is all. There is no totting up of points or holes where a bad performance could cast a shadow over proceedings.

There is a formal dinner on the Saturday night at which a ballot is made for Sunday morning fourballs. The distinguishing feature of these is that a member of the host club is required to be partnered by a member of the visiting club so that yesterday's fierce rivals become today's uneasy allies. And after all that, and lunch, those who can go home, do.

The first Royal match played against Royal Liverpool at Hoylake in 1997 provided its own happy footnote. As Captain, Ian Valentine invited Jimmy Armour to participate and play on the course where he had won the British Boys' Championship exactly fifty years before.

Since that day in 1947 when he defeated Ian Caldwell 5 and 4 – the latter a considerable golfer who would later be both English Amateur Champion and a Walker Cup player – Jimmy Armour had not been back to Hoylake. However, his hand would appear to have lost nothing of its cunning for in the Royal match he won both his Saturday foursomes and his Sunday fourball and the stableford prize.

The Club's Crests

The Centenary year of 1978 saw the second change in the design of the Club Crest, which was brought about by the granting of Royal Status in that year. The motto "Tam Arte Quam Marte" was retained as was the snake entwined around five golf clubs, however, two crosses and a ducal coronet were added to the design. There is a theory that the five clubs represented the five original holes and that there was a leather thong which was used to keep the clubs together. The thong was superseded by the serpent.

The first Secretary, Dr John Highet was a great driving force in the formation of the Club. It is thought, that the snake featured in the design of the Crest, was included as a mark of respect to the Doctor since the snake has long been the symbol of the medical man.

The initial Crest was simpler in style and was certainly in place prior to 1886 at which time it appeared on the Dinner Menu to mark the completion of the then new and modern Clubhouse.

The design of the second Crest around 1888 survived for ninety years until 1978 when the aforesaid refinements had to be incorporated.

The translation of the Motto "As much by Skill as by Strength" is as appropriate now as it was originally.

Original Club Crest

Second Club Crest

New Club Crest

THE CLUB BECOMES ROYAL

To All and Sundry whom these presents do or may concern,

WE, Sir James Monteith Grant, Knight Commander of the Royal Victorian Order, Writer to Her Majesty's Signet, Lord Lyon King of Arms, send Greeting: WHEREAS, Major Bertram William Sydney Boucher-Myers, Companion of the Distinguished Service Order, Captain, and Archibald Hamilton Bruce Alexander, Chartered Accountant, Secretary, ROYAL TROON GOLF CLUB, Craigend Road, Troon, having by Petition unto Us of date 10 October 1978 for and on behalf of the said Club, Shown; THAT Troon Golf Club was formed on 10 March 1878 under the Captaincy of James Dickie, the land on which the course was constructed having been acquired from His Grace William John Arthur Cavendish, 6th Duke of Portland, who became the first Honorary President of the said Club; THAT in 1923 the said Club acquired by purchase the land on which had been constructed the three courses, videlicet:— the Old Course, the Relief (Portland) Course and the Ladies Course; THAT Her Majesty the Queen has graciously pleased to approve the inclusion of the appellation "Royal" in the name of the Club, which is now Royal Troon Golf Club; AND the Petitioners having prayed that there might be granted as for the said Club such Ensigns Armorial as might be found suitable and according to the Laws of Arms, Know Ye Therefore that We have Devised, and Do by These Presents Assign, Ratify and Confirm unto the Petitioners for and on behalf of Royal Troon Golf Club the following Ensigns Armorial, as depicted upon the margin hereof, and matriculated of even date with These Presents upon the 120th page of the 59th Volume of Our Public Register of All Arms and Bearings in Scotland, videlicet:— Azure edged Or, five ancient golf clubs, one paleways and four of a like likeness and shape of a collet serpent of the Second, the whole surmounted of a ducal coronet of the Last, in chief two crosses ouchée of the Third. And in an Escrol below the same this Motto "TAM ARTE QUAM MARTE" by demonstration of which Ensigns Armorial the said Club is, amongst all Nobles and in all Places of Honour, to be taken, numbered, accounted and received as an Incorporation Noble in the Noblesse of Scotland, In Testimony Whereof We have Subscribed These Presents and the Seal of Our Office is affixed hereto at Edinburgh this 20th day of August in the 28th Year of the Reign of Our Sovereign Lady Elizabeth the Second, by the Grace of God, of the United Kingdom of Great Britain and Northern Ireland, and of Her Other Realms and Territories, Queen, Head of the Commonwealth, Defender of the Faith, and in the Year of Our Lord One Thousand Nine Hundred and Seventy-nine.

Ensigns armorial

The Amateur Championship of 1978

THE Amateur Championship of 1978 was every bit as much an examination of physical endurance as of golfing skills. In a week full of lashing rain and gales, Peter McEvoy of Copt Heath emerged victorious. On his way to the title he had played 141 holes of golf and vanquished eight rivals, notably Paul McKellar, who he met in the final. By his own fine play, he once again thwarted Scots hopes of having a homebased winner.

The eventual margin of four and three in McEvoy's favour looks substantial enough but it is a little deceptive. McKellar was three down at lunch but he got two holes back and, momentarily, McEvoy looked as if he might falter before once again pulling away from the tall East Renfrewshire man. In winning the Amateur in 1978, McEvoy became only the fifth golfer to defend the title succesfully, the others to that point being Harold Hilton, Horace Hutcheson, Lawson Little and, spoiling the alliteration rather, Michael Bonallack.

McEvoy had another major distinction to his credit in that he was the first British Amateur ever to complete four rounds in the Masters at Augusta, Georgia. In conversation with him, I asked him had he ever seriously contemplated turning professional. He said, in an answer entirely free from false modesty, No; he thought the step up was a trifle too demanding. He also pointed out that as an amateur he had been given the chance to play with or against almost all the top-ranking American professionals.

Two Royal Troon members performed admirably in the Championship. Ian Hamilton made it through to the last sixteen, with further progress halted by Allan Brodie of Balmore the reigning Scottish Amateur Champion, a title he had won at Troon the previous year. His clubmate, Alan Sym progressed one stage further, to the last eight, where he lost to David Suddards of South Africa. Suddards would lose in the semi-final to the eventual champion, Peter McEvoy

This is his account of a well thought out Championship campaign.

1978 Amateur Championship
BY PETER MCEVOY

My memories of the 1978 Amateur are very clear. I felt very comfortable during the whole week. There were a number of reasons for this but the overriding one was that I knew the area through close family connections. My mother is from Ayr and I had Aunts in Prestwick and Ayr. Indeed, I had lived the first 10 years of my life not far down the road in Gourock.

In addition to these local connections I stayed all week in Ballantrae where my parents had a holiday cottage. This meant an hours journey to the course each day but it also meant home comforts and real relaxation in the evenings. All of this combined to give me a very comfortable feeling during the championship.

Royal Troon itself suited me right down to the ground. At that time I was playing a lot of golf, not quite full-time and I was doing my solicitors articles but I was still able to practice my game extensively. At that stage in my golfing career I had quite a facility to hit the ball low under the wind. As Royal Troon was a classic out and back links and the wind blew strongly into our faces on the return home all week I felt that I had a certain advantage. Without meaning to sound conceited I felt that while there were a number of players who could match me going out I really felt if I was all square after nine I had an excellent chance of victory against anyone coming home.

THE CLUB BECOMES ROYAL

Peter McEvoy with runner-up Paul McKeller and Club Captain, Major B. W. S. Boucher-Myers, 1978 Amateur Championship

As for the details of the matches themselves I remember best very nearly losing to John Glover, who was to become Rules Secretary at the R&A, only surviving because he uncharacteristically took 5 from the centre of the last fairway.

As the championship progressed I was conscious of the presence of two very good South Africans in my part of the draw. I duly met Gavin Levenson in the quarter-finals and David Suddards in the semi-final. Fortunately for me the wind blew and the conditions suited me better than them. I was very thankful for this as either player would have been formidable if the conditions had been more to their liking rather than mine.

The final itself was notable for the very windy weather. My opponent, a very dogged Scot, Paul McKellar, drove the 1st and the 3rd in the afternoon round, this will give those who know Troon an idea of the strength of the storm.

Given that Paul McKellar was relatively local, his home club was East Renfrewshire, the crowd were almost exclusively on his side. While this is an obvious advantage I learned a lesson that day. Paul's start in the afternoon was electric. As I mentioned before he drove the 1st and 3rd to win both holes with birdies, while reducing my lead to 2 holes. On the 4th he really got the crowd roaring with a bunker shot that hit the flag and stopped 4 feet from the hole leaving him a great chance of another birdie. I was lucky enough to hole a long putt for a birdie and Paul missed. The silence was deafening. In a stroke his home advantage had worked against him.

This is no criticism of the crowd it was just that their disappointment was unconcealable. My spirits rose and I hung on for victory.

Troon is obviously one of the classic tests of golf and one always favours a course where one has had success. My fondness for the course is enhanced by the fact that it suited my game at the time of my success. In considering it a wonderful test one has to realise that I am not really being completely impartial but my view is in common with pretty much everybody in the world of golf.

Once the championship was over my extended family and I went for a meal to the Marine Hotel. It was a cause of great celebration for us all. I remember being woken from in front of the T.V. in the lounge at about 9.30 in the evening. I'd popped out to see the news and fallen asleep. The wind and the long weeks of golf had got to me. Waking up was the start of the best bit of winning an Amateur Championship, it was the start of reflection.

Peter McEvoy receives Winner's Medal from Club Captain, Major B.W.S. Boucher-Myers, 1978 Amateur Championship

119

Being a Member of Royal Troon

By Sandy Sinclair

HAVING been a member of Royal Troon since the club celebrated its centenary in 1978, I have had a great deal of pleasure in playing this great links course. The differences with its great neighbour, Prestwick, are fascinating for anyone who loves the game.

Troon is the traditional links course par excellence, nine out and nine back as opposed to the two concentric nine holes of Muirfield. It is much more a "what you see is what you get" course than its famous neighbour. It has no Himalayas (the 5th) or Alps (the 17th) as has Prestwick. The modern professional golfer wants an open course with predictable bounce, the traditionalist may side with the poet John Betjeman when in his poem, 'Seaside Golf' he says:

"In spite of grassy banks between I knew I'd find it on the green".

In the 1962 Open at Troon, Gary Player was reported to be unhappy with the capricious bounce of the ball on the sun-baked fairways (it is interesting to record that, despite the jibes about Scotland's weather, only the Wesikopf Open of 1973 has been played in truly adverse weather conditions with the exception of one day in the first Troon Open of 1923). The club reacted decisively by installing an excellent sprinkler system which greatly lessens the chance of the wicked bounce which leaves the golfer appealing (usually in vain) to Higher Authority for justice.

A noted feature of the Royal Troon course is that the Gyaws Burn supplies from its narrow but deep recesses almost all the water required for the sprinkler system, crossing as it does the 3rd and 16th fairways.

Royal Troon has the enormous advantage of having two courses, the Old Course and the Portland course. The latter is very different from the senior course but it complements it and its existence not only facilitates the holding of major championships but also provides the opportunity for visitors to play two rounds in the day, separated by a memorable lunch since Royal Troon is renowned for its food.

And what is it like to play the last few holes? General opinion now seems to be that a really good course should afford a comprehensive view of the last green from the clubhouse. Royal Troon most certainly provides this. The proximity of the players on the 18th green to the lounges has an inhibiting effect on me personally. A missed putt or a chipping indiscretion is sure to be commented on unfavourably by the discriminating onlookers in the lounge.

The gravel path immediately below the windows is out of bounds which means that there is a tendency to be short of the pin with one's second shot. Once inside the clubhouse the members are most congenial, despite their natural desire to win and the staff, both inside and outside, are invariably friendly and welcoming.

My association with the Club has been long. I have attended every Open played at Troon with the exception of Arthur Havers win in 1923. In various capacities I saw Bobby Locke win in 1950 and the triumphs of all his Troon successors right down to Justin Leonard in 1997.

And finally, for it is often the small things that make you warm to a person or organisation, after a round at Troon my golf shoes do not require cleaning!

The 1980s

OCCASIONALLY the Club was called upon to adjudicate on questions of membership of the other two clubs. Early in 1980 a case arose of a lady member who became a professional golfer. The Club informed the Ladies that a professional golfer was not eligible for membership. Only the same facilities could be offered as would have been accorded a male professional, namely permission to practice occasionally on the Old and Portland Courses.

In August 1980, the Club was the venue for the British Youths Open Amateur Championship, which comprised seventy-two holes stroke-play over the Old Course. Gary Hay of Hilton Park won the title at the second hole of a sudden-death play-off, against Philip Walton of Malahide, both players having a four round aggregate score of 303. In the play-off, Hay survived the first hole when Walton missed his putt from seven feet for victory. At the second, Hay pitched close from the back of the green for par, Walton missed his putt for a half and the Scot was champion.

The wider world continued to impinge. There was a request that the Club should stage the British Ladies' Championship in the still distant 1983 but the request was reluctantly turned down, because the Open Championship and the Scottish Ladies were both scheduled for 1982. No doubt the Committee were aware of the stern injunction of old Andrew Kirkaldy when Sunday golf was mooted: "Even if the golfers don't need a rest, the course does".

The Scottish Development Agency suggested that senior American executives should be offered Associate Membership and that this might be a powerful bargaining card in attracting visitors to set up industries in Ayrshire. The Club was not insensible to this argument but was reluctant to relinquish the control which the normal admissions procedure gave them. The reply was that perhaps such candidates could be welcomed as temporary members.

Much of the attention of Committees at this stage was taken up by the coming on the market of the adjacent house and grounds of Craigend. Should the club buy it? If so would the members approve the transaction, for their approval was most certainly needed. The negotiations were protracted and convoluted and are dealt with elsewhere.

It was felt that the club should offer Honorary Membership to two golfers who had greatly distinguished themselves at Troon – Bobby Locke, winner of the Open in 1950 and Arnold Palmer whose success had come in 1962. Both were favoured because in the words of the citation "neither was in contention for future championships and both men would be very acceptable to members". Arnold Palmer at once accepted but Bobby Locke was never able to make the trip.

Wing Commander Derek Graham

Derek Graham was born to an English mother and a Scottish father and was brought up in the steel town of Consett in the North of England. Educated at Consett Grammar School he learned to play his golf locally. On leaving school he joined the RAF training as a navigator before leaving flying to become an Air Traffic Controller and eventually in 1978, the Station Commander at RAF Prestwick.

On being given a posting to the Ministry of Defence, Wing Commander Graham, as he now was, opted to leave the RAF after thirty years service and applied for the Secretaryship of Royal Troon in the run-up to the 1982 Open Championship. He began a dual monarchy with Archie Alexander in October

1980 but confesses that he found, as in flying, that going solo could in the end be easier. He speaks particularly highly of the work of the Club's Championship Convenor, Tom Holden, and is emphatic that the successful running of the 1982 Open Championship brought much prestige to the Club.

A particular interest of Derek Graham was the valuable artifacts belonging to the Club, some of which were casually stored away in cellars, which were liable to flooding at the time of the neap tides. By his efforts some valuable books and photographs were saved. One book in particular was the History of the Musselburgh Links which the American golfer Ben Crenshaw, a devotee of golfing history, was keen to buy.

In 1983 family illness prompted a recall to the South for Derek Graham and the following year he returned to England to take up the post of Secretary/Manager of Denham Golf Club, in Buckinghamshire a position he would occupy for twelve years before retiring back to Consett in 1995.

Given his choice he would have happily seen out his time at Royal Troon, which he describes as *"the greatest of Scottish Clubs"*.

The Scottish Ladies Championship of 1982

This was the championship in which the younger generation of Scottish women golfers came to the fore and indicated to their elders politely that perhaps it was time that they moved over.

The format of the championship was that there should be two rounds of medal play after which 32 players would compete in match-play for the title. It was widely expected that Belle Robertson of Dunaverty and The Ladies' Club would come very close to annexing a record-breaking seventh title and when after the medal rounds she shared top place on

Wing Commander Derek Graham, Secretary 1980-1984

a 148 aggregate with Gillian Stewart there seemed no reason to change that opinion. Wilma Aitken of Old Ranfurly with a second-round of 73 had served notice of her intentions.

The development of the championship provided many interesting features. Gillian Stewart, already a championship winner and Curtis Cup player was eliminated by Winnie Woolridge, who under her own name as Winnie Shaw had had a distinguished lawn tennis career which had culminated in selection for the Wightman Cup. She had come to golf comparatively late in life but almost immediately showed a considerable aptitude for her new chosen sport. She would get as far as the semi-final where she went out to Jane Connachan of Royal Musselburgh 4 and 3. Her early and lamented death would deprive both tennis and golf of a keen competitor and a great lady.

The other semi-final between Belle Robertson and Pamela Wright of Aboyne was one of the greatest piquancy. The former was going for the record number of wins as noted and 23 years before Belle McCorkindale, as she then was, had been defeated in the final by Pam Wright's mother, Janice Robertson as she then was. There had been no prior case of mother and daughter winning the national championship so stakes on both sides were high. Pamela however would have to go some to equal her mother's four titles.

In that semi-final, a kind of war of attrition developed, both ladies playing well below their best with holes being generously tossed at opponents. Clearly it was likely to be settled by a mistake rather than any surpassing stroke of brilliance on the day and victory went to Miss Wright although it did not arrive until the 22nd hole.

The weather at Troon that week had been indifferent to say the least and this greatly handicapped Jane Connachan at the start of the final. Playing in glasses she was soon three holes down.

Gradually the Musselburgh girl hauled herself back into the game and applied fierce and unrelenting pressure. Again Pam Wright found herself going beyond the home hole but only for one extra, Jane Connachan nipping in for a notable victory. She had come into the championship very short of good recent competition but after a tentative opening she had steadily improved in the course of the week.

The papers had no hesitation in describing her as a coming star and the *Sunday Standard* was particularly complimentary *"She has perhaps the fastest pair of hands ever seen in women's golf and she hits the ball like any young professional"*.

The combined ages of Pamela Wright and Jane Connachan were 35 and their example was noted in Ayrshire. In the early 1990s, just up the road from Royal Troon, the West Kilbride Club would provide a Men's Champion and a Ladies Champion with a combined age of 28! To the best of our knowledge that remains a mark to be shot at and a token that youth will be served.

When the British Ladies came back with a proposal to play their championship a year later in 1984, the club was happy to accommodate them.

Jane Connachan and Pam Wright on the 18th green, 1982 Scottish Ladies Close Amateur Championship

The Open Championship of 1982

MOST golfers win Open Championships but just occasionally a golfer will have an Open thrust upon him. Tom Watson certainly believed this had happened to him in 1982 at Troon, both then and for a long time afterwards. By this time the Open had finally settled down to being the masterpiece of organisation which it is today.

Tom Watson came to Troon with three Open successes in Scotland already under his belt and he also came as U.S. Open Champion. With him came Arnold Palmer whose visit to Troon twenty years earlier had both revived the Open and sown the seeds of a British renaissance – although that was a long time in coming. This time he was made an Honorary Member of Royal Troon and he hinted at his own mortality by stating that he would not return beyond the limits of his automatic exemption.

Three other stalwarts made their farewells, each of whom could write Open Champion after his name. Henry Cotton, now 75 years old, Fred Daly, some five years younger and Max Faulkner played the last eight holes in a touching ceremonial and, as they holed-out on the last green, they passed into golfing history.

It is always interesting to read the views of participants on the course. It is no great surprise to learn that those who have just returned a 65 think the course sublime while those flirting with 80 are of the party which thinks new venues should be sought. Thus, at the end of the Troon Open of 1982, Sam Torrance – one over par for four rounds – thought the course "an excellent test of golf". Meanwhile Bernard Gallagher had a guarded "perhaps I'll eventually change my feelings about seaside golf but at the moment it's not exactly my favourite game".

In the seventies and probably to this day there was a school of thought that blind tee shots or approach shots to a green are undesirable from a players viewpoint. It will come as no surprise to learn that prior to the 1982 Open Championship the Club received a request from the Royal and Ancient Golf Club to consider altering the ninth and tenth holes on the Old Course to eliminate the blind element of play. To seek the best way forward the Club again sought advice from Frank Pennink, with the final proposals involving the construction of a new ninth green to the right of its present position and the removal of a section of the sandhill between the Championship Tee and the fairway on the tenth. The creation of the new ninth green was assisted by the work on the tenth, as the sand removed was used as the base for the new green. In addition to the new Mackenzie green, the fairway on the ninth was moved to the left creating a more pronounced dogleg with two fairway bunkers built on the left-hand side of the fairway at driving distance. Part of the hill, which protected the old green, was also removed giving players a clear view of the green for their second shot. It is worthwhile highlighting that had the work on the new ninth green not proceeded, the old green required to be lifted and relaid.

The work on the tenth was much simpler, involving the removal and reshaping of the right-hand side of the sandhill, which would enable players to see the mound to the right side of the fairway from the Championship tee. Work on both holes was completed well in advance of the Championship with the total costs of the project paid for by the R&A. A new Championship Tee was also built at the seventh hole.

In the consciousness that preparation had been thorough and all conceivable contingencies foreseen,

1982 Championship Committee

the members and general public settled down to enjoy the week. The fireworks came early. A young American, Bobby Clampett, was off to a flier and led the field by two strokes. He was comparatively unknown this side of the water but did not deserve to be as already he had narrowly missed out on four very prestigious events in the U.S. In moderate conditions he blazed around the course in 67, two shots ahead of Nick Price, another young man with a reputation to make.

Watson was level with Price – nicely-placed, ready to pounce but with the crushing pressure of leadership removed – and he would oscillate between third and fifth for much of the Championship. As always there were some prominent names who had dealt themselves out by a dismal start and both Jack Nicklaus and Tony Jacklin would find opening 77's irretrievable. The cognoscenti looked at the leaderboard when all were in at the end of the first day and they pondered. Not to take too much account of Clampett's score, that was sure.

Someone always had a first round like that and then was heard of no more. The second round would find him out.

It didn't. Clampett improved on his opening bid and his 66 gave him the best two opening rounds since the just-departed Cotton had returned 67 and 65 at Sandwich in 1934. Could it be that this youthful American was indeed too young to feel decently nervous? He had finished his second day at six under for the round and it could well have been a truly miraculous round for at one time he was nine under. He dropped a stroke at both the 1st and 17th but just when eyebrows were being arched knowingly he struck back with a brave birdie at the last.

Despite a scintillating 66 from Sandy Lyle, a new American name on the cup seemed a foregone conclusion. Tom Watson, seven strokes behind, was beyond catching Clampett if the latter played half-way steadily. Put it another way, if Clampett played the last two rounds in level par then, to have a chance, Watson had to break 70 twice. Even Nick Price, two strokes closer to Clampett, would have to go some.

On the morning of the third day, Clampett seemed to have bolted the door firmly. Recovering well from an early dropped-shot, he stood on the 6th tee 12 shots under for the competition. It is a quirk of Open Championship golf that Royal Troon until 1999 possessed both the longest and the shortest holes in the entire rota. The shortest – the Postage Stamp – we have already discussed. The longest – the sixth, Turnberry – at 577 yards has temporarily been supplanted by the sixth at Carnoustie by all of one yard. Under threat from Carnoustie, then St. Andrews and, more menacingly Hoylake, Troon by 2001 had re-established yardage supremacy for an individual hole. The sixth at Troon was to be a Flodden for poor Clampett. Bunkered three times in the course of the hole he did well enough to scrape an eight.

Normally that would have been that but Watson and Price failed to press their advantage and Sandy Lyle had most cause to be pleased with a 73. Now he was only two shots adrift and perhaps a British success loomed. Clampett could console himself that his 78, as bad a round as he could recollect, nevertheless kept him undisputed leader even if the margin was the slenderest possible.

It had been a very odd sort of day because scoring had been pretty high despite the excellent playing conditions. Price and Watson, both with 74's, could scarcely be said to have taken advantage of

Clampett's fall from grace. As against that, the golfers immediately fore and aft of Watson on the leaderboard, Des Smyth ahead, the Japanese golfer Kuramoto and Peter Oosterhuis behind, were comparatively untested in this particular furnace.

The principal question as the last day began was which, if either, of the two young golfers – Clampett and Price – could keep it together and give the Claret Jug a new name. Or could Watson, with a blazing round, overtake them? Part of the question was soon answered. Bobby Clampett could not last the pace. Before three holes had been played he had dropped three strokes to Price and was tottering to a catastrophic 77. His last 36 holes would cost him 22 more strokes than his first 36. At the turn on the final day Price led by a stroke.

At this point Watson, on the 11th, played what many onlookers described as the shot of the championship, a three iron to within a yard of the pin and he clinched his eagle. That would perhaps get going a round which, with only one birdie to date, was rather lacklustre. The importance of the eagle was lost for a moment as Price had a fine spell from the 10th to the 12th which left him two strokes to the good.

Two strokes ahead with six holes to play – steady would do it. All the advantages were with Price save one. Watson had metaphorically been over this course before and had resisted the almost overwhelming mental pressure that such a situation brought. Price dropped a stroke at thirteen but this scarcely seemed to matter when Watson did the same at the fifteenth. As the sixth had destroyed Clampett, so Price allowed the lead to slip with a mortally-wounding six at the, fifteenth where he took two in the pot bunker on the hill short and right of the green.

The denouement was swift. Price bogeyed the short 17th while Watson covered the last three in par. Price needed to finish with only the sixth birdie on the 18th all day and he never really looked like getting it despite a brave attempt at a 12 yard putt. Watson had taken the lead at the only time it really mattered, the last hole. Quite unnoticed, Peter Oosterhuis had come

Bobby Clampett and Nick Price during the 1982 Open Championship

up at a great rate on the blind side and his splendid 70 gave him a share of second place.

It was a mark of Tom Watson's consummate professionalism that he was almost dismissive of his win; "I didn't win the Open", he was quoted as saying, "Nick Price gave it to me." Understandable that such a great golfer would wish to triumph simply by his own exertions but he had worked hard to keep himself in contention and to be in a spot from where he could make his last spring.

Anyway, he had made two pieces of golfing history. He became only the fifth player to be Open Champion of the U.S. and of Great Britain in the same year. He thus joined the aristocratic ranks of Bobby Jones, Walter Hagen, Gene Sarazen and Lee Trevino. His other achievement worthy of merit was that he had added Troon to Carnoustie, Turnberry and Muirfield as Scottish courses on which he had won the Open. The following year he removed all self-doubt about his performance at Troon when at last he won the championship in England, Birkdale being the venue.

Open Championship 1982
Final Leaderboard

T. Watson (U.S.A.)	69 71 74 70 = 284
P. A. Ooosterhuis (England)	74 67 74 70 = 285
N. Price (South Africa)	69 69 74 73 = 285
N. Faldo (England)	73 73 71 69 = 286
D. Smyth (Ireland)	70 69 74 73 = 286
T. Purtzer (U.S.A.)	76 66 75 69 = 286
M. Kuramoto (Japan)	71 73 71 71 = 286

Golfing brilliance sometimes seems to be on loan from the gods, rather than an outright gift. For Bobby Clampett it was, in the words of Robert Browning, "never glad, confident morning again". One hopes he took for consolation the certain knowledge that those first two rounds at Troon would stay happily in the mind of each spectator fortunate enough to see them.

The Open Championship of 1982

By Tom Watson

My first experience at Royal Troon was during a visit to the Scottish West in 1981. A very good friend of mine, Frank (Sandy) Tatum, a former USGA President, arranged a golfing sojourn to a number of great links courses before the playing of the Open at Sandwich. We started our golfing journey at Ballybunion on the rugged west coast of Ireland. We then traveled east to play Old Prestwick, Royal Troon, and finally Royal Dornoch.

I mention these courses in light of the great respect I have for all of them as true links tests, which the typical American golfer has a hard time understanding. In fact, I was just learning the intricacies of links golf at that time and, even today, am still learning every time I step onto a links course. That day, when I played Old Prestwick in the morning and Troon in the afternoon, is one of my fondest memories and will be told to my grandchildren and to all those golfers for whom I have the greatest respect, for it was a day of great camaraderie and joy.

The story of my meeting with Royal Troon really begins with the morning round at Old Prestwick. We started on the first tee with my caddie suggesting a 5-iron, which – for this professional's ego – seemed too conservative. But after playing it and then seeing the complications which could have been encountered if I had not heeded his advice, I zipped my ego into the pocket of my golf bag and left it there for the remainder of the round, while listening to my caddy's every word. Sandy and I had a wonderfully spirited competition, and after completing the round were asked to stay for lunch, which we gladly accepted. We ate and drank our hearty fills and then proceeded to Troon where on the first tee I, for the first time in my life, had the sensation that I might not get the ball airborne, since the effects of the lunch and that last glass of Kummel were taking their tolls. I managed to spray the ball straight right but barely in play. My next shot was a lucky shot that resulted in a fortunate birdie. For the next nine holes, every shot I made was spot-on, so when standing on the 11th tee, I was seven under par! Then the effects of the Old Prestwick lunch must have worn off or, more correctly, the difficulty of the homeward nine made the remainder of the round a challenge that I was not capable of meeting. I finished the round with a 68 with which, I was very pleased. But the memory of the final holes remained. Their difficulty imprinted on my mind ever so strongly, and I knew that to win the Open at Troon the champion had to negotiate the hazards of the incoming nine successfully. The next year's events at The Open were to prove my initial observations concerning the incoming nine eerily correct. It was, in fact, the final nine holes that simply proved the deciding factor in who won and who lost.

Tom Watson receives the Trophy from Captain Sir Robert Fairbairn, 1982 Open Championship

The 1982 Open played at Troon will always be remembered for who lost the tournament, not who won. Bobby Clampett had a huge lead midway through the tournament, only to see it disappear in a series of mishaps that none but a sadist could enjoy to witness. Then on the final day Nick Price seemingly had the tournament won if he could negotiate the last few holes in just two over par. But the treacherous 13th, 15th, and 17th holes reached up and took the claret jug from him leaving me one shot the clear winner.

I had played the last nine under par but not until the last hole had I thought that I had much of a winning chance. My eagle on the long 11th gave me just a glimmer of hope. But a bogey on the long 15th made me think this was not my year since Nick was at that time well ahead of me. The rest is the aforementioned history.

I still look back on that last nine and still think of the first time I played Troon and the thoughts I had of it as having the most difficult finish in Open golf. And I think how fortunate I was to have – luckily – won there after all.

A few years later I again had the pleasure to play Troon before the 1984 Open at St. Andrews. This time I brought with me three close friends from the States who had never experienced links golf. This particular day was bright and blustery, the wind at our backs on the outgoing nine. On the first tee I told my friends, all of whom had handicaps of 10 or less, that we were going to play two distinct courses. The first nine was to be somewhat benign, but the incoming nine a real bear. After playing the first nine in 39, 40, and 41 strokes, their spirits were best described as somewhat overconfident. Not one of them broke 60 on the final nine, and it took a rather long time after that for their spirits to return to normal.

Such is Royal Troon and her great links test. I am forever in her debt for reminding me that she will always be the winner when our egos get the best of us. Royal Troon, thank you for letting me be your champion and for all the wonderful memories.

The British Ladies Championship of 1984

There are various ways of winning major golf championships but shooting 90 in the first qualifying round would not seem to be one of them since so good a golfer as Wilma Aitken had returned a 76. The young American Jody Rosenthal was undaunted although she did permit herself a "there goes the medal". She had the consolation of knowing that the weather, driving rain and a gale force wind, could not possibly be worse though it might very well be just as bad. Her 76 second round was a noble effort but even then she had to participate in a play-off in order to qualify.

The Scots would be particularly dangerous with Wilma Aitken, a Troon member the real threat. National pride had been hurt by the fact that no Scot had been found worthy of Curtis Cup selection. Clutching at straws it was noted that Miss Rosenthal came from Edina, Minn. That was something. In the widely-drawn field she cruised past Cecilia d'Algue of France 2 and 1, it was actually a little easier than the results suggests, and then in the quarter finals the Swiss girl, Regine Lautens, was on the wrong end of a 6 and 5 trouncing.

So to the semi-final where Wilma Aitken awaited her. It was somewhat flowerily described in *American Golf* as "beloved Wilma against the colonist". Beloved Wilma succumbed but only after a protracted battle which saw her edged out by 2 and 1. There were still hopes that the title might remain in Britain since the other finalist was an English girl Julie Brown but Rosenthal was never in bother. Early in the inward half she unleashed a triple-decker, birdie-eagle-birdie and that was that, to the tune of 4 and 3. The following morning the Club flag was observed to be at half mast and one of the American girls on enquiring why was told that "Wilma died on the 17th yesterday".

Jody Rosenthal had struck another blow for American college golf. She was one of the mainstays of the Tulsa, Oklahoma side and at the time of winning at Royal Troon she was also the Minnesota Amateur champion. She was but the latest American girl to profit from a system which produced quality in depth.

Back with the Club

Meantime the usual tidying up of loose ends and the day to day business of the club went on. The links with Atlanta, Georgia remained strong. The Athletic Club of that city had decided to dedicate a Royal Troon Room in their clubhouse to commemorate Charlie Yates' win in 1938. The room rests with the St. Andrews, Hoylake and other rooms commemorating Bobby Jones' major victories. They wrote to see if any memorabilia could be spared for its decoration. The Scottish end responded suitably.

Links with other clubs had become even more important with the conferring of Royal status. A very enjoyable match had been played against Royal County Down and approaches for regular matches were accepted by Royal Lytham, Royal Birkdale and Royal Aberdeen.

The position of Captain was causing some little concern. There was a definite feeling among the membership that holding the office of Captain should not be the automatic prelude to Honorary Membership. In 1986 it was minuted that future captains should only serve one year. This is the perennial captaincy dilemma, the virtues of continuity struggling with the laudable wish to let the honours go round. Before long it was found that continuity had it and in a very little time captains were once more eligible for re-election.

There was a feeling also that clubs within the Club were a bad idea in that they encouraged divisiveness and in the words of the mover, Dr J. L. Hastings, "were not in the best interests of the Club nor of its membership". On a happier note, the club presented two silver goblets to its first-ever Walker Cup player, a young Colin Montgomerie who would go on to become the leading player in European professional golf. The new Walker Cup player would use Royal Troon briefly as his attachment when he turned professional.

Membership of the club continued to be highly prized and to keep numbers manageable there had to be periodic cullings of waiting lists. Golf clubs look for different virtues in their applicants but one thing that those desirous of joining Royal Troon had to have was patience and lots of it. By 1988 it was taking on average seven years to attain membership. The memberships were fixed at 450 Ordinary members, 350 members of the Ladies Golf Club and 120 Portland Club members.

Already the 1989 Open was looming ever more imminently. The correspondence was beginning to flow. The R&A would deal with traffic access, using the expertise gained elsewhere. For the duration of the Open Championship the Club would get 150 free seats each playing day for the stand at the 18th. The Birthday Honours List of 1988 brought an item which delighted the membership. The Head Greenkeeper, Norman Fergusson had been awarded the British Empire Medal. The club showed its gratitude in a tangible way by underwriting the recipient's expenses for the investiture.

Major Developments in the 1980s

Even (perhaps especially) in Ayrshire the best laid schemes of mice and Committees occasionally gang agley. Such was the case with the purchase of Craigend House. The Eighties and Nineties saw considerable expenditure by the Club developing and improving both playing facilities and those in the Clubhouse.

The first major expenditure was the purchase of Craigend House and gardens, an old property situated in what today is the Visitors car park.

From the first idea of purchase to conclusion took around 6 years, with a degree of controversy arising from time to time.

In June 1980 Craigend House was placed on the market at an upset price of £110,000. There was discussion at Committee who agreed to offer £110,000 conditional upon Members approval at a Special General Meeting in August 1980. The seller accepted this and took the property off the market.

At the Special General Meeting the proposal to purchase was rejected by 128 votes to 102. The Committee was unhappy with the result which largely was occasioned by some unexpected suggestion to the Members about the future use of Craigend House, for example creating a Craigend Club for overseas visitors to stay and play the Courses. Despite pleas that the important issue was to acquire the property and land adjacent to the Clubhouse and consider the use thereafter, the proposal fell. However, within days the Committee received a requisition that a Special General Meeting be held (a) to acquire Craigend and (b) to increase the borrowing powers to effect the purchase. The Special General Meeting was called for 30th August 1980 with the Committee making it clear that they were not involved in the requisition but favoured the motions. Alas, Craigend was sold to developers on 29th August and so the S.G.M. was not held.

In August 1981, an approach to the Development Company who had purchased Craigend was made seeking additional car parking space for the Club. The Developer responded by stating that they proposed to create time share flats and if their Clients had "special privileges" they would offer Royal Troon Golf Club access to the leisure facilities of squash and swimming pool. This was rejected unanimously by the Committee.

In April 1983 the style of development was turned down by the Scottish Office after the usual planning appeal process.

In August of the same year, a new planning application was made for 29 flats and garages. However, in March 1984 the Developer asked for a meeting with the Club. At the meeting held in April 1984 their representative was advised of the Club's interest in the site and further advised that he had to investigate and prepare plans for the site.

In March 1985 the Club were advised that the Developer would sell Craigend to the Club for £150,000.

A Special General Meeting was held on 13th April 1985, attended by 213 Members plus Committee, when approval was given to purchase by a vote of 144-78. The eventual transaction was funded by Members Loans of £100,000 (more than half the Members waived their repayment rights over a period of time) and an interest free loan of £75,000 from the R&A repayable over 10 years.

The story wasn't over yet as there was a further Special General Meeting called by Members proposing that a working party be set up to consider developing Craigend/Clubhouse and grounds.

The Special General Meeting was held on 5th October 1985 where the Committee presented a report, with costs from an independent firm of surveyors, to the effect that demolition of the house (now empty and unheated for over 5 years) would cost £7,500 whereas to reinstate the house and create inhabitable "semis" would cost £220,000!

The Members' motion was swept aside by a large Majority in respect of all their resolutions and, at the conclusion, a further Special General Meeting was convened where a resolution to demolish Craigend House was passed unanimously.

Thereafter the Visitors car park was created and would house the facilities for the R&A at the 1989 Open. It was recognised, after the Open, that a proper road access from Craigend to the Clubhouse should have been effected and this was done after the Open with a new entry to the Club off Crosbie Road. It is of interest to note that there are still to be seen, against the wall adjoining the Marine Hotel, the gravestones of family pets of the previous owners of Craigend!

With Craigend House disappearing as an issue, the Committee were concerned in 1986 that the Clubhouse roof and some stonework were giving cause for concern. Initial thoughts were that the entire Clubhouse roof required to be reslated and it was thought, in February 1988, that this might cost £100,000. By April 1988, a full tender revealed that the costs would be £206,000 but could be done in 5 phases. The work started in September 1988 and continued into 1993 where, as is inevitable with a roof on a 100 year old building with so many pitches and thus additional work, the final costs were £250,000 and around £50,000 had to be spent on renovating and strengthening stonework. All of the costs were met without recourse to the Members for loans or levies.

Colin S. Montgomerie
Amateur Days

"I first set eyes on Troon when I was four years old and I've been playing there off and on ever since. At first it was just the kiddies' course and later on Troon Portland because you can't play Royal Troon, officially, until you are 18.

I became a member in 1984 and as an amateur competed in about a dozen or so medals but I have never broken par. I've been level – that was in my last competition there as an amateur in the Summer Meeting – but never better with a card in my hand. I've played all the Championship courses now and I love Troon and always will. It may not be the best of them but it is certainly the toughest. The overhead conditions see to that."

EXTRACT FROM GOLF MONTHLY: JUNE, 1989

Such has been the distinction of Colin Montgomerie's professional career, most notably his almost total monopoly of the European Tour leadership, that it is easy to forget that his amateur career was both protracted and equally illustrious.

It was protracted because, reversing the modern trend, he thought long and hard about his ability to make the transition to the professional game, unlikely as that may seem more than a decade on. As an amateur he would win most of the distinctions open to him but he first came to notice on the back of a defeat. In the British Amateur Championship of 1984 at Formby he reached the final but went down 5 and 4 to an eighteen-year old who equally would leave his mark on the professional game – José Maria Olazabal.

His, Montgomerie's, time as an amateur was going to have to stretch to take in his period as a student at Houston Baptist University. In 1985 he won the Scottish Amateur Open Stroke Play Championship over Dunbar and North Berwick while entered from Royal Troon. His aggregate of 274 for four rounds established a record which would only be bettered by Barclay Howard with 271 over Monifieth and Panmure in 1997.

In his time as an amateur, Montgomerie won 13 caps against the Home Countries; France, Germany and Sweden. He was in the Scottish sides which played in the European Team Championships at Halmstad in Sweden in 1985 and at Murhof in Austria in 1987, two years in which he also found favour with the Walker Cup selectors. He also represented Great Britain and Ireland at the World Amateur Team Championships at Hong Kong in 1985 and Caracas in Venezuela in 1987.

Colin Montgomerie

He himself says that the event which convinced him that transition to professionalism was feasible was a rather less glamorous tournament, the Scottish Amateur Golf Championship played over Nairn in 1987 when he took the title by swamping A. W. Watt of Barassie by a resounding 8 and 7. His professional achievements need not be recorded in detail here but have been and are likely to be such as to force him to postpone yet further the time when he will gratify a strong and abiding wish to have a few rounds with his father, James, over Royal Troon.

His long apprenticeship in the amateur ranks and his father's determination that he should see something of life as most people lived it – a gruelling summer was spent stacking shelves – meant that when he made the final transition he was not only physically but mentally toughened. His early caps in Scottish golf at the lower levels also meant that he had to overcome the drawback of being regarded rather as an Anglo-Scot, a comparable situation to the one pertaining in Association Football and which caused such metaphorical giants as Denis Law and Billy Bremner some grief.

When he played in the World Amateur Team Championship at Hong Kong and Caracas he played out of Royal Troon where his handicap was plus three, early evidence of an exceptional talent. In 1988 he had his first full professional season and although his subsequent career is more properly recorded elsewhere his astonishing Ryder Cup career is certainly worth noting. For almost two generations another Scotsman, Eric Brown, had shone like a beacon in the wreckage of successive Ryder Cup encounters. Four times he emerged undefeated from such frays, often winning the only point that came Great Britain and Ireland's way. In successive Ryder Cups he beat Lloyd Mangrum, Jerry Barber, Tommy Bolt and Cary Middlecoff. This is a superlative record but it has been surpassed by Colin Montgomerie (admittedly with much more backing from his teammates than Brown ever had). His opponents were of top calibre, Mark Calcavecchia, Lee Janzen, Ben Crenshaw, Scott Hoch and Payne Stewart.

It is possible to make two seemingly contradictory prophecies about his future career. The first is that he will spend more time from now on in the United States. He has always liked the American lifestyle, a liking fostered from the time of his university days in Houston. In addition he may find the rule which makes defence of European titles mandatory to be increasingly burdensome.

Pulling in another direction, it seems unlikely that the captaincy of the Ryder Cup team would not be available if he wanted it. He always could handle the playing pressures and with maturity has come the ability to lead and not forsake diplomacy in so doing. This may be some way off as increasingly it is impractical to have anything but a non-playing captain and he will rightly regard himself as still having several years left at top level.

The Open Championship of 1989

"We are not dogs. We can play a bit too" U.S. GOLFER TOM KITE

TOM Kite's slightly nettled response had its roots in what many saw as a subtle shift of power in top-class golf. By the end of the 1980's Faldo, Woosnam and Lyle would be showing themselves capable of winning in America and the infusion of European players to the Ryder Cup side would make an engrossing contest of what had become an archaic embarrassment.

This revival of the competitive side of British golf intensified home interest in top-class matches. Before the 1989 Open got under way, it was estimated that the event would bring close on £10m to Ayrshire and that the police would have to deal with 15,000 traffic movements per day.

For the 1989 Open Championship a new tee was built at the eighteenth hole. This new Championship Tee was nearly thirty yards further back and with the addition of a new bunker short of the two existing bunkers on the left hand side resulted in a much tougher finishing hole. Consideration was given to building another bunker on the right hand side, but this was thought to be too penalising.

The competition was played in a heat wave apart from a dull couple of hours. There was little or no wind worth considering. Norman Fergusson, overseeing the preparation of the course for the last time before retiral, remembers the still, misty, early mornings as he cut holes under the direction of Alan Turner, the R&A's man.

There was much speculation about the outcome, not least among the players. Tom Watson at 40 felt that he could do it again and this would prove to be no wild vision. His rivals considered Greg Norman to be all the more dangerous for coming into the Open on the back of comparatively indifferent form and many considered that the undemonstrative Nick Faldo would be the man to beat. The proven top golfers were looking for wind on the grounds that they could handle it and the less experienced men might not be able to.

The members of Royal Troon as ever hoped for two things – a worthy champion and a stout defence from the course itself. This seemed unlikely when on the first day no fewer than sixty players returned par or better. Lee Trevino, Fred Couples and Paul Azinger all proved Tom Kite's point for him by recording 68's one ahead of the hitherto out-of-form Greg Norman. Three British players were on 69, Mark James the big name among them. It seemed a normal opening day

Nick Faldo, 1989 Open Championship

until Wayne Stephens came in and scattered the field with a 66.

Stephens had gone out in 32 – spectacular, but everyone knew the outward half was the easier and you had to post a score there. Stephens found the inward half scarcely more difficult and covered it in 34 strokes, though the absence of wind made it perhaps rather easier than usual. Stephens came from Jersey, not a bad golfing stable as Harry Vardon had come from there and so too, briefly, had Tony Jacklin.

Nick Faldo had returned a rock-solid, unobtrusive 71 with no shots dropped and a lone birdie. He had done all that was asked of him and saved par with two great recoveries at the last two holes. He would be a threat, so too Fred Couples. And perhaps Wayne Grady would be worth keeping an eye on. It was early days though as the sun beat down and not a few of the Troon gallery decided just to sit it out under sunshades. Mark Calcavecchia had returned an opening 71 which was very creditable but did not immediately mark him out as a possible winner.

The second day is often that on which most sparring takes place but perhaps unusually a decisive move was made first by Tom Watson who of all the top players was perhaps the best at watching and waiting. How would he now fare from the front? It was not, however, the very front because Wayne Grady had put a 67 alongside the previous day's 68 and led by two strokes. Watson had been joined by the individually-clad Payne Stewart whose 65 was a magnificent round. The home players had wilted and, in so far as there was a British challenge, it was being sustained single-handedly by Faldo who was round again in 71. It was, once more, a round in which solidity was the key characteristic and in which there were, to quote J. M. Barrie, "No drums, no trumpets".

Wayne Stephens had by no means collapsed – nothing wrong with a 72 – but, by the halfway stage of the Royal Troon Open of 1989, there were 14 Americans among the 26 leading competitors. It seemed certain that Troon would have to wait a while yet to produce the first home winner on the course since Arthur Havers. As often happens in really good

Payne Stewart, 1989 Open Championship

weather, nobody slaughtered the course with the possible exception of Payne Stewart. Those who could read the runes noted that Greg Norman's recovery of form seemed to be enduring for he had a second round of 70.

Who had dealt themselves out? There were as ever some prominent names – Tom Weiskopf, Gary Player, Tony Jacklin and Arnold Palmer – but they did tend to represent the previous generation rather than current threat. Nick Price was still there and he had been runner-up to Severiano Ballesteros at Royal Lytham the previous year.

At the end of the second day there were some deductions to be drawn. Payne Stewart would be very pleased with life since, because of re-alignments at the last hole, his score of 65 constituted a course record. Watson had come through what might have been a difficult second day very calmly and remained well-placed to observe, rather like a U-boat skipper deciding which ships in a convoy he would pick off. And Mark Calcavecchia had moved up nicely with a

68 although there was still nothing particular which would tag him as eventual winner.

On the third day there was the sense of anticipation that this would be the time when some of the top guns would break free with a really special round. Wayne Stephens returned a 76, which rather put him out of consideration but he could be abundantly pleased with his performance in the midst of the great.

Perhaps the other Wayne (Grady) would be the man. His third round 69 took him to twelve under, one ahead of Watson. The latter felt he could win at Troon.

"When you have won on a course it is easier to win the second time because you have the same feeling".

A Watson success would be very popular with the Scottish crowds given that a home victory was not feasible. Watson, with his previous success and vast experience, appeared to be in the optimum position. Faldo had been despondent when, after having gone out in 32, he could do no better than 38 on the return but he seemed rather more dispirited than a good round had warranted.

The final day acquired an added piquancy due to the fact that Calcavecchia was an imminently expectant father and throughout the Open had declared himself ready to abandon the competition and return to the States at a moment's notice should the situation warrant it. Fortunately, from his point of view, the baby co-operated. The initial fireworks that day came from another source.

Greg Norman's third round of 72 had seemed certain to assign him to the ranks of the respectable finishers – a substantial cheque but nothing more. He now proceeded to play one of the great Open Championship rounds of all time. He started with six consecutive birdies and his gallery, modest at first, swelled as birdie succeeded birdie. Messrs. Grady and Calcavecchia could listen to the roars or block their ears as the fancy took them.

No golfer, no normal golfer, can keep up such a run of success and inevitably there came a dropped stroke, at the Postage Stamp. Norman was, of course, no normal golfer. He reached the turn in 31 and when he added three more birdies on the inward half, a 63 or even a 62 seemed possible.

He did not quite manage that but his 64 was two things: a course record and one of the golfing rounds of all time. Grady and Watson set off together some ninety minutes later and both were entitled to be shell-shocked. There could be no greater testimony to their abilities than the fact that, in the wake of this tidal wave, both men birdied the first.

Watson of course had something else to play for – a sixth Open, which would mean that he had equalled the record total achieved by Harry Vardon and he would have won five of them in Scotland. But he was the first to falter and slowly his position eroded and he dropped out of contention. Grady was outright leader at the ninth. He still faced the difficult inward half but he had already covered it in 33. He could take heart from that and when, with twelve holes played, he led by two strokes it seemed as if Norman's pyrotechnics would have been expended in a glorious but losing cause.

The play-off trio Mark Calcavecchia, Wayne Grady and Greg Norman, 1989 Open Championship

The Third Man, so to speak, – Calcavecchia – had a moderately satisfactory front nine of 35 and was about to play himself into a strong position, oddly enough following some quite indifferent golf. At the 11th he was all over the place but a 14 yard putt saved his par. At the next hole, perched high on a bank left of the green which was fast and sloped away, a four seemed the height of his ambition. From a grassy lie his pitch hit the stick on the full and disappeared into the hole like a descending lift.

Another birdie, more orthodox, followed at the 16th but over the last two holes he needed one more if he was to catch the tall Australian. He got it at the last with an eight iron to just over a yard and it was now up to Grady, following behind, to win it for himself if he could. He faltered and dropped a shot at the short seventeenth but, needing a par at the last hole to tie, he got it bravely and honestly. The three men: Norman, Calcavecchia and Grady – would have to play off.

Over the years the R&A, had reduced the time allocated to play-offs. There was a time when it had needed 36 extra holes to make such a decision. That figure was then halved. There was a real feeling that sudden-death was to be avoided at any cost and therefore at Troon in 1989, the distance was over 4 holes – the 1st, 2nd, 17th, and 18th. This four-hole version was a recent introduction, so recent in fact that almost until the moment of teeing-off Mark Calcavecchia was convinced that he was about to engage in sudden-death play-off.

Surely Norman must win on the back of the momentum which his great final round had generated. It certainly seemed like it early on as he added to his superb day with two more birdies at the first and second. Grady, with two pars, was by then struggling but Calcavecchia, by birdieing the second, had given himself some chance, however faint. With the honour on the 17th, Norman sought the shot that would put the championship out of reach of the others. His shot was stopped by the collared fringe at the back of the green which gave him the dilemma of chipping or putting. He took the wedge, was too strong and missed the return putt. Grady also bogeyed and he was definitely out.

Mark Calcavecchia playing his second shot at his fourth play-off hole, 1989 Open Championship

If two or more of the golfers were level after the four holes, the title would be decided on sudden death and this seemed the probable outcome as the three players came to the last tee. Calcavecchia hit a barely-satisfactory drive which was cut and, while the lie was tolerable, he was a considerable distance from the green. Norman then proceeded to lose the championship by means of a drive that was almost too good. Perhaps the sight of Calcavecchia's less than perfect tee shot impelled him to go for broke. In any case his ball reached a seemingly out of range bunker and nestled against the face. The face had been straightened prior to the Open to make it impossible to reach the green. Calcavecchia now had the final counting shot of the championship. He was equal to it and a dismayed Norman saw a 5 iron shot from an unpromising position roll to within seven feet of the flag.

It was the end. Norman extricated himself from one bunker but found another and his second recovery shot flew out of bounds at which stage he picked up.

Rubbing salt into the wound the young American holed what by now had become a pretty superfluous birdie putt.

It had been one of the great Open finishes, at times of almost unbearable intensity and Royal Troon had been privileged to stage it. Golf has its own severe and just logic. Only three players had broken 70 in three rounds of the championship and they were Calcavecchia, Grady and Watson.

Greg Norman's course record, 1989 Open Championship

The 1989 Open Championship at Royal Troon
By Greg Norman

I started the final round of the 1989 Open Championship seven shots off the pace set by my close friend and countryman Wayne Grady. Even though winning from that position would have been seemingly impossible, as I went to bed the night before my overriding thought was that if I got off to a fast start anything could happen. I dreamed of three 3s that night and I interpreted that to mean I would start the day with three straight birdies. I could not have even dreamed that I would have gone 3-3-3-4-2-4 to start the day – six consecutive birdies.

I finally made a par at No. 7, and felt very comfortable going to the tee at the Postage Stamp. I hit a nine-iron into the bunker and then two-putted for my only bogey of the day. I added three more birdies and finished at 13-under. After signing my card, I remember thinking that with 20 guys left on the course, somebody would surely top my 275. I waited nearly 90 minutes for Wayne and Tom Watson to complete their rounds. But nobody made a move, and when Wayne finished, I had somehow tied for the lead after he could only manage 71. I felt at that point that I had put myself in position to win another major.

But as I stood there all afternoon watching the leaderboard, I never even thought Mark (Calcavecchia) would be a factor until he staked an 8-iron out of the rough on 18. It was a great pressure shot and one that would ultimately win him the Championship. When Wayne and

Mark and I headed into the four-hole playoff, I felt my game was as sharp as anyone's and that I had a better than equal shot at winning.

I hit one tight on the first hole – a little punch-and-run to about six feet and I made birdie. The irony of it all is that 1989 marked the first time in the Open history that a four-hole playoff was used rather than sudden death. Had it been sudden death, I would have celebrated my second Open on this day. But on we went and I hit another one close at No. 2. I had Mark one-down at No. 3 when I hit a 3-iron about 45 feet over the back of the green. I couldn't get up and down, and Mark made three to tie. I still felt good about things when we reached the 18th tee, and to this day I contend that the fairway bunker I hit it in was out of my range. The fairways were so hard and fast that I hit it about 350 yards off the tee into a bunker that I didn't even consider when I lined up the shot. I hit driver there all four times previously and never came close. I drew a horrible lie against the lip, but I had to go straight for the flag after Mark hit a great shot just a few feet below the hole. I hit it in another bunker and then out of bounds just over the green from there. I was finished and Mark capped it off by making one of the few birdies of the day at 18.

1989 Championship Committee

Obviously I was disappointed that I didn't win, but it was Mark's first major and he and Sheryl were expecting their first child at any time. I was very happy for him, and looking back, it just seems he was destined to win.

One stark statistic exemplifies, better than any other, the Open's progress to become one of the great world sporting occasions. In 1962, which may fairly be taken as the last of the old-fashioned Opens, Troon attracted 37,098 spectators with pretty spartan and rugged provision for spectators. Twenty-seven years later those numbers had risen to 160,639 – an indirect tribute to the organisation involved.

The Open Championship of 1989
By Mark Calcavecchia

I first played golf when I was six years old in the small Nebraskan town of Laurel where I was born. My Dad had laid out a nine-hole course and we played on that. With the Nebraskan winter it was a short golfing season, beginning in April and ending sometime in October.

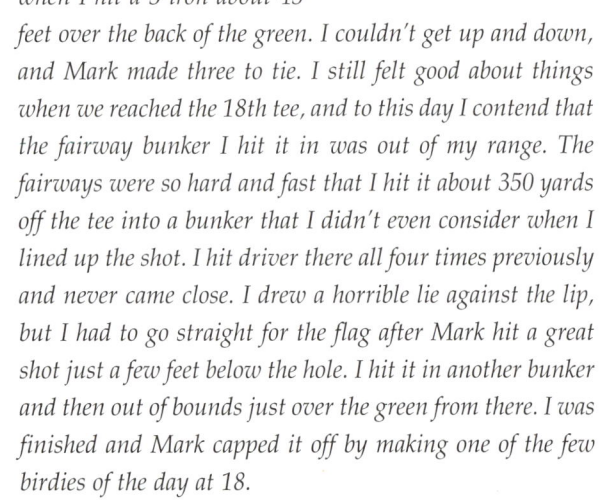

**Open Championship 1989
Final Leaderboard**

M. Calcavecchia (U.S.A.)	71 68 68 68 = 275
W. Grady (Australia)	68 67 69 71 = 275
G. Norman (Australia)	69 70 72 64 = 275
T. Watson (U.S.A.)	69 68 68 72 = 277
J. Mudd (U.S.A.)	73 67 68 70 = 278
F. Couples (U.S.A.)	68 71 68 72 = 279
D. Feherty (N. Ireland)	71 67 69 72 = 279

When I was 13 the family moved to Florida on account of my father's health and we settled in North Palm Beach. My brother took me to a tournament at Doral in 1973 and once I saw the top-flight players I knew that this was what I wanted to do.

It took me a couple of years to accustom myself to round the calendar golf and I spent much of the first "winter" phoning my buddies back in Nebraska to tell them that I was playing golf or tennis. I'm not really sure how much they appreciated that!

In 1986 I had my first win on the professional circuit. Another followed in 1987 and then in 1988 I began to play really well. I won a tournament in Boston followed by the Australian Open and then in early 1989 I won tournaments in Phoenix and in Los Angeles. Altogether I had four successes in four months.

Coming into the Open of 1989 therefore I felt pretty good. My short game was particularly strong and any tournament, which I entered I believed I had a good chance to win.

My preparation was nothing out of the ordinary. I played in a little pro/am in Switzerland to get the jet lag out of the way and landed at Troon on the Sunday night. In all I played three practice rounds. In one of them I was accompanied by Mark O'Meara, Curtis Strange and Arnold Palmer and if my memory's good I clipped Arnold for £50 that day.

Troon was my third Open and the links was much as I imagined it. I'm a huge fan of links golf. It's fun to play a different kind of golf. Normally we play through the air over here (the U.S.A.) and normally everything is so green and watered.

There was a pretty good drought going when we got to Troon in 1989 and the fairways were dry and bouncy. In my first Open at Muirfield in 1987, a course, which I loved immediately, I did well enough to finish somewhere about eleventh. The following year at Lytham I had a terrible time and of course that influenced my opinion at that stage. But, as Tom Watson says, you have to talk yourself into liking links courses otherwise you'll be frustrated by the bad bounces you will get.

When I first saw Royal Troon I thought it was awesome. I loved it and it is my favourite course in the world, and not just because I won the Open Championship there. It is the great variety of holes that attracts me, short and long, easy and difficult.

The key round of my Open Championship was the third one. I had a birdie at the seventh after being in a pot bunker. I didn't play particularly well but somehow scrambled a 68.

The keys to the last round were the 11th and 12th. On the 11th I was all over the place, left bush, right bush, left bush. When I reached the green I didn't even clean the ball but just hit the ball and it went in. At the twelfth a chip went in on the full for a birdie. I hadn't hit a good shot between the seventh and the 12th but I got great momentum from the chip and hit it well for the rest of the round.

Greg Norman had started off with six straight birdies and I was three or four groups behind and I knew very well what he was doing. When he followed by birdieing the first two holes in the play-off I thought "Wow, he's going to birdie 'em all!"

Up to the last minute I had no idea that the play-off would not be sudden death. I admit to feeling surprised when we were taken over to the first and I remember thinking "That's an odd way to decide an Open

Mark Calcavecchia receives the Trophy from Captain D. H. D. Forsyth, 1989 Open Championship

Championship, over the easiest hole on the course." Then I realised that Greg, Wayne (Grady) and I would fight it out over four holes.

And, as I say, Greg birdied the first two and I had to hole a 25-foot put on the second to stay in contention. Playing the last hole, the fourth in overtime as it were, the tournament lay between Greg and myself. I hit an indifferent drive at the last and Greg opened out. I knew from earlier that this particular bunker was reachable from the tee and while Greg's ball was in the air I remember thinking "If this thing kicks a little bit right it can end up in the trap" and it caught the corner of the trap.

I then hit a great five iron second shot to the heart of the green, which came up eight feet away from the hole. This left Greg needing a miracle shot and he found another bunker from which he went out of bounds. I holed a pressure-off putt for a birdie.

The Presentation was a blur, I didn't really know what to say but the crowd was magnificent, not a single one left their place on the grandstand and fairways. Immediately after coming off the course I spoke to my wife who was expected to give birth at any time. Indeed she had thought she was going into labour in an elevator in New York City just before I came over but in the event the baby was two weeks late.

We went back to the Caledonian Hotel in Ayr, my caddy, some friends and I and all week I had been saying "I'll bring the Cup back here and we'll have a party. They said "O.K., sure…" kind of doubtfully but I did and we all had champagne.

What else? I remember working with Peter Kostis, now of C.B.S. T.V. who changed me to playing with a fade and gave me a swing I could play with. We were lucky with the weather. It was amazingly warm and the wind never rose beyond ten miles an hour. How lucky we were as we realised when we came back to Troon in 1997. Then you absolutely had to make your score on the front nine and be three or four under as you would certainly be four or five over on the way back.

In a strange way winning the Open means more now than it did then even although the immediate result of winning a major is that you are treated as one of the best half dozen players in the world at that time. You are in demand and golfers like to travel, it's really neat to get a change of pace and experience different cultures. As I say I like links golf but would not necessarily want a steady diet of it.

Nevertheless talking to Colin Montgomerie who will win a major, has to, he's such a good ball-striker, I realise what a wonderful place Troon was for a keen young golfer to grow up in. As for me, I will remember Royal Troon in 1989 as the place and the time when the course, the weather and my game all came together for one glorious week.

James D. Montgomerie

IN coming to the Secretaryship James D. Montgomerie was uniquely qualified. He was born in Glasgow and educated there at Shawlands Academy and later at Glasgow High School. His twin sporting loves were Association Football and golf. From the first he acquired a very impressive knowledge of Partick Thistle sides and a capacity for enduring reverses cheerfully but it was golf which was to rule his life.

His 'prentice years on the golf course were those at the very end of World War Two and he vividly recalls a charity match at Killermont which featured Henry Cotton, Hector Thomson, Donald Cameron and Bill Shankland. He had already played some golf at Ralston and joined Haggs Castle as a junior member. Shortly after going up to the Royal Technical College (as Strathclyde University was then known) he became a member of Pollok.

A subsequent generation of Montgomeries would gain a wider golfing recognition but James Montgomerie's own record was anything but negligible. He had been a semi-finalist in the Scottish Boy's Championship in 1946, he played to a handicap of three and, during his time at Pollok, he reached the final of the club championship. He joined Troon in the mid 1950's when he was working in Hillington in Glasgow.

Promotion took him to England, as so many other Scots, and his lot fell among pleasant places in Yorkshire, Ilkley to be precise. His application for membership was eventually successful (it was the time of very long waiting lists) and he proved a decided acquisition, being Club Captain in 1979. In 1984 the concern for which he worked was taken over and he decided to return to Troon. With perhaps a prescient glimpse towards such a future, he had retained his membership while in England. He had scarcely moved back when he was sounded out about the possibility of Secretaryship and he assumed this office in July 1987. He served for some eleven years and was in post for two Open Championships although a serious illness limited his participation in the preparations for the Championship of 1997.

J. D. Montgomerie, Secretary 1987-1997

James would say that much of his skill in man management was acquired among (normally) good-tempered Glaswegians at Hillington while from Ilkley, in addition to the golf, he brought away a very keen appreciation of Yorkshire cricket and names such as Bob Appleyard and Brian Close fall readily from his tongue. Son Colin showed a fair degree of promise at this other game while at school at Strathallan.

It is inevitable that James' over-riding priority should have been that strict standards be observed on course and off. His background had been in orthodox clubs and he learned the reasons why certain things were done in certain ways.

For him there were two overwhelming priorities. The first was to carry out the wishes of the General Committee meticulously as minuted and the second was to look after the well-being of the members. From time to time the Secretary might have to act as a kind of interpreter between Committee and membership.

The Public Relations aspect of the job became especially important when expensive projects were taken in hand. Their execution might be vital to the well-being of the Club but the benefits, as for example in the ceaseless battle against coastal erosion, would not always be immediately apparent. Again, a fine greenkeeping staff would merit more than the traditionally Spartan quarters allocated to them by many Scottish golf clubs.

He oversaw the upgrading of the Course and Greenkeepers' Compound and regarded it as very much part of the job to be in daily communication with the greenkeeping staff. In looking ahead he foresaw that in time the Club's whole coastline would have to be safeguarded against further erosion.

Royal Troon is an Open Championship course and over the years James Montgomerie came to have a considerable admiration for the R&A officials. When asked if the Course was effectively taken over by the R&A during the Championship he replied in the affirmative after the slightest of hesitations. He explained this by mentioning that he had been informed by a St. Andrews' man and a security officer that should it be necessary to evacuate the grandstands during the Championship because of a perceived bomb threat, the decision on evacuation would be taken by him, James Montgomerie!

His pride in Royal Troon is manifest and nothing gives him greater satisfaction than the universal reaction of approval when its name crops up among golfers abroad. He is famous as the father of Colin, the most protractedly successful Scottish golfer ever. He sees Colin as his own bridge to the wider world of tournament golf while Scots always wanted to talk about him and wish him well. Sometimes these good wishes got in the way of work but the interest was almost universally kindly.

But not, surely, in the United States? Here the past Secretary made an interesting point. He pointed out that trouble was most likely to arise when Ryder Cup, Walker Cup or Solheim Cup matches were held near big American centres of population such as New York or Chicago. Then non-golfing galleries were attracted, devotees of more exuberant sports such as basketball, baseball and American football where emotions were expressed much more overtly, hence the asinine cries of "In the hole!" or "You're the man!".

In character, even when Colin was being given a particularly hard time of it, James Montgomerie's predominant thought was that there should be no attempt at crowd retaliation when next the Ryder Cup came to Europe.

Interestingly the three players who had most impressed him as people were all Americans. He cited Davis Love III as a golfer and a man and Mark O'Meara as someone who had bridged very well the "gap years" between being 40 and the oncoming of eligibility for Seniors' events. He made the point that, with the firm establishment of the Senior Tour, an outstanding player could quite easily have an earning span of more than forty years. He also admired the ill-fated Payne Stewart for his unassuming behaviour during a visit to Royal Troon.

A recurrent strand in his thinking is that when something requires to be done in the Clubhouse or around the Course then it must be done to the very highest standards available. This is a positive duty in the matter of bequests.

James Montgomerie was prepared to agree that as a city boy it was more difficult to join a club at an early stage. In his own case, his father already was a member of Pollok and with so many men away on service it was easier to get into a golf club than it would have been even three years later. He saw retaining young golfers in the game as a problem which might prove increasingly severe.

Normally the admission of young golfers had to be structured since golf was perhaps the most demanding game for learning social and sporting etiquettes.

He remains a popular elder statesman at Royal Troon, firm in his conviction that he chose the most social of games.

Secretary/Manager James Montgomerie retired in August 1997 to be succeeded by Jan Chandler.

Justin Leonard

CHAPTER SIX

The 1990s

The 1990s

THE Ladies Minute Book presents a historical curiosity at this time. In October 1990 a Greenlees Jamboree was held to celebrate the Golden Jubilee of the Greenlees Tournament, a highly valued competition in Ladies' Golf and one played on an inter-club basis. Count fifty years back and the conclusion is inescapable that the League must have had its origins in October 1940 and that would have been a highly optimistic time to start any golf competition.

The serious as ever mixed with the peripheral. Early in 1990 bad erosion problems were made worse because of severe and prolonged gales in conjunction with high tides. There was major erosion of the first three holes while the safety margins at the level of the dunes were no longer acceptable. Armour stone was to be used in reconstituting the dunes to a higher and safer level and the estimated cost of this work was £150,000. This was all the more worrying in that subscriptions had already passed the £350 mark. It was agreed that the possibility of a grant from the local authority should be investigated.

The Committee took time off from this weighty problem to turn a stern avuncular gaze on the subject of the Prize-giving, which had been too protracted for their taste. Henceforth speeches would be confined to the champion and he would be advised on the need for brevity, which if nowhere else, would be the soul of wit in Troon.

On the subject of dinners, the regal empowerment had meant that there was now a proliferation in the number of dinners where it was expected that Royal Troon would be represented. Three Royals had their centenaries at almost the same time, Johannesburg, Ottawa and Porthcawl – and although Ganton was not a Royal Club, there was no doubt that the centenary of the Yorkshire club was a major occasion and normally for these there was no lack of volunteers.

Sometimes the club's links with the past created problems and such was the case with the Adam Wood clubs. These are among a number of interesting things belonging to the Club, and are probably the the oldest set of golf clubs in existence. The clubs – there are eight of them – were discovered in a boarded up cupboard in Maister House, High Street, Hull, along with a newspaper dated 1741. This is a very old house, and was rebuilt in 1745. It was the residence and Counting House of the Merchant Burgess family of Maister. It is thought that the clubs were very old when they were boarded up. The late Lord Balfour, who was an expert in golf archaeology, gave it as his opinion that the clubs belonged to the time of the Stuart Kings.

Adam Wood, Captain 1893-1897

It was not possible to handle these old clubs, as they were in a sealed glass case in the lounge, so they could only be admired from a distance, which is probably just as well. We have been unable to trace how the donor of the clubs got possession of them. They were gifted to the Club by Captain Adam Wood in 1915.

The difficulty with the clubs was of course that they were almost literally priceless. To keep them on show in the clubhouse was to create a major security risk for already in the United States and indeed in the United Kingdom, there had been cases of golfing memorabilia being stolen almost to order. In addition, the cost of insurance was likely to be prohibitive. A satisfactory if temporary solution was found in the negotiation of a three-year loan of the clubs to the British Golf Museum at St. Andrews where they were put on show. The Club had additionally commissioned the making of replicas of the clubs and these are now on display in the hallway.

Many of the most senior members must have cast their minds back to 1938 and the near miss of J. B. Stevenson. A happy way to keep green J. B. Stevenson's memory was the institution of the trophy which bears his name and was presented to the Club by his widow. Its format, foursomes in which a member and visitor play together with another pairing is a recognition of J. B. Stevenson's liking for and aptitude in that particular format of the game.

The Committee was irked by a *Glasgow Herald* article on women's rights. This swerved in direction to a suggestion that golf clubs that did not toe the line in this regard might find themselves disadvantaged when it came to the renewal of liquor licences. It was agreed that a lofty silence was the optimum response. More agreeable was the edition of *Golf Magazine U.S.A.* which ranked Royal Troon 25th in order of the world's courses, a rise of eleven places from the previous year.

In June 1991, the Club hosted its first Scottish Amateur event in fourteen years, when the Scottish Amateur Stroke Play Championship was played over the Old and Portland Courses. In very testing conditions, where a driver was frequently used for the tee-shot at the par three 17th, Andrew Coltart of Thornhill with a four round total of 295 won the title by two strokes from David Carrick of Douglas Park. Five strokes behind the leaders after 36 holes, the champion's outstanding third round of 72 gave him a three-stroke lead starting his final round and the cushion of victory. Coltart would turn professional shortly afterwards and has achieved considerable success in the paid ranks.

The number of international members had by now risen to 13. These, as the name would imply, were men from other nations, mostly other continents who were recommended by senior members and who were distinguished in various fields of activity. In 1994 the Troon club honoured, with Honorary Membership, Tom Weiskopf, who had won the Open Championship of 1973 and in 1996 Colin Montgomerie who was on his way to becoming arguably the finest golfer that Scotland has ever produced.

It is easy to lose sight of the primary purpose of a golf club which is, unsurprisingly, to allow people to play golf. In recent times one can read ten pages of Minutes before any mention is made of actual play but the club was playing more matches. To take a month in 1998 three matches were played and resulted in a nice equipoise in that the match against Royal Lytham and St. Anne's was won, that against Portland was lost and the game against the Champion's Club of Texas was halved.

The world was shrinking fast. A Captain in the 1950's would attend dinners of nearby Ayrshire clubs and perhaps the occasional one in Glasgow. Now Captain and Immediate Past Captain went off to celebrate the centenary of Royal Harare. This was followed up by making sure that Royal Troon had a presence (Captain and Vice Captain) at the Centenary functions of the Atlanta Athletic Club in Georgia, very much a command performance in view of the long-lasting ties between the two golf clubs.

The Adam Wood Clubs

Major Developments

THE next bad news impacted in November 1990 – see "A Decade of Coastal Protection". This was financed without recourse to Members although the R&A contributed a grant of £50,000. The Scottish Development Agency also contributed a similar sum. Enterprise Ayrshire later granted a loan of £35,000 to assist with the 1993 erosion problem in view of the Club's contribution to tourism in Ayrshire.

In 1991 the Captain Jimmy Armour, asked his Vice Captain, Mike Houston, to chair a Sub-Committee, called Group 2000, to canvass Members for their views on the strengths and weaknesses perceived by Members on the state of the Courses, Clubhouse and facilities. A survey of Members drew a heavy response from them and their views helped to determine a strategy for the years ahead.

In the autumn of 1991 the Greens Committee turned their attentions to improving the utilisation of the Practice Ground. Following consideration of the options the Committee agreed that the best way to accommodate the members' needs would be to consider introducing a Driving Range facility incorporating equipment to collect, clean and dispense golf balls. It was decided at an early meeting that good quality golf balls would be purchased, although this would mean replacing them on a more frequent basis. Like all such schemes, finance was a major consideration, the proposed option being to make a small charge for a basket of balls, the monies generated contributing to the running costs of the improved facility.

As this was viewed as a major operational change for the Club the Committee decided to seek the views of the membership and circulated a paper outlining the proposal. When the feedback was reviewed, a small majority was against the proposed change, however there was one main reason for rejecting the proposal. They did not agree with having to pay to practice. The Committee took note of these comments and decided that whenever the facility was introduced, no charges would be made, the initial and on-going costs being met from club funds. However, before the new facility could be introduced, the implementation had to be postponed due to the erosion problems of January 1993, at the rear of the 6th green.

The new Driving Range facility commenced in May 1994, the process being expedited as a result of a chance comment at the 1993 U.S.P.G.A. Championship. James Montgomerie, the Club Secretary had been discussing the project with his son Colin and had mentioned that the purchase of the equipment had been delayed due to the extension of the erosion protection measures. Colin enquired

Main entrance hall after refurbishment

The Smoke Room

about the cost involved, as he would like to donate the equipment to the Club. The suggestion was put to the Committee, agreed, the equipment purchased and the first balls struck in anger in May 1994. It is interesting to note that in the first month of operation a total of 60,000 balls were hit, greatly exceeding the conservative estimates and proving the immediate benefits of such a facility. In later years, the watering system was extended to improve both the teeing and landing areas and the practice greens. The later introduction of tuition by the Club Professional and his staff on Saturdays during the summer months provided further benefits to the membership.

During Jimmy Armour's Captaincy, it began to be apparent that the Old Course irrigation system was on its last legs and it was resolved that the entire system be replaced. Mike Houston diligently led an investigation into the most up to date systems and suppliers. At the end of the day, the Committee agreed to stay with Watermation who had installed and maintained the original system. The cost amounted to £250,000.00 and the work was carried out in the winter of 1994 and early 1995. The new system has "twin tracks", i.e. the fairways are irrigated by sprinklers on either side of the fairway, as against the original system of a single track up the middle of the fairway which was not too efficient as the effect of wind on the water from one sprinkler reaching both sides of the fairway dissipated a lot of the benefit.

Again the R&A, anxious to assist in improving the standards and quality of Open venues, assisted with a grant of £50,000.

Ian Valentine and Mike Houston determined that the Clubhouse urgently needed improvement and Ian, as Vice Captain, started the ball rolling by

The Dining Room

seeking ideas and thoughts. It was made clear that the Dining Room and Smoke Room would not be changed under any circumstances. It was envisaged that the renovations would take around two years – from January 1995 to January 1997 – with the absolute proviso being that all works be completed for the 1997 Open Championship.

The alterations to the Entrance Hall, renovation of the Club Bar, demolition and replacement of the old toilets and showers and renovation of the Ailsa Lounge were all completed within budget and to timetable. The costs of around £500,000, including carpets and furnishings, provided the Members with a greater degree of comfort including air conditioning in the Ailsa Lounge, a more visible Caddie Master's area which improves security and modern shower and toilet facilities. The design and quality of the woodwork, being in sympathy with the age of the building, has been favourably commented upon.

Although the Clubhouse was receiving a lot of attention, there was continued investment in greenkeeping machinery following the policy of replacement and upgrading. However, the greenkeepers' sheds were in poor shape, there being only one shed built in 1987 worthy of retention. The Committee decided that a greenkeeping staff so often commended by visitors deserved working conditions commensurate with their abilities.

A Decade of Coastal Protection

The sea is the eternal enemy of Royal Troon Golf Club. Up to 1990 any coastal protection work on Royal Troon's 2100 metre long Western seaboard had been carried out by the existing greenkeeping staff as and when required. This work had consisted mainly of chespale fencing and in a few instances, mainly adjoining the 2nd & 3rd tees, of stone-filled containers buried in the face of the dune embankments.

In November 1990 a severe westerly storm swept away these protection works and damaged both the 2nd & 3rd tees. A protection scheme comprising gabion wire baskets and mattresses packed with stone was proposed by specialist gabion contractor C.R.C. Gabions Limited at a cost of £70,000 the work being carried out in January 1991.

Shortly after the above work was completed another severe storm seriously eroded significant lengths of the 1st and 2nd fairways completely eroding the shallow dunes separating the beach from the mown fairway. Action was taken to continue the construction adopted at the 2nd and 3rd tees and in May/June 1991 work was undertaken to protect approximately 470 metres of coast along these two fair-ways. The overall cost amounted to £119,000.

Mainly for budget reasons this protection stopped some 70 metres short of the 1st Tee. Following another storm in January 1993 this unprotected section was eroded and it was decided to complete this length at a cost of £20,000.

The same storm also caused serious erosion of the 8 metre high dunes behind the 6th green. Adopting the same protection method successfully used at the 1st and 2nd holes approximately 120 metres of gabion protection was built on the approximate line of the original dune and the slope of the dune reinstated and protected by a plastic Geogrid mesh to minimise further wind erosion of the sand surface and stop blown sand on the greens. This protection allowed the newly planted marram grass time to re-establish. Grass is now well established and is assisting the re-establishment of the dunes. This contract was carried out in May/June 1993 at a cost

Storm Damage – the 2nd tee, 1991

of £60,000. Planning permission was required to undertake this final phase of the erosion protection measures, as its location was in a section of the Old Course designated as a Site of Special Scientific Interest (S.S.S.I.). The area designated as a S.S.S.I. stretches from the Gyaws Burn to the Pow Burn and includes both the Old and Portland Courses.

All of the protection schemes constructed over this period have successfully withstood any subsequent storms since then and with marram grass now well established and covering much of the area they are relatively inconspicuous. Regular monitoring is carried out and to date the schemes are undamaged and show no signs of movement.

It is unusual for two severe storms to happen within 2 years of each other and the damage to many areas on the West Coast of Scotland has been well documented. Since then other storms have struck the coast as recently as in 1998 and 1999 and it would appear that this part of the country may be in a period of strong storms. Protection schemes that work successfully to withstand the elements should be considered for any areas which might be at risk to safeguard the asset concerned.

Storm damage – rear of the 6th Green, 1993

The Post-war Green Superintendents

Norman J. Fergusson BEM

IT is no exaggeration to say that Norman Fergusson has been a Troon Golf Club man since he drew his first breath which was on 26th July 1927. He was born within the confines of the course, in Gyaws Cottage which the club had built for his father, William Fergusson, who was at that time the Head Greenkeeper. If the Troon professionals were a long-lasting little group, the greenkeepers were even more so. Three only would have spanned almost the entire twentieth century and these three were Charles Marr, William Fergusson and Norman himself. William Fergusson was in his limited spare time a very fine golfer. Norman mentioned in an interview that he (William) stopped playing over Troon Portland with a very definite finality when he overheard another Portland member complain of his continual success.

The Fergusson dynasty ranks in importance alongside those of the Jenkins and the Fernies. Greenkeeping had been a Fergusson way of life for at least three generations. Norman's grandfather was Head Greenkeeper at Prestwick St. Nicholas and when Norman's father and uncle went to work at Troon, aged fourteen, they used to walk from Prestwick to Troon every day before commencing their day's work. Norman had a brief flirtation with the shoe industry before starting work with the greens staff at Troon in August 1942 and most fortunately for the club he managed to see the rest of the war out as an employee before reaching the age of call-up.

During the wartime years his ingenuity and industry did much to keep the club going and some of the other greenkeepers were taking up their peacetime jobs again by the time Norman went off to do his National Service in the Middle East. Back in Scotland he had the misfortune to lose his father, William, who died quite unexpectedly in 1953. William knew all that there was to know about the course, having tended it for some 26 years. The vacated post inevitably drew many applicants when advertised but there was no doubt in Committee that the man for the job was already among them. Norman Fergusson took over as Head Greenkeeper in 1953 and before his time was done he would have been in charge of

Norman J. Fergusson BEM with Captain M. G. F. Houston and Honorary President A. H. Galbraith at his presentation to mark 50 years service to the Club, 1992

four Open Championships after he had tried his 'prentice hand helping his father with the Open of 1950. Highly respected and much liked by the members, his wry account of a round of the course from a Greenkeeper's point of view, delivered at his testimonial dinner, reveals a fluent and original mind. It is reproduced here.

1st Hole

I arrived at the First Green one summer evening to change the pin position, ready for the next day's Medal and I was aware of two men walking over from the direction of the Marine Hotel, one tall and one very short.

I had just decided where to cut the hole and was taking the plug out when the short man came on to the green and asked me if I could explain what I was doing as they were really curious about it. I explained to him some of the finer points of pin positioning – was it reasonably level, well away from any previous pin position, free of plug marks, was there any chance of a strong crosswind next day (keep to the other side), was there any chance of flooding (keep out of the hollows).

He looked at the plug I had just cut out and said, "and what do you do with that?". I explained that I would use it to fill the previous hole in the green as two holes might be a bit confusing! He said that was all pretty amazing as he had never realised that the pin position on a green was ever moved. It would appear that Willie Carson knows as much about golf as I know about riding winners at Ayr.

2nd Hole

One early morning during the practice rounds for the 1950 Open, I was raking the left hand greenside bunker, when I was approached by a competitor who asked me if I would tidy up after him, if he had some practice shots from the bunker. As there was nobody else about, I said yes, this would be OK, whereupon he reached into his back pocket and gave me what I imagined would be a pound note, but which in fact was two fivers.

Frank Stranahan playing in the 1950 Open Championship

This was more than a week's wages for me at the time, so I was well pleased with his generosity. When I told my Dad about this at lunchtime, he said maybe one of the fivers was meant for him, but I said, "No, I don't think so".

The following morning he met me again while I was working at the Second and after chatting for a minute, he asked me who would be changing the holes for the Open and I said that this would be my job, whereupon reaching for his back pocket, he said could I give him a list of the pin positions. This was years before the R&A began giving lists of pin positions to everyone on the First Tee.

I don't think Frank Stranahan, who was the leading American amateur at the time, would ever have been contender for Sportsman of the Year. I didn't offer to give him his £10 back, he might have taken it.

3rd Hole

During the war years there was a naval gun emplacement to the right of the fairway off the drive and a small arms range just over the burn.

The sailors who were my next door neighbours in the Gunnery School in Sun Court Hotel would practise firing at a drogue being towed up and down behind a light aircraft over the sea.

It could be a bit off-putting, trying to cut a fairway when all hell was breaking out just a few yards away, but the good news was that I never had to take evasive action – nobody ever fired back!

4th Hole

Working at the sheds one day, I heard the sound of an aircraft in trouble and ran out in time to see a Mustang fighter disappearing down on to the Fourth fairway. I arrived over there to find it had come to a stop at the green, which at the time was opposite where the shelter is now, and had caused surprisingly little damage. The pilot was totally relaxed about the whole thing and asked if that was the Marine Hotel he had just passed.

This was another noisy fairway to work on as the Army used to come ashore on a fleet of landing barges, on foot, and in trucks and bren carriers and take up position in fox holes all along the dunes and fire over my head at another lot advancing from the Portland Course. There were channels cut through the dunes all along this stretch as far as the Fifth green to enable the traffic to drive from the beach up on to the course.

5th Hole

Number five, Old Troon was the home address of a caddy who lived down a hole behind the green during the war years.

He answered to the name of "Kilwinning" and apparently preferred this lifestyle to being in the Army.

6th Hole

This was another noisy area during the war years. The Commando Unit who were based in Troon used the big hill on the right for hand grenade practice.

I can remember when the old Sixth had a huge sleeper faced bunker right across the hill face on the approach. This was filled in years before the green was moved, but the bunker to the right of the green was very unpopular with a lot of the members and there was a time when we were filling it in one winter and digging it out the next on a pretty regular basis.

Although we had tried altering the shape once or twice, it had always given us a problem with sand blowing on to the green, and when the decision was finally taken to move the green to its present position, I made the mistake of moving the old bunker down to the new green and, of course, it just went on blowing out!

7th Hole

The first warning we had that something very weird was happening at the far end of the old course was when we started getting problems with bursts in the water main crossing the Seventh fairway. One time the pipes seemed to have moved apart at a join, leaving a gap. Another time, the pipe seemed to have been forced up and split open.

This was a 3" metal pipe which, by this time, was pretty ancient and prone to leaks, but this was something we had never experienced before. The clue to what was happening finally came to light at the Eighth.

8th Hole

A new water feature appeared in the hollow to the south side of the tee. This began to take on massive proportions and led to enquiries which established the cause as being due to the collapse of mine workings from Glenburn Pit.

After negotiations with the committee of the time, the Coal Board accepted responsibility for this and brought in earth moving machinery with which they

The 8th Hole, The Postage Stamp

raised the whole area to above the water level using a hill which sat behind the present Ninth Championship tee.

Some time after this it became obvious that the Eighth green was on the move and the back edge was now much lower than the front. This was a complete lift and re-lay job with the back having to be raised two or three feet.

I can remember, when the Pit was in operation, seeing miners unloading from buses in the field beyond the caravan site and walking down a tunnel, which was apparently a short cut to the coal face.

9th Hole

The first attempts to change the blind shot involved building a green which was visible through the gap on the left. By the time the green was ready for play it had tilted to one side so badly that the whole thing was abandoned and we went to plan B, which involved taking a bit off the top of the hill, so that the top of the pin was visible.

It is anybody's guess how much the shape of the course altered at this time, but I can remember as a wee boy, asking my Dad what were the two things I could see behind a hill at the far end of the course, looking from our living-room window. He explained that these were the chimneys of Colonel Staunton's house (St. Andrew's House). In later years, the whole house became visible from the same window.

10th Hole

In all my years under fire, I was only hit with a ball once. This was while changing the pin position on the old 10th green, which was a blind shot to the hollow to the right of the present green.

I don't know what this says about the accuracy of the Troon members because I'm quite sure a lot of them were trying to get me over the years.

I got a letter telling me to report to RAF Padgate just after the war ended and when I got back three years later the green had been moved to its present position.

Like the 9th, the 10th had a new green which was built but never used. Nothing to do with subsidence this time – after a great many hours of hard toil, building the whole area up from a deep hollow and working to an architect's plan, it was decided that the shot to the green would be so difficult that the whole thing was abandoned. It is still there if you would like to try it. It is the flat area between the green and the steps to the 11th Medal tee.

View of the 11th Hole

11th Hole

Before the alterations, the drive to Eleven was from a tee which is now in the rough to the left of the 10th approach, right over the top of the hill.

It was the caddies' job to perch on top of the hills at the 10th and 11th to watch for the drives landing. I think nowadays, they would want a crash helmet and danger money for a job like that.

12th Hole

I was cutting the green one day during the war when I became aware of a tank heading in my direction. I nipped off the green pretty smartly and stood watching while it rumbled on to the green and then took a sharp left turn and continued on its way down to the 9th. Years later I would get overheated if I saw somebody getting a bit too near a green with their caddycar.

The tank regiment was stationed on the course for most of the war years. The tanks were ranked in rows all over the present practice ground and the tents were on the Children's Course behind the houses. Their training ground was all the land from there to the caravan site which at that time was a Polish Army camp.

13th Hole

When my Dad and his brother started work at Old Troon, they would walk to and from their work every day from their home which was the Greenkeeper's House on St. Nicholas.

My uncle told me that they would walk up the 13th Fairway, on summer mornings, gathering balls which had been lost the previous night by members playing into the sun on to a fairway completely white with daisies.

I was always very pleased that I managed to eliminate daisies from the course and would ask if anyone who sees one would get a map reference and report it to Billy McLachlan.

14th Hole

Absolutely nothing of any importance ever happened at the 14th, unless of course you got an ace there, in which case I'm very sorry I did not get to hear about it.

It gives me a chance to tell you about my own hole in one. Although I have been playing since the age of four, I never quite mastered the game and mostly played for my own amazement! The highlight of my career came one summer's evening on the Children's Course. I introduced my father-in-law to the game. He had worked as a dairyman all his life and had a genuine agricultural swing. I was 4 up at the 4th, when my tee shot at the 5th bounced once and then vanished. "It's in the hole!", I shouted, and he said "Oh right, I'll have this for a half then!".

15th Hole

Raising the level of the fairway hollows finally cured the flooding problem. It was so bad at one time that it was known to the members as Loch Brander after the then Secretary.

The alteration we made on the approach partially cured the problem of the blind shot to the green, but an earlier attempt to sort this was less successful.

Again working to an architect's plan, we built a new green behind and slightly left of the present green. This would have added an extra 30 yards to the hole and proved to be so unpopular that it was never completed.

16th Hole

I was working at the green on one of the Open Practice Days, when Gary Player came over and asked me what depth of sand was in the bunkers.

I told him that as far as I knew it stretched from there to Australia as I had never seen anything to prove different. I hope you find this answer funnier than he did!

17th Hole

After a lifetime of battling with the rabbit damage problem, there were a few areas which were pretty well cleared. I had cleared Craigend of the shrub roses and whins right of the 18th and at the 1st tee. The only remaining area on the top section of the Old Course was in the whins at the front tee to the 17th. I spent months with this problem. I would pump gas into the burrows and block them off and everything would seem OK the next morning, but two or three days later, there would be fresh scrapes on the 17th fairway and the burrows would be open again.

This was one of the lowest periods of my life. Can you imagine how it feels knowing you are being completely outwitted by a rabbit?

18th Hole

Some course alterations are more popular than others, but I have yet to meet one that was universally approved. One Monday morning, the Greens Convenor asked me to take away the slight ridge that runs diagonally across the 18th Green. I was a bit worried about this as it was late April and there was a real danger that the turf would dry out. This was in the days before mechanical turf cutters and sprinkler systems.

We got the job completed alright, trying our best to answer questions such as "What the hell are you doing now?". A few days later the Convenor came out and said would I please put it back the way it was.

On the final day of the 1989 Open, I was in the crowd at the 18th feeling a great sense of relief that the week had gone so well with no big problems, when it was announced that there would be a play-off over the 1st, 2nd, 17th and 18th. I was thinking of taking a walk up to the 1st Green, when it suddenly hit me that I had told the lads to take in the pins as the last match cleared each hole. I commandeered an R&A buggy and got to the sheds and back just in time. You would have heard about it if I hadn't!

The 18th Green

William (Billy) D. T. McLachlan

Ayrshire born and bred, Billy stayed in Barassie until the age of sixteen, when his family moved house to Troon. He attended Barassie Primary and Marr College but had no great desire to pursue an academic career and left school in the summer of 1980, at the age of sixteen. In December of that year he started a work experience programme with John Menzies, but after three months decided he preferred the outdoor life. In the spring and summer of 1981 he devoted his energies to playing golf.

Although an accomplished golfer, he never felt good enough to turn professional and through the father of his golfing partner, a close friend of Norman Fergusson, he learned about a vacancy for an apprentice greenkeeper at Royal Troon. He decided to enquire about the vacancy and went to see Norman Fergusson. He remembers knocking at the back door of Norman's house and this tall man appearing at the back door, where the interview took place. He was offered and accepted the job on the spot. He started in September 1981 and became Royal Troon's first apprentice in ten years and the youngest member of staff by a similar margin.

He was the first Royal Troon apprentice to attend Elmwood College and he excelled among his cohort of sixty trainees. In his second and third years at College he was the second placed student in his year, the coveted top place going to a mature candidate who was already a Green Superintendent. Even at this early stage in his career Billy's abilities had been recognised and were being carefully nurtured by Norman Fergusson. As his career progressed, Norman's confidence in Billy's abilities increased and his skills were increasingly utilised on the critical jobs on the links, verti-draining, key tasks on the greens and the application of feeds, fertilisers and weed-killers. Naturally, this trust was reciprocal and under his mentor's guidance his skills and knowledge were honed. Billy and the rest of the Green staff all wanted to do their best for Norman Fergusson, due to the nature of the man and the great boss he was.

In the summer of 1992, Jimmy Armour as Captain, Mike Houston as Vice-Captain and David Smyth as Green Convener met with Norman Fergusson to discuss his thoughts on retirement and possible successors. Norman indicated that in his opinion Billy McLachlan was a strong candidate and with Norman's agreement Billy was appointed Deputy Superintendent, commencing this new appointment in August 1992. With Norman Fergusson's retirement looming, and with his strong support, the Committee agreed to the appointment of Billy McLachlan as Green Superintendent on a two-year probationary

Billy McLachlan, Greens Superindendent

period. To ease the transition Billy was appointed to the post in September 1993, which permitted a four-month hand-over period. Norman Fergusson retired at the end of December 1993, with Billy taking over on his own from the 1st of January 1994. Although never doubting his abilities there was a certain degree of trepidation in taking over from the "Big Man", as he was affectionately known by his staff. As one would expect, the initial move for one of the boys to top man was difficult, but Billy would proceed with confidence, knowing that Norman was always available for advice, if required. In fact to this day Billy still enjoys visits from Norman as it allows him to show the Master the latest equipment at his staff's disposal and any alterations or additions which have been made to the courses.

The Committee's confidence in Billy's abilities was demonstrated, when his appointment was confirmed after only one year of the probationary period.

In common with Norman Fergusson, whose youngest brother Willie was a greenkeeper at Royal Troon, Billy's youngest brother John is a member of his staff, being appointed by Norman in 1990. John is currently the Team Leader for the Portland Course.

Billy McLachlan has now been involved in three Open Championships at Royal Troon, two as a member of the green staff and one in charge in 1997. When asked the difference between the two roles, he replied, "As a greenkeeper I worked closely to Norman Fergusson's instructions. As Green Superintendent I spend more time planning the setting-up of the course and preparing staff workloads and rotas." The plaudits received about the course during and after the 1997 Championship bear testament to his and his staffs' abilities. He enjoys the buzz of the Open, but when asked what he enjoyed most about the Championship, he replied smiling, "When it is over!"

During his employment at Royal Troon, the major advances he feels have been in the machinery at his disposal, the upgrading of the staff facilities and the replacement and development of the automated watering system. He is extremely proud of the position he holds and enjoys the challenge of looking after Royal Troon's three courses. In his own words, "Royal Troon is a great Club, with a good Membership and I am very privileged to hold the Top Job". His future ambitions are to see further improvements in the courses under his control and to continue, where possible to extend the period during which the courses are in peak condition.

Married with four children, he enjoys nothing more than playing a few holes on a summer evening with his eldest son on the Par 3 Course. His opinion is that McLachlan Jnr. will be a better player than his father.

His relaxation is spent on the links, playing to a high standard, his lowest handicap having been ONE. His current handicap is two, which is a reduction from the four it increased to when he took over from Norman Fergusson. This was a re-assurance to Royal Troon's Committee of his dedication and his intention of getting to grips with his new role. He plays most of his golf nowadays on the Portland Course, where he is a member of the Club. He was the Portland Club's Champion in 1989 and on three occasions has scored a scratch 66 in a medal competition, once with a ball out-of-bounds at the 7th hole. Previously a Member of the Troon Welbeck Club, he was their Club Champion in both 1983 and 1989 and also won their Open Competition in 1989. He has been the beaten-finalist in the Troon Links Championship on four occasions and in 1985 lost to David Smyth, who eight years later would be Green Convener when Billy was appointed to succeed Norman Fergusson. Both strongly deny any connection between the two events!

Although not a keen football supporter, he keeps an eye on the progress of Ayr United F.C., in case Norman Fergusson comes to visit.

The Greenkeeping Staff, 1997 Open Championship

The Open Championship of 1997

A GOLF COURSE is seldom in a static state, rather it is continually evolving. Those competitors of 1997 who had played in the previous Open Championship at Troon in 1989 would have noticed some fairly major changes. There was a new Green Superintendent, Billy McLachlan, taking over from Norman Fergusson. He had of course experience of the Championship in 1982 and 1989 under Norman's direction and would prove an extremely capable replacement.

There was a new watering system which had cost £250,000 and covered greens, tees and fairways. On the latter there were two banks of sprinkler heads which made it possible to overspray the rough. The other major work on the course had been the coastal protection measures. Out at the ninth the two-tier green had been slightly reshaped with the back tier being flattened out. The green now had small mounds both on left and right approaches. The fairway had been realigned so that it was rather more left and while this made the hole more of a dog-leg, there was compensation in the fact that a player could see the whole of the flag from the normal landing area for his drive.

Further surgery had been carried out on the 11th hole which, in 1989, had been widely held to be much too easy a par five. Perhaps it was the effect that was major rather than the surgery itself because, by the modest device of lopping 18 yards from the hole's 481, the hole changed from being a very probable birdie to being a fiendishly difficult par four. At just over 7000 yards, a par of 71 might be seen as pretty demanding.

At the 15th work had also been carried out to ensure that a well-hit tee shot had its reward with a view of the whole flag for a drive played down the left hand side. A ridge that traversed the fairway some 120 yards from the green had also been lowered, proving that the question setters were not totally without compunction.

There can never have been an Open Championship which threw up so many plots, sub-plots and counterplots. Troon in 1997 had everything. There was the emergence of the inordinately gifted Tiger Woods who evoked the enthusiasm earlier commanded by such as Arnold Palmer and Severiano Ballesteros. Tigermania became a fashionable

1997 Championship Committee

affliction. There was the heart-warming story of the Scottish amateur, Barclay Howard, who would come back from golfing obscurity to finish as the leading amateur and in doing so play three splendid rounds. And there was the sad sight of Ian Baker-Finch, Open Champion of a few years previously, now seemingly incapable of putting two shots together. Add to this the presence of H.R.H. The Duke of York and few, if any, ingredients were wanting for a quite exceptional championship. The Duke played off eight and had put it on record that his favourite golf course was Machrihanish in Kintyre.

There had been a huge entry – 2133 had at least gone through the initial stages of formal application. Four courses were pressed into service for the qualifying rounds both Gailes courses, Bogside and Barassie. As the players assembled, special thought was being given to security. Inevitably this involved Tiger Woods and the line taken was that security would be thorough but not obtrusive. What always happens when an especially charismatic golfer emerges is that he brings a fresh public to the game whose boisterousness, rather than any malice, can cause problems of crowd control. Michael Bonallack, Secretary of the R&A referred to this when he said: "A new element has started following golf in the U.S.A. and they were getting a bit rowdy at the U.S. Open last month."

Scottish golfers told themselves that they were above such antics and bathed in the warm words of Jack Nicklaus on arrival: "Of all the countries in which I have been fortunate enough to play golf Scotland is my favourite." Nicklaus, not the most patient of mortals would have been glad of the measures announced for the speeding up of play. There would be one penalty-free warning. A second warning would incur a penalty stroke, a third two strokes and the fourth would result in disqualification.

A good number of golfers would be making their first Open appearance, but among the more experienced there were great hopes that a man with strong local affiliations, Colin Montgomerie, could come through on his own turf. His past experience had not been propitious since he had failed to make the cut in four of the last five years. He had, however, just come second in the U.S. Open. Could he go one better on a course which he thus vividly described?

"You're really hanging on from the seventh tee onwards"

Arthur Havers had earned himself £75 for his 1923 win. The victor this time would take away a cheque for £250,000. All the major threats for the title were in unusually good form coming into the championship. Woods had won five tournament events, including the Masters by an almost indecent margin. There was a kindly interest in him and, in some quarters, an ignoble desire to see him fail. He was to play three ordinary rounds – not all that ordinary but burdened by the isolated 6, 7 or 8. Nevertheless, the grizzled veteran (of the kind that infests Scottish golf courses) who muttered "Aye, ye'll no' reduce this course to a

Justin Leonard on the last green, 1997 Open Championship

pitch and putt" was forced to reconsider in the light of an awe-inspiring 64.

As ever at Troon the weather would command most attention. The first day's play took place under grey lowering skies and the blustery winds that remind Scots that they are not put into this world for pleasure. Only five players would better 70 all day. Accepted wisdom on Open golf is that you cannot win it on the first day but you can lose it. With a 76, Montgomerie was not quite out of it but had given himself a heavy burden. Woods had returned a 72, containing one disfiguring hole, and it was only a bad round to those who had come to see him shoot four 65's. Two young players, Darren Clarke and Jim Furyk, had returned 67's and as ever the running was made on the front nine. Indeed, in the miserable conditions, Jesper Parnevik was the only player to match par on the inward half where the eighteenth was universally acknowledged to be unreachable.

Elsewhere the Scottish amateur Barclay Howard had returned an excellent 70 but there is seldom, if ever, an obvious winner after the first round. For one man there would be no second round. Ian Baker-Finch had seen his game disintegrate completely and he was also suffering severe back pain. He debated long and hard whether to play at all before informing Michael Bonallack that he would. He recorded a heart-breaking 92 – 44 out and 48 back – before retiring from the Championship and, to all effects, from major competitive golf.

The attitude of his fellow professionals was interesting. There was a good-mannered reluctance to comment at all and the expression of commiseration was widespread and perfectly sincere. Yet there was also an expression of unease, as if even to discuss the subject might bring on the heads of others the ailment – whatever it was which had terminally damaged Baker-Finch's career. Like all professional sport, golf calls on its practitioners to be self-absorbed most of the time although, as we shall see, exceptions can be found.

Day two was such that the weather seemed from another country: sunny with a gentle breeze. Darren Clarke put one excellent round on top of another and led on 133 with Justin Leonard two behind him and Parnevik three. Clarke suddenly seemed a very credible winner and he was quick to acknowledge the help that Montgomerie had given him from his unparalleled local knowledge. All three players – Clarke, Leonard and Parnevik – had gone round in 66. Leonard's round was, perhaps, the most meritorious in that he had to complete it well after the other two were safely in. At that time, Leonard still had the inward half to play, well-described by Peter Masters in *Golf Illustrated* as "a mad scramble for the sanctuary of the clubhouse."

Woods was not totally eliminated from contention although his 74 included an 8 at the tenth which owed something to a sudden flare of temper. But he was still there and the same could not be said of Ballesteros, Player, Price, Lyle, Torrance, and Azinger, though most of the great deeds of these men had been in times past.

Day three saw the fine weather continue and 29 golfers took advantage of it to beat par. When the dust had settled Woods had shown what an exceptional golfer he was with a round of 64 – 32 out and 32 back. It was possibly a shade too late – to win he would have to do as well again or even better, but still he had to be watched. The new leader who would be watching him was Parnevik who led from Clarke by two strokes, rather disappointing for the latter in view of the favourable conditions. Many of Clarke's friends had made the short sea crossing to Troon to see if he could become the first Irishman to win the Open since Fred Daly in 1947. A few seasoned veterans would also warrant a cautionary glance. Fred Couples had come in with a 70 which, unusually, had an eagle but no birdies. But Parnevik still seemed to be the man to beat and he led, despite his 71, by two strokes from Clarke and five from Leonard.

In the crisis, Leonard kept his head remarkably well. Clarke faltered after an early shank and shed strokes and Parnevik then looked the winner down to the last half dozen or so holes but had two bogeys over the last three where Leonard had two birdies. He

Open Championship 1997
Final Leaderboard

J. Leonard (U.S.A.)	69 66 72 65 = 272
D. Clarke (N. Ireland)	67 66 71 71 = 275
J. Parnevik (Sweden)	70 66 66 73 = 275
J. Furyk (U.S.A.)	67 72 70 70 = 279
S. Ames (Trinidad & Tobago)	74 69 66 71 = 280
P. Harrington (Ireland)	75 69 69 67 = 280
F. Couples (U.S.A.)	69 68 70 74 = 281
E. Romero (Argentina)	74 68 67 72 = 281
P. O'Malley (Australia)	73 70 70 68 = 281

was home and hosed and added more belief to the notion that golf was becoming a young man's game by becoming the third 'twenty-something' to win a major title that year. Woods at 21 had won the Masters, Ernie Els the U.S. Open at 27 and now Leonard had annexed the Open with a round that was at once brilliant and disciplined.

And what of Woods, who had needed something breathtaking? As often happens, the round was good but early chances for birdies were missed and he absolutely needed birdies. When he got two consecutively at 4 and 5, it seemed that this might be the kick-start that his round needed. In his catch up position he could not afford to drop strokes anywhere and the Postage Stamp wrote finis to his ambitions when he ran up a triple bogey six there. Nevertheless he had demonstrated his credentials to the British public and justified the advance hype and publicity.

My Performance at Royal Troon in 1997
By Tiger Woods

The record will show that I placed 12 strokes behind the winner, Justin Leonard, in the 1997 Open Championship at Royal Troon with rounds of 72, 74, 64, and 74 again. My scores in all but the third round were ruined by a few high numbers such as 7 at the 11th hole in the first round, 8 at the 10th hole in the second round, and 6 at the par-3 eighth hole in the final round.

The frustrating thing was, I was hitting the ball really well but getting nothing out of it. I was able to turn things around for one day, when I shot 64 in the third round to equal the course record. I knew I would be all right if I could just eliminate those high-scoring holes, and that's what happened.

I went out in 32 and came back in 32, having one eagle, seven birdies and two bogeys. The eagle-3 was on the 16th hole, where I played a two iron off the tee to be short of the burn that crosses the fairway. I then had 280 yards to the hole, and I played a driver off a bare lie in the fairway, and finished 15 feet from the hole with my second shot.

For a while there, I thought I might contend for the Claret Jug, but it was not to be in this, my first Open Championship as a professional.

Tiger Woods' course record, 1997 Open Championship

There had been, for those who enjoy these things, a remarkable oddity on the second day when three Scandinavian golfers – Edlund, Olsson and Fulke – all achieved holes in one and even more oddly each did it in a losing cause since none of them survived the cut. Jack Nicklaus had survived and rolled back the years on the last day by going to the turn in 35 before bowing out with a 40 on the inward half.

There remained certain questions for the golf enthusiast. Jesper Parnevik had abandoned a winning position and moreover had done this for the second time. He was certainly his own man so the question was: Did he have a streak of eccentricity that in the last analysis stopped him winning at the very top level? Justin Leonard was much more organised and his sister Kelly remarked that he was the kind of fellow who "made lists of lists".

Barclay Howard could be well pleased with his week's work. His first two rounds of 70 and 74, excellent scoring, had been followed by a slight sag to 76 and in the circumstances one would have looked for a final round in the 80's. Not a bit of it: Howard in his final round returned a superb 73 to finish on 293 and take the Silver Medal. His labours of course had no pecuniary implications although it is worth noting that he would have received £5,750 had he been a professional but he had, for a golfer, the much greater satisfaction of having gone stroke for stroke with Nicklaus over the four rounds.

One other development has to be mentioned. Aware of the need to popularise the game amongst the young, the R&A had taken the decision to allow free admission to under-18's provided they were accompanied by an adult. It was a bold gesture and there were those who had grave doubts as to its wisdom but it was as successful as such a bold gesture deserved to be. There will be more to say on this later.

Two men stay in the mind from the week – Baker-Finch and Leonard. Only a few days before the Open, Baker-Finch had taken the clubs over to Ireland and had returned a 3 under par 68 over the European Club. He must have nourished hopes that whatever affliction had been laid upon his game was on the point of lifting. It was not and, instead, the onlookers came to realise on what precarious terms top golfers lease their genius. There was real sadness in his remark:

"When you're bogeying or worse you start to notice the cameramen on you and all that stuff."

Leonard made his own little bit of Open history in 1997 by becoming only the third man to overhaul a five stroke deficit, the others being Jim Barnes at Prestwick in 1925 and Tommy Armour at Carnoustie in 1931. The feat has, therefore, never been accomplished outside of Scotland to date.

Troon had had a great week's golf and at the end of it had crowned a most deserving champion. The young American had won in conditions alien to him and well described by the experienced Curtis Strange:

"Links golf usually means hard, fast fairways, lots of wind and playing the ball along the ground instead of in the air. You must guard against saying "Good shot!" until the ball stops rolling. You're going to get some lies and breaks you think you don't deserve. But that's all part of links golf. You just aren't going to hit many greens on the back nine and you must rely on your short game to help you score."

Sound advice, duly taken by Leonard, so well taken in fact that in the entire four rounds he was never bunkered. Tiger Woods was similarly to be bunker-free in the Open during his memorable week at St. Andrews in 2000 but Leonard had got there first though to considerably less acclaim. He is above all a methodical golfer, one who thinks his way round the course. In his own memories of the 1997 Open he lets us see the amount of preparation which led to his eventual triumph.

The Open Championship of 1997
By Justin Leonard

My fondness for the Open Championship began in 1993 while playing as an amateur at Royal St. Georges. It was my first time at the Open, and after playing in the U.S. Masters and U.S. Open that same year I felt I was ready for the challenge. I was so young then. I came away from that week, after missing the cut, with a new interest and future love, links golf.

I returned to Scotland in 1995 to qualify successfully at St. Andrews, then the following year at Royal Lytham. I learned some invaluable lessons during these two years of qualifying and playing. I had a better understanding of how to prepare myself to play a links course under Open Championship conditions. All of the oddities, the different weather conditions, the little bounces here and there, and the types of shots to play around the greens can be overwhelming.

So many Americans who travel to Scotland to play links courses believe that you have to hit the ball low in any and all conditions. I began to realize after my third Open that you do have to hit the ball low, but you need to know when to do it. The way I play the game, course management is not an option, it is a necessity. That aspect of the game becomes even more important on a golf course such as Royal Troon.

In preparing the week before the event in 1997, I spent time working on many things. I knew that I needed to lower my ball flight to keep shots from being affected as much by the wind. When hitting practice balls, I found the tightest lies possible, sometimes hitting from bare ground to prepare myself for the hard ground in Scotland. I worked on driving the club down into the ball, almost squeezing it against the ground to simulate the tightness of the turf. I worked on similar lies around the greens, trying to pinch the ball rather than sliding under the ball as we so often do in America. I practiced putting from off the green, over knobs and through valleys, knowing this can be very important around the greens.

Since this was my first year to be exempt from qualifying, I decided to arrive on Sunday, giving myself four practice rounds rather than only two if I had needed to play in a qualifier. I also decided that my best preparation once in Scotland would be to actually play the course rather than using the practice grounds. I played four full practice rounds Sunday through Wednesday, plus eight extra holes late Tuesday afternoon. I felt that playing as much as possible would help me to learn a few extra things about working my way around the course. I also wanted to be very comfortable with my club selections from tees due to the number of holes on the front nine that required irons. In fact, the only drivers I hit all week on the outward nine were on holes 4 and 6, the two par fives. By Wednesday night, I felt confident that I had done all I could to be prepared to play a very difficult golf course.

I awoke on Thursday to the sounds of the wind. Playing in the afternoon that day, I knew it was going to be very difficult, and patience was going to be the key. A player has

Justin Leonard receives the Trophy from Captain I. B. Valentine, 1997 Open Championship

to take advantage of the outward nine when it is downwind, as it was the entire week. The scoring had to be done early in the round, as the back nine is one of the toughest in Open history. I remember not being particularly happy with my outward half, knowing how difficult the inward nine was playing. I proceeded to miss every green in regulation on the inward nine that day. As horrid as that statistic sounds I managed to shoot even par. I remember standing on the 18th tee at two under par. The wind was blowing so strong that I was unable to reach the fairway with my tee shot, and had to chip forward out of the rough. I then hit a six iron to about 12 feet, and made the putt for par to shoot 69.

The conditions on Friday were much kinder, and scoring well became very important. It is difficult to make up ground in the Open, so it was crucial to stay in touch with the leaders. After a solid start, I hit a four iron second shot to the par five 4th. I made the 15 foot putt for eagle, then followed that with a 20 foot putt for eagle at the par five 6th. At the end of the day, I had shot 66 and found myself in the final group on Saturday.

Paired with Darren Clarke, the third round did not go as well as the first two. Darren made some incredible saves on the back nine, while I seemed to play tentatively, leaving putts short most of the day. I remember looking at the leaderboard on the 17th hole, and realizing that I needed to make a birdie to play with Fred Couples on Sunday. I hit a solid tee shot to the par three, and made the putt for my first birdie of the day. I was disappointed with my round, but excited about playing with Fred, knowing I would enjoy his company.

That night while having dinner near Jack and Barbara Nicklaus, I was reflecting on my day. Barbara walked over and patted me on the shoulder and said, "If you can get your putts to the hole tomorrow, you can still win this." I knew exactly what she meant. I needed to play more aggressively to make up five shots and catch Jesper Parnevik. I sat in my room late that night, thinking about a tournament the previous month that I won by making up five shots during the final round. I was rejuvenated. I now had a mission.

Rather than thinking about what Saturday could have been, I was thinking about making Sunday something to remember.

While warming up on the practice ground on Sunday, I was hitting 1 irons off of a side-hill lie. I hit seven or eight of the best shots I had ever hit, and I knew then that it could be a fun day. After 14 holes, I was four under for the day, and one shot behind Jesper. I missed the 15th fairway, and hit a poor approach short and right of the green. I then hit a mediocre chip fifteen feet short of the hole. While I was reading the putt, I told myself that in order to have a chance to win, I needed to make it. This is probably not the best line of thought to have, but I made the putt regardless and maintained my momentum. I faced a similar putt on the par five 16th after a poor third shot. I calmly made the birdie putt to climb into a tie for the lead. After a solid 3 iron at the par three 17th, I read the 35 foot putt as though it were the last one I would ever hit. As the ball neared the hole, the hair on the back of my neck stood up as it was tracking dead center. Just after it disappeared, the gallery roared with approval, and chills went up my spine.

On the walk to 18th tee, I tried to regain control of my emotions, and focus on the job at hand. While standing on the tee, which is adjacent to the 16th green, I heard a loud moan from the gallery as Jesper had missed his birdie putt. Now I was a stroke ahead, and hit a three wood to the fairway. Not wanting to take any chances, I hit a six iron to the middle of the green and two putted from 35 feet to cap a round of 65. As I was walking to the scorer's tent, my caddie told me that Jesper had made bogey on 17, and that I had a two stroke lead.

After signing my scorecard, the press secretary from the R&A told me of the procedures for the awards ceremony. It did not hit me that I had just won the Open Championship until the middle of my acceptance speech. At that moment, it all came upon me what I had accomplished, and I struggled to regain my composure. After finishing, it was a whirlwind of congratulations, interviews, and photos.

That night, after speaking with my family and friends, I began reflecting on the day and what it meant to me. I walked out to the 17th green with my caddie and some people we became friends with during the week, and talked about the day. It was a special time and place to let it all soak in, and enjoy the setting. I had won the battle, the battle that so many of the world's best had fought, and only the best of those had won.

One of my fondest memories is meeting my family after the return trip home with the Claret Jug and seeing how happy they were, letting them hold the trophy, talking about the whole experience. It was a wonderful time in my life, and continues to be to this day.

I returned to Royal Troon during the summer of 2000 in preparation for the Open Championship. I played a round with my father, Larry, and my instructor Randy Smith. As we played, we talked about certain shots, or I *showed them where I hit a chip from, or where I made a certain putt, and we would hit the putt over again. It was a wonderful day, and the hospitality shown to us by the membership made it even better. I was able to see my name on a locker in the Captains' and Champion's Locker Room, even though I was not supposed to be there. It was a chance to share Royal Troon and all its splendors with my family, and they were able to see just how special a place it is, and why it holds a special place in my heart.*

Thank you for the opportunity to review and remember these very special times in my life.

Out-takes from the Open Championship of 1997

There are few utterances more revealing than those that a golfer makes in the Press Tent when the Championship is behind him. For several years David Begg had the difficult job of persuading the players to distil their thoughts for general consumption. Here is Jack Nicklaus, having made the cut and having performed perfectly respectably yet still, in the phrase of Dylan Thomas, "raging against the dying of the light". It absolutely encapsulates the man, amiable but with an underlay of spikiness. He was asked by David Begg if he had enjoyed the ovation from the crowds in the stands at the eighteenth as he came up the last fairway:

"It's always very nice. I love to come up the 18th but I'd love to come up four or five hours later when there are a lot more spectators in the grandstand and I am in contention ... I do not come to play in the Open to walk the 18th fairway at 2 o'clock in the afternoon. I do not walk up the 18th to get an ovation for my golf of the last 30 years. Making the cut is decent but it is not competitive. Competition is the chance to win the tournament. I'm not here just to play four rounds of golf."

In that speaks the consummate professional and the unwillingness to settle for anything other than top grade that was so instrumental in prolonging Nicklaus's winning career.

Colin Montgomerie, who had played well without ever really threatening, revealed a balanced

Barclay Howard receiving the silver medal, 1997 Open Championship

equanimity and a wry sideways look at the expectations laid upon him by his fellow countrymen:

"It's a pleasure to play with a crowd that are as much behind you as that. But I did not play to my potential this week. This is the best support I've ever had. Sometimes I have not had the support you would expect in Scotland, for example in the Dunhill Cup. Here, though, the support has been fantastic."

Mark Calcavecchia had done it all before of course but was far from blasé:

"It sure as hell beats the U.S. Open. Everyone in golf is here. I'm the opposite to Monty (Colin Montgomerie). The U.S. Open is his favourite tournament but the British Open is mine. I'll be back."

Perhaps the most poignant remarks came from Barclay Howard who a couple of years before had virtually dealt himself out of good class amateur golf. Now he found that, over four rounds in the Open, he had matched Jack Nicklaus shot for shot and was about to win the Silver medal for leading amateur.

"Every day it's got better and better. My scoring hasn't but I was delighted with a 73 today because I was really

uptight. But Tommy Tolles, the Ryder Cup player was brilliant to play with. He talked to me a lot on the first two holes, settling me down.

He said things like, 'Come on, you're not playing for money, don't worry, the crowd is right behind you.' And at the last, what a gentleman, he waited back to let me go up first. I can understand why some players don't sign autographs because they've been doing it for years but to me it's a novelty and if people are taking the time to ask me, I'm only too delighted to sign it for them. I'll maybe go and hit a few balls now just to loosen down a bit then I'm going to sit and rest."

On an earlier occasion at Troon when Tom Watson had won his lovely laconic sense of humour came through. The questioner was congratulating Watson on having overcome his first attack of the yips, some years before and saying how difficult it must have been when every one foot putt presented a problem.

Most sportsmen when being interviewed tend to agree with the questioner. On this occasion Watson stonily pointed out that he had no such problem:

"Even at my worst I could always hole twelve inch putts. At fifteen inches though, I'm thinking, I'm thinking."

The Hosting of the Open Championship of 1997

The invitation extended by the R&A to host the Open Championship is, at one and the same time, the greatest honour and the greatest responsibility that can befall a club. It is true that much of the organisation is taken care of by the R&A but each Open Championship brings its own problems and normally a club will accept the invitation with great joy but with considerable trepidation.

When the invitation to stage the 1997 Open Championship was made to Royal Troon, there had already been six previous Opens at Troon. It is fair to say that only the Opens of 1982 and 1989 gave any guide to the staging of a modern tournament. The triumphs of Arthur Havers in 1923, of Bobby Locke in 1950 and even, perhaps, of Arnold Palmer in 1962, and Tom Weiskopf in 1973, were gained in a more informal arena and one which was on a much smaller scale.

It had been public knowledge since 1993 that the Open would be coming to Troon in 1997 and senior office-holders at the Club had known it for a little longer. The hope was that all members would find themselves involved in the world's most prestigious tournament when Troon would be the focus of attention for the golfing world.

The onus for the success or otherwise of the competition would rest locally with the Captain, Ian Valentine and on the Chairman of the Championship Committee, David Smyth. Both men were experienced. In the last Open played over Troon – that of 1989 – Ian Valentine had been Chief Marshal, a post specifically identified by the R&A as being crucial to the success of any championship. David Smyth had also experience at the sharp end being a Sector Controller in 1982 and 1989 on the marshalling side. The Troon Championship Committee had made a visit to Royal Lytham during the previous Open of 1996 and had made some useful contacts both within and without the R&A.

The general strategy was that David Smyth would do most of the liaising with St. Andrews and while Ian Valentine would also be heavily involved, he should be left as free as possible to discharge the demands of hospitality which would be so much part of the Open Week. Both men knew what it was like to be at the sharp end of things during Championship week.

There were certain disaster scenarios which had to be taken into account. What if the weather was so bad that there had to be a postponement on to the Monday? What implications did this have for Clubhouse accommodation if things turned out this way? What were the arrangements for a play-off if this became necessary? There had been a play-off in 1989 and Ian Valentine will be forever grateful that, as Chief Marshal, he had insisted on a clear-cut plan of action to cover that eventuality.

Taking the improbable but not impossible a step

further, what was to happen if the play-off resulted in stalemate and the necessity arose for sudden-death play-off? In 1989 sudden-death would have meant playing from the first, but following observations in the Championship Committee's Report in 1989, the R&A accepted the advice about crowd safety and now sudden-death is over the 18th until a winner emerges. Over the winter of 1996-7, various officials from St. Andrews came through to supervise progress – the R&A would not formally take possession of the course until the Friday immediately preceding the week of the Championship.

The collective wisdom of the Open Clubs is to expect the unexpected and Royal Troon suffered a heavy blow when, at this time, the end of August 1996, the Secretary – Mr James Montgomerie, fell ill and required hospital treatment. The wisdom of leaving Ian Valentine free to tackle problems as they arose was now demonstrated as for the next few months the Captain became the *de facto* Club Secretary.

By late autumn, David Smyth was organising bonding sessions for his committee which took the shape, the very agreeable shape, of a match with Royal Dornoch. Time off the course, or at least some time off the course, was devoted to instilling a sense of team spirit within that same committee. It was in the month of March that nearby residents would first have been visually aware that a major event was pending.

There was a series of dinners, the first being with the major T.V. companies who would be covering the event. Since Arnold Palmer's time in the early 60's, the Open had become much more significant in the United States and this was reflected in the amount of transatlantic television coverage. Interest in Asia was almost as keen and the major Japanese networks were well represented.

Life would be markedly easier if relations with the media were good and the Club was determined to implement all reasonable requests. On the evening of Press Day, when the writers would themselves discover some of the hazards of the course, a dinner was held in the Marine Highland Hotel which officials of Royal Troon and the R&A attended.

By this time television camera positions had been decided upon, not a long job since there were so few changes since 1989 and no radical ones. Communication requirements were changing almost from day to day and a state-of-the-art telephone system was installed by B.T, almost a century after the first hand-cranker had been placed in the clubhouse.

The Open had come back to Troon at a time when security had reached an almost unimaginable level of strictness. This time there would be two complicating factors: the presence of Tiger Woods and the certainty of a royal visit since H.R.H. The Duke of York was known as a keen follower of the game. Any notion of laxity would be unthinkable but there was always the danger that a security system would be set up that was so rigid that it would affect the enjoyment of spectators and indeed antagonise them.

Naturally, there were places where spectators would not be encouraged to go. To stand on the gabions would certainly, improve their view, but the risk of damage to these stone-filled wire baskets, which were such an integral part of Troon's coastal defences, was much too high to be risked, to say nothing of jeopardising the safety of those spectators.

After Press Day there were other golfing visits to be fixed, notably those of the five leading suppliers of the event. Here again a balance had to be struck if at all possible. Royal Troon could never forget that in the run-up to the Championship, two courses were being used and three sets of members inconvenienced. It was the duty of Messrs. Valentine and Smyth to maximise returns from the championship while, at the same time, depriving members of their beloved course for the shortest time possible. There were still an unreconstructed few who believed that having to give up their customary fourball was too big a sacrifice to make, even for the world's best.

The R&A saw its role as that of facilitator although it drew the line strictly sometimes. St. Andrews funded a part-time Secretary to be based in Troon and handle matters directly related to the Championship.

THE 1990s

The Royal and Ancient, with the wisdom gathered from over one hundred Opens, was a careful steward. This was best illustrated by the case of the additional Diesel Cushman which David Smyth declared to be necessary to help the work of the greens staff. The R&A felt unable to purchase a piece of equipment the use of which, on their behalf, would be for a very limited time. Following amicable discussion with David Smyth, they agreed that there appeared to be nothing in the rules which debarred the governing body from paying for the hire of such an implement during the weeks immediately preceding and following the tournament.

The small pieces of the administrative jigsaw were being filled in and not the earth-shaking issues which were unlikely to be overlooked. Police, fire, first aid, sign-posting, traffic control were all taken care of as the actual vision of a deserted course was suddenly replaced by the notional one of up to 40,000 people running hither and yon. A greens staff working all the hours that God sends would need a portaloo exclusively for their own use. A strong PGA recommendation would have had a provision of showers for the caddies but although discussions and visitations took place with Portland, it was not found possible to produce a satisfactory outcome.

Then, suddenly, the cat was among the pigeons with the announcement that the R&A was desirous of trying a very bold experiment. It was nothing less than the free admission of under-18's, even if unaccompanied by an adult. This was a real problem. Royal Troon could scarcely oppose such a step. They were in full agreement with the R&A that young people must be encouraged to come into the game as there was a disturbing falling-off in the number of young players coming forward. Royal Troon was also aware that any unthinking opposition would play into the hands of the news reporters (there was nothing to fear from the golf writers) who had made up their minds that here was a stuffy Club which

Aerial view of the Course during the 1997 Open Championship

could be expected to put obstacles in the way of the young.

The Club wished to do nothing of the kind but was aware of the concerns of some of its more conservative members on the matter. If things went wrong the enjoyment of many adult spectators would be affected and any chance the initiative might have had would vanish. The suggestion the Club made through the Captain was that any unaccompanied juniors should write to the R&A for a free ticket which would admit them to the course by a special junior entry gate. The notion worked like a charm. The young people came, behaved admirably and, just as important, enjoyed themselves.

No one could have foreseen the growth of the Open. In 1923 Arthur Havers won £75 of a total £225. In 1962 Palmer won £1,400 of £85,000 – he actually lost money by competing. By 1997, the Open we are discussing, Justin Leonard would win £250,000 of £1,600,000.

The R&A had of course the expertise which comes from continual involvement and this expertise was freely available to the club on such things as the condition of the ground. The single most important responsibility of the club was that of marshalling. Recruits for this were garnered by letter to the other Ayrshire clubs asking them to supply a team which would be responsible for stewarding and crowd control at a nominated hole. Wherever possible the notion of 'split holes' was avoided; things went very much better if Barassie had the third hole and Bogside the ninth. Love of the game and the opportunity of a round at Troon for the two members of each club who would be controlling the hole and their members at the Open ensured an adequate number of volunteers.

As in every other walk of life, experience taught lessons. In 1989 the Chief Marshal's Team had shared a portacabin with the Head of the Security Guards. It had not been an entirely happy marriage and as the Chief Marshal of 1989 was now the Captain, the arrangement was not repeated.

The club was also responsible for supplying the scorers and this was one of the areas where the Ladies were given preference. The other was Players' Registration and Reception where it was felt that the Ladies were more likely to give a favourable first impression of Troon. The problem of litter was dealt with, most enthusiastically, by the pupils of Marr College, Troon as had been the custom for several years. It was thanks to their efforts that the course was not submerged under the piles of litter that 40,000 spectators at a golf tournament can generate.

People were needed as runners, to drive the medical buggies, to help photographers, for a hundred and one tasks.

The Clubhouse

Ian Valentine's task in the clubhouse was not simply to dispense hospitality like a medieval magnate. Again the problem was one of balance – how to do justice to your guests without making your own members feel superfluous? Unless well handled, it is a situation in which egos can be bruised. Fortunately the fine weather made it unnecessary to restrict entry to the clubhouse on the scale that would have happened had it rained.

The Captain greeted his royal guest, his fellow captains from other Royal clubs, overseas guests and those captains from clubs such as Prestwick, Western Gailes and Pollok with which there had been a long tradition of inter-club matches. He also welcomed past captains with their wives and (an especially happy touch) widows of past captains.

Only the correctly badged could gain admission to the clubhouse and there were different passes for different days, rather like a Buckingham Palace Investiture. There were special passes for the Captain, the Secretary, the Championship Committee, the President and the Club Professional.

The locker rooms were the exclusive domain of the players and the press and there was a rather unfortunate incident when some of the latter attempted to get too close to Ian Baker-Finch after the player's highly distressing round. Baker-Finch had to be spirited away by a side entrance. The sensible and sympathetic handling of the Press – essential but not always easy – also fell within the Captain's and Chairman of the Championship Committee's remit. They would deal not so much with the golfing press as with the news reporters seeking general comments.

Movement of spectators had to accommodate television. Club members had been given 140 seats in the stand on the 18th green. Which entailed being seated by 4.30 pm on Saturday and Sunday as the leading golfers started to come in and, if nature abhors a vacuum, then television certainly abhors shooting empty seats. There were 41 camera positions and photographers numbered 650 of whom 400 were foreign.

And suddenly it was over. The long work of dismantling the stands began almost at once. Letters of thanks which were complimentary and sincere arrived from the R&A, broadcasting organisations, the Press Associations and H.R.H. The Duke of York.

The members re-emerged and began to arrange games. It was decided that the week after the Open should be exclusively for members and their guests. There was a feeling in some quarters that this was the real business of the club.

Ian Valentine and David Smyth accepted the congratulations of their friends and the warning that they would fall asleep on their feet in the almost immediate future. Both did, David Smyth lasting a day longer. Both men claim to have enjoyed the experience.

Club Captain Ian Valentine and Championship Committee Chairman David Smyth on the Monday after the Championship

New Arrival – Senior Member

Jan W. Chandler

NO man, it is said, can serve two masters and yet there are times when a Secretary/Manager must feel called upon to serve many more than that or at least to make the attempt. A recent survey, taken to be precise in the summer of 2000, found that the average length in office of Club Secretaries in the Greater Metropolitan area of London was a mere 18 months. It must have been a similar club that M. E. H. had in mind in a brilliant article in The Golfer's Handbook of 1970. Writing as a beleaguered Secretary he had this to say:

"The number of members in a club may be 250 or 1250. They all as individuals, know how to do the job better than the Secretary. They are experts in administration, accounting, green keeping, the law, staff control, housekeeping, car parking, slow play and fast play. They all know how to produce fast, true greens, deal with vandalism, make a profit, keep beer in top class condition, know where to buy wines at low prices and are able to cook and serve excellent meals at one third of their present cost. They, however, do not know how to pay their subscription on time, deal tactfully with visitors, mend pitch marks on the greens, rake bunkers or understand the rules of golf or the handicapping scheme. They are therefore a very special breed who need careful administration and control. However, it is surprising how many of them are so friendly and pleasant and how good it is to work on their behalf. As most Secretaries know, club Members are appreciative people and it is a privilege to be among them."

The last two sentences must be true of the vast majority of Royal Troon members since longevity has been a key characteristic of their Secretary/Treasurers, Secretaries and perhaps Secretary/Managers.

Jan Chandler, the present incumbent is an Ayrshire man, born in Saltcoats and educated at Ardrossan Academy, and later at the Universities of Strathclyde and Glasgow. In discussing the job he agreed that there were various ways of doing it – the tyrannical, for example, which was going out of fashion or the Sir Humphrey, where the secretary could use his advantage of continuity to ensure that he was the real power in the land. A club where the Secretary is a martinet, although efficient, will obviously send out a different message from one where the atmosphere is relaxed and friendly.

No matter the ambience certain basic administrative tasks have to be done. Accurate minutes have to be taken from the General, Green and House Committees, and they must, above all, be a true account of what the Committee felt at a certain point of time and what it had therefore decided to do. In Jan Chandler's opinion, the job of Secretary/

Jan Chandler, Secretary/Manager

172

Manager is one that today requires the successful candidate to have had some recent top-level financial or industrial experience.

Visitors and catering form a significant part of the modern golf club of the first rank. It is not enough that visitors are allowed to play, they must be welcomed given that the decision has been taken to have them. It will not do, for instance, to have visitors told that there are no changing facilities available in the Clubhouse but that they may change in their own cars.

In the matter of visitors the Secretary must invariably have some discretion in exceptional circumstances which may arise on the day. Golf clubs are today fairly large-scale establishments illustrated by the fact that at certain times of the year Royal Troon will employ 50 people with all the implications that has for PAYE, National Insurance and the requirements in regard to current employment legislation

The ideal Secretary, Jan Chandler thinks, will be a conciliator by nature but a conciliator with a steel core. Members will, left to themselves, wish to play 365 days in the year. Occasionally this will not be practicable. Someone on the spot has to give a ruling. There is a sense in which he has to know almost as much about green-keeping as the green-keeping staff itself. Variegated as his own job may be, he has to know as much about the jobs of others as will prevent him being hoodwinked.

Despite what M. E. H. had to say at the top of this section, Jan Chandler says that mingling with members and hearing their views is for him the most rewarding part of the job. Club Secretaryship is essentially a job that people come to having done other things, he did and has no regrets.

The Secretary has to bear in mind that to a member his (the member's) problems are always immediate and must take priority over the rest of the Club business, even if he (the Secretary) has been interrupted in the preliminary planning for the next Open to come to Royal Troon. He must also bear in mind that small but articulate minority who would rather that the Open did NOT come to Royal Troon to disturb the even tenor of their ways.

Jan Chandler is aware that Royal Troon is a club with a long history and therefore change comes slowly if it comes at all. He finds this totally understandable, indeed agrees that it puts a certain responsibility on him to be a sounding board. His instinct, when confronted with a rule that seems questionable or unsound is to say, "What was the original intent behind this piece of legislation?"

He believes that since Secretaries are usually there while Captains change – though not invariably so! – they have a certain continuity which they can bring to bear. If a Secretary can act as a good sounding board it can cut the feet from the many rumours which from time to time assail clubhouses. An instance at Troon was where the dryness of the course in the summer of 2000 led to a claim that the watering system had broken down and another that the company providing the technical spare parts equipment for the watering system had ceased to function. There was then a third rumour that the Committee had taken a decision not to water so that the course would be played as it had been in the infancy of links golf. Good liaison meant that the unspectacular, truthful version of the situation emerged, namely that there had been no rain for a fortnight.

As in other jobs the *"soft answer that turneth away wrath"* is often of great use. The member raging because there is no caddie for him at the appointed time may have forgotten, or never known, that the caddies are self-employed and that effectively there is a limit to how far Caddie A can be directed to carry for Member B.

In a sense one has to be in the job to learn it. In the musical *'Damn Yankees'.* in a song called *'You Gotta Have Heart'* there is a phrase, "There's nothin' to it but to do it" and it fits here. In 1997, Jan Chandler had a brief handover period working with the then Secretary, James Montgomerie, in the lead-up to Justin Leonard's Open.

There are facets of the job that apply to every golf club, along with some which are peculiar to Royal

Troon. The recognition factor is important to members although it is obviously much easier for 750 members to recognise one Secretary than the other way about. An additional complication is the Scottish custom of giving surnames as forenames, memorably captured by Billy Connolly in a sketch about B.B.C. Scotland:

"I say, Cameron, have you seen Finlay?"
"Yes, he's over there talking to Campbell"

Despite this additional hazard, the Secretary is pretty sure that he can put name to face for the overwhelming bulk of the membership.

Another task that has to be undertaken, on account of the structure of the Troon courses, is a constant and friendly liaison with The Ladies' Golf Club and Troon Portland. There are formal annual meetings with the club officials which are preceded by more informal meetings of the Secretaries. Many things have to be done conjointly, not least the calendar of events for the three courses.

The job is so fascinating that it could easily absorb the office-holder seven days a week round the clock.

Post 1997 Open Championship Developments

In 1998, the Committee took the decision to appoint a Club Archivist. Andrew Taylor agreed to take on this challenging post and his help in the preparation of this book and the location of memorabilia pertaining to the club has been invaluable. The preparation of this History has enabled the Club to learn more about its distinguished past.

With the Clubhouse refurbishment completed for the 1997 Open Championship and the new watering system installed, one would have expected that all major upgrades would be finished. However, there still remained work to be done. The first priority was the final phase in the upgrading of facilities for the Club's greens' staff. This involved the construction of a new building, which included a re-equipped workshop, toilet and showering facilities, a canteen area and chemical storage facilities. Work on this final phase of the Greenkeeping complex commenced in February 1998 and was operational by May of that year, the total investment being in the region of £150,000.

It had been the objective of Green Committees over the years to provide two courses in championship condition for the enjoyment of members, their guests and visitors. In the late 1990s a succession of dry summers had taken their toll on the Portland Course's fairways, which resulted in a programme of verti-draining, reseeding and feeding to re-establish a good coverage of indigenous grasses. The final piece in the Portland jigsaw would be the installation of fairway watering, as both the greens and tees were already covered by the current system. In October 1998, the Committee approved the expenditure of £160,000 to install fairway watering on the Portland with the work being carried out during the winter of 1998/99. This extension now provides full coverage on both the Old and Portland Courses and like the former, some twenty-three years earlier, this additional investment has transformed the Portland fairways. However, it has placed a greater

Andrew Taylor, Club Archivist

reliance on the Gyaws Burn, with subsequent committees investigating alternative sources of water.

On the subject of membership, it was noted with deep satisfaction that Dr A. M. Mathewson was the third member of Royal Troon within the last 20 years to have been Captain of the R&A.

The bond between Royal Troon and Charlie Yates was further cemented when he wrote to the Club Captain David Smyth suggesting that the American Walker Cup team, under the Captaincy of his nephew Danny Yates, had a stop over practice round at Troon prior to their match at Nairn in September 1999. After their round the team were entertained to lunch by the Captain and Past Captains.

An interesting footnote is that the American Walker Cup team in 1938 played in the Amateur Championship at Troon then lost at St. Andrews. After their visit in 1999 the American Team lost the match at Nairn. Perhaps Troon has a jinx over American amateurs that should be noted by the R&A for future Walker Cup matches in the Scotland!

Senior Member

Russell McCreath is the longest serving playing member. Those of us brought up on the marvellous golfing stories of P. G. Wodehouse – *The Heart of a Goof* and *The Clicking of Cuthbert* come to mind – will remember the oldest member of that fictional club who perpetually sat on the veranda and gave his views on all golfing topics with Olympian detachment.

Visit of the U.S. Walker Cup Team and Officials with the Club's Honorary President, Captain and Past Captains, 1999

Olympian detachment is not the style of Russell McCreath who has in his time performed many duties for the Club, including a comparatively brief spell in which he shouldered the burdens of Secretaryship. His time in the office came between the tenures of Alistair Sweet and Archie Alexander. In an honorary capacity he was much involved with the staging of the 1973 Open Championship at Troon.

He bears the unusual distinction of being a man who has holed out in one on no fewer than ten occasions, four of which have been on the Old Course, three at the Postage Stamp and the other at the 17th.

This seems to run clean counter to the thrifty precepts of the Bank Manager he had been for most of his working life. On at least one occasion the wind was tempered to the shorn lamb as his hole in one at the 17th was achieved on a day when the Ayr Gold Cup was being run and many chums who might have been hovering expectantly at the bar were off at the races. Most of his other "singles" were collected across the fence at Prestwick where he also had a long-term membership.

The Ladies' Golf Club

The original Ladies' Clubhouse, and afterwards, the Portland Clubhouse

FOR well over one hundred years, the Ladies' Golf Club of Troon has devoted itself to the twin objectives of running an efficient organisation and producing good golfers, with the occasional great one thrown in for good measure.

The Club's start was spasmodic. Founded in 1882 with the active encouragement of the Duchess of Portland, the club was initially loosely structured, with no official Captain and indeed no course, the men's course being used when available. This was an arrangement which in the long term would suit neither party and in May 1882 it was agreed that the ladies could have the Craigend hole on the men's course and part of the neighbouring land for their exclusive use. Much as the men's course had done, the Ladies course became larger by instalments and in 1886 two holes were added to the north of the Gyaws Burn.

When the Relief Course, later known as The Portland, was opened in June 1895, the intention was that the Ladies should be allowed to use it. However, they were not prepared to come third in a race of three as they would have had to yield priority to members of The Portland Club. They persuaded the men to approach the Duke of Portland who granted the Troon Club the use of the field between Gyaws Burn and Craigend. The ground was rough but a sandbank was removed from opposite the Ladies' Clubhouse – a modest enclosure that would eventually be taken over by The Portland Club when the Ladies acquired new premises and gradually the terrain was licked into shape.

In the sphere of women's golf, Troon was one of the foremost clubs in the field and from the very beginning, the Ayrshire club made its mark. As we have seen elsewhere, it was the final of the Ladies' Championship of 1904 which first brought the Troon Club to the general notice and proved that women's golf could be not only a participating sport but a spectating one as well.

The course acquired quite a reputation for protracted finals in the Ladies' Championship. In 1925, Joyce Wethered (later Lady Heathcoat-Amery) overcame Cecil Leitch after 37 holes and even that was topped by the 1952 final in which Moira Paterson (Mrs J. C. Milton) beat Frances Stephens ((Mrs F. Smith) at the 38th hole.

On the distaff side Troon was much more than a good social club. The standard of women's golf was frighteningly high. In the leading inter-club competition in

Joyce Wethered and Miss Cecil Leitch at Troon, 1925

176

THE 1990s

The Ladies' Golf House circa 1900

the West of Scotland, the Greenlees Trophy, Troon was almost invariably in contention for the title. Most of the leading women golfers in Ayrshire were members at one time or another but a commendable sense of loyalty and old affiliations was retained. This meant that such fine golfers as Jean McCulloch and Betty Singleton tended to enter external competitions from their earlier clubs of West Kilbride and Prestwick St. Nicholas respectively.

In the inter-war period it would indeed have required a superlatively strong side to get the better of Troon in a club match. We will shortly notice the achievements of Helen Holm, who, in addition to the two lieutenants we have just mentioned, could also count on the assistance of Mrs Walter Greenlees, Mrs G. Coats and Mrs J. B. Walker.

The collective record was formidable. Mrs Greenlees, Mrs Coats and Miss McCulloch were all West of Scotland champions and, going a step further, Mrs Coats was a losing finalist in the Scottish Ladies

Scottish Ladies Championship, 1907

177

and Miss McCulloch had been Scottish champion three times. Mrs J. B. Walker was also a national champion – of Ireland in her case – and she had a very notable success in 1935 when she added the championship of Australia to her honours list. Three times she achieved the ultimate in selection when she was chosen to play for Great Britain against The United States in the Curtis Cup.

No wonder that some of the other Greenlees Trophy Clubs were just a little despondent when this particular Troon caravan rolled up to the clubhouse door. There must have been times in the 1930's when The Ladies Golf Club of Troon side would have been predominantly, if not exclusively, composed of international players.

Helen Holm

Of all the women players in the years of Troon's existence, the most gifted beyond any doubt was Helen Holm. Pictures of her from the 1930's are strangely modern in appearance. She was tall, slim, good-looking and her preference for trousers when playing golf makes her look much more modern than her contemporaries. Only Joyce Wethered, and even then only possibly, had as graceful a swing. Helen Holm won her first two Scottish Championships playing out of Elie and Earlsferry but it is with Troon that she is indelibly associated. Oddly enough, while playing out of the Fife club, she met a Troon player in the final of 1932, Mrs G. Coats.

Since it was the Troon Ladies Jubilee year it would have been highly appropriate had Mrs Coats won and she almost did. Newspaper critics did not spare the Ladies in those days and the *Glasgow Herald* was in its most schoolmasterly mood.

"Had the final finished, as at one time it looked like doing, in Mrs Holm's favour by a hole or two. it would have been one of the dullest on record for the golf up to that point had been neither interesting nor exciting. But from the fifteenth to the fifth extra hole which she won, it was one long thrill. Eight holes were halved and marvellous recovery shots played when all seemed lost."

This dogged victory marked the beginning of a stellar career for Helen Holm. She was a major figure, not just in Scottish or indeed British golf but she was a leading performer on the world stage. She trounced Pam Barton by 6 and 5 at Royal Porthcawl in the British Ladies final of 1934 and two brief years later Pam Barton would be champion of the United States. The Ladies' Club presented Helen Holm with a diamond brooch and the honours due to a returning Caesar. Her car was towed through the streets of Troon to her home and railway fog signals served as fireworks. These marks of favour would be in evidence again in 1938 when she beat Miss E. Corlett at Burnham.

She was by now a national heroine since her Open win in 1934 was the first time in 23 years that the title had come to Scotland. In her first experience of competitive European golf, she won both her foursomes and singles in a match against France at St. George's Hill.

The *Bulletin* newspaper summed things up neatly with its headline *"East, West Holm's Best"*. Of the girls, she had defeated in the Ladies Championship at Burnham, Elsie Corlett was the only working girl in the 1938 Curtis Cup team, an eloquent social comment on the time required to travel to away matches in those pre-war days. Even then, Elsie Corlett was a journalist and in one of the

Helen Holm

Cartoon British Women's Championship, Royal Porthcawl, 1934. Winner Helen Holm

few professions where publicity would be useful to her employer.

In the 1936 Curtis Cup Helen Holm had greatly distinguished herself. She had won singles and foursomes in the first match in which the British Isles had managed to draw with the United States. She comfortably defeated the highly thought-of Patti Berg by 4 and 3 and, partnered by the other wonderful Scottish golfer of the time, Jessie Anderson, (Mrs G. T. Valentine) the all-Scots combination defeated Mrs Hill and Miss Glutting 3 and 2.

Now, in the States again in 1938, Helen Holm was the player the Americans feared and there were flattering comparisons with a Scotsman the Americans held in high regard. *"She is not a killer such as Jack McLean was in his great days. Rather does she brush aside opposition in the manner of Jones."*

Looking back, there is a strange air of fragility pervading those immediate pre-war years and there was an eerie chain of events in the 1937 season. In the Home International series, held that year at Turnberry, the event was scarred by the sudden and totally unlooked-for death of one of the English team, Bridget Newell. After some hesitation the matches continued and an inspired English side beat Scotland 6-3 although Helen Holm won her match. Later during the Ladies' Championship of that year at the same venue she defeated Pam Barton, then the U.S. champion by 5 and 3 although the English girl, who would herself be killed in a flying accident during the war, had severely twisted her ankle just after the turn. She soldiered on bravely before a gallery of 500 and then conceded with a very Thirties gesture. Let the *Glasgow Herald* tell it:

"When they had reached the fifteenth green and the position was obviously hopeless, the beaten U.S. champion wrapped her arms round her opponent's neck and kissed her".

Helen Holm would then be beaten 3 and 1 by the fast-emerging Jessie Anderson who went on to take the Ladies' Championship.

By this time in club competitions Helen Holm was playing off a handicap of plus four. She was a most graceful mover and her 1938 Scottish final against Jessie Anderson at Nairn in 1938 is worthy of mention. The players were round in under two hours, Jessie in 72, Helen Holm in 77 with two holes the margin of victory.

If anything were lacking in her career, it might have been the fact that she never won the Scottish on her own course at Troon. All of her five victories were away ones and, indeed, in her post-war career she herself always thought she was never quite as good after 1945. She reached two Troon finals but sustained heavy defeats from Jean Donald and Marigold Speirs.

In the first of these finals, in 1949, against Jean Donald, Helen Holm ran into an opponent in incredible form. She herself went to the turn in 38, more than respectable, but found herself four down. There was no letting-up and 6 and 5 was the margin of victory. It was followed by a Helen Holm touch as, smiling she unpinned her red rosette with the thistle emblem and pinned it to the blouse of the victor. Helen Holm's progress to the 1957 Scottish, again at Troon was nerve-racking in its late stages. In the fifth round she edged out Janette Robertson by one hole and then beat her old adversary Mrs. George Valentine (Jessie Anderson) at the first extra hole. Marigold Speir of St. Rule did not seem to present such an obstacle in the final but was an emphatic winner, admirable for a four handicap player.

Her last Scottish success came twenty years after her first and she was a stalwart of the Scottish international side on either side of World War Two. Perhaps more importantly in an amateur game she was a joy to watch and to play with or against. She had the approval that mattered most, that of her sporting contemporaries.

Since her death in 1971 her memory has been kept green by the tournament known as The Helen Holm Trophy, a most imaginative competition. Her son, Michael Holm, presented The Ladies' Golf Club of Troon with her favourite club, a jigger, to which were attached her many championship medals. From the outset this tournament, 54 holes of medal golf played over the Old Course and the Portland Course, attracted a distinguished entry. Nothing more needs to be said about this when the reader learns that the initial competition, played on the 28th and 29th April 1973 was won by one of the greatest women golfers Scotland has ever produced, Belle Robertson, a member and later Captain of The Ladies' Golf Club of Troon. There was a pleasing connection with men's golf in that the special prize awarded for the best score by an under-21 player was won by Cathie Panton, daughter of the famous John. For twenty years or so after World War Two, it was he who with Eric Brown had so ably carried the banner of Scottish professional golf.

The Helen Holm Trophy is now known as the Helen Holm Scottish Ladies' Open Stroke-Play Championship played for annually. It still takes the form of two rounds over the Portland Course and one over the Old Course. The competition is run by the Scottish Ladies Golf Union and attracts a significant international entry. In future years it would be won by some of the finest young women players such as Alison Gemmill of Kilmarnock Barassie, Catriona Lambert of Stirling University and Mhairi McKay of Turnberry.

It is only fitting that it should for Helen Holm was ever eager to assist young golfers. Mrs Jean Anderson (perhaps better known to golfers as Jean Donald) liked to tell of how she was asked by Helen Holm how her game (Jean's) was just before the Scottish Ladies at Nairn in 1951.

"Not good," said Jean and was astonished when Helen suggested a visit to the practice ground for a spot of diagnosis. Jean pointed out that they might well meet in the Championship to which the senior golfer replied "that makes no difference, it is more important to me that you should play well".

Helen Holm and Teddy Dawson playing in a match, West of Scotland Ladies v Men at Pollok Golf Club

Belle Robertson

Helen Holm was a golfer of quite outstanding ability but it would be quite wrong to represent her as having carried The Ladies' Golf Club single-handed. Throughout the 1960s there were stellar performances from other people and occasionally even Mrs. Holm faltered in the final stages. In the Scottish Ladies Final of 1963 Belle Robertson was favourite to beat Joan Lawrence but the latter retained her title in winning 2 and 1. Moreover she was never behind at any stage in the final, a final which, unusually for Troon was influenced by a strong east wind, a circumstance uncommon enough to be worth remark.

In 1966 the youngsters were given their chance to shine with Scotland beating England 5½ - 3½ in the Girls' International. The championship itself was won by Gillian Hutton of Dunfermline who defeated Dinah Oxley of West Byfleet in the final.

In 1969 Troon produced a new champion when Heather Anderson won the Scottish Ladies' Championship at West Kilbride by defeating Kathleen Lackie of Montrose by the comfortable margin of 5 and 4. In the 1968 Home Internationals at Porthcawl Heather Anderson won her singles against Wales and both singles and foursomes against Ireland and England.

Another distinguished Member of The Ladies' Club is Phyllis Wylie who as Phyllis Wade won the English Ladies Amateur in 1934 at Seacroft and was runner-up to Wanda Morgan in 1936 at Hayling. Following these achievements she played in the Curtis Cup at Essex Country Club, USA, halving her foursomes match but did not play in the singles. She also represented Great Britain against France on four occasions, toured Australasia with the Ladies Golf Union side in 1935 and represented England in many Home International Matches and also against France.

She joined The Ladies' Club in 1950 when she moved north to live in Ayrshire and won the Ayrshire Championship in 1954 and was a stalwart of many Greenlees Trophy teams. For many years she has played a key role in organising and encouraging the Juniors and is still present every Monday, when their competitions are held in the school holidays, despite being in her 90th year.

So the Ladies' Club continued to flourish and passed proudly to its Centenary in August 1982, the event being marked by a Celebration Lunch at which the Ladies' Golf Club was presented with an ornamental clock by the Captain of Royal Troon Golf Club. There were fourteen past Captains present and the oldest there, Mrs Y. Greenlees, could boast a membership which went back 70 years.

Truly the game of golf had magical powers for Ayrshire Ladies. Jean McCulloch, the celebrated golfer from West Kilbride lived to attend a dinner given to her to mark the 75th anniversary of her first Scottish championship and from the East Mrs Charlotte Beddows was to claim that at 79 years of age her swing was better than it had ever been.

And at the other end of the scale the Ayrshire Ladies Championship of 1997 was an all-Troon affair with Roslyn Kennedy beating Sharon Lambie 2 and 1.

Currently on the ladies' side the highly promising Suzannah H. Laing, currently on a University scholarship in the United States, may be the next Troon Lady to make international headlines.

Suzannah is a third generation Troon golfer and

Helen Holm Trophy

her grandfather, who possibly does not count as an outside agency, wanders down and gives a word of counsel from time to time. He is Douglas B. Fraser who is currently the Honorary President of Royal Troon. Suzannah like many Troon girls started on the Par 3 course as soon as she could walk and on several occasions won the Bentinck Girls' Championship.

So far her path has been one of smooth and unhurried progression. She was a girl international from 1997-99 and in this last year she was on the winning Scots side at Mullingar in the Republic of Ireland. She has won the West of Scotland Girls twice and had the tremendous distinction of being the top qualifier in the Daily Telegraph Competition in 1998.

Being in the United States has by no means daunted her and in golfing terms she appears to travel well. She is at the University of San Francisco and in collegiate circles this year has had five top ten finishes.

She has made a recent team of the top ten from the West Coast Universities who will be playing in the PAC 10 Tour Asia which will take in Japan, Korea, Hong Kong and China.

The combination of her own ability and the energy and advice from the grandfather-President should ensure that hers is a name which will become very familiar in a few years time. The future appears to be in very safe hands.

Troon Portland Golf Club

TO expect three clubs of very different origin and provenance to co-exist peacefully on the same tract of ground might seem to be asking more than fallible human nature can achieve. Yet, for the great majority of the time, Royal Troon, Portland and The Ladies' Club of Troon manage this particularly well and have done so for the past century.

In the early days there was some dispute as to who could play of right over the course. It was not referred to as the Old Course at the outset since there was no other. The obvious answer might have been that members were so entitled and no others but there was a fear that, just possibly, local residents might have the right to play golf and other ball games over the ground which Troon Golf Club had acquired. There were such prescriptive rights in some of the East Coast burghs, notably Musselburgh and St. Andrews. Perhaps in an endeavour to avoid uncontrolled trespass or perhaps with the notion of gratifying the then Duke, approximately 40 residents of Troon, the Residenters, were allowed to play over Troon within certain restrictions. These were that they must always give way to full members and would not be allowed to play on Saturdays.

This could only be a temporary solution. It was still necessary to ensure that no one outside the magic 40 availed themselves of the course and in order to achieve this, Strath and Fernie – the first two professionals – had to divert themselves from more useful work to root out 'strange golfers'.

A more enduring concordat had been worked out by March 1885 whereby the landlord agreed to grant a lease not only for the existing course but for a new one to be called the Relief Course (the name Portland would not come into use until the 1920s).

Henceforth Privileged Players (as the Residenters were more commonly being called) would confine their play to the New Ground where they would have the same privileges as ordinary members. The solution had been put elegantly by Provost McKay to the former Captain, Adam Wood, at a retiral dinner in June 1897.

"The young men of Troon, rightly or wrongly, conceived that these links held by us at a nominal rent ought to be opened for their use. To solve this knotty problem, to avoid collision with the people of Troon and to meet the wishes of His Grace, The Duke of Portland, the club secured a lease of ground for the Relief Course where natives of the place are now allowed, at a moderate payment to enjoy the pleasures of golf, etc, etc."

Much of the initial expenditure was borne by the Troon Club and, as elsewhere in the world, this had some effect on the tune that the Burgh piper played. The privilege of playing over the New Course would be restricted to a membership of 150 and all nominations for membership of the new club were subject to scrutiny and approbation or otherwise of the Troon Committee.

Thus, from the outset, the complete control of the Portland Course and Club has been in the hands of Troon Golf Club. This arrangement was further codified in 1921 when the club at last persuaded the Duke of Portland to sell both courses. This purchase, of course, cancelled the provisions of the lease and when title was granted there was no reservation in favour of any right conferred on any person outside Troon Golf Club to play over the courses.

The new course was up and running on 29th June 1895. It had been designed by the Troon professional, Willie Fernie, who must have rejoiced that he had less far to travel than when constructing another of his courses, Spa in Belgium. The official opening was by that same Troon Captain, Adam Wood, and he presented a silver medal to be won in handicap competition.

This is a history of Royal Troon Golf Club, not the Portland but the relationship is so unusual that it deserves to be developed at some little length, even if with as much brevity as may preserve accuracy. In the early years the ground rules had to be spelled out, some might say worked out. There was resentment on the part of Portland members (we will anticipate use of the name) when they were not allowed to introduce friends to the new course. It had to be pointed out that Troon Golf Club's lease from the Duke expressly prohibited such an allowance.

At this stage the Portland Club were ekeing out an ascetic existence in a little wooden clubhouse which had formerly belonged to The Ladies' Club of Troon. It was grotesquely inadequate and to replace it was a matter of some urgency. With that optimistic view of life that no doubt the pyramid-builders had when they approached Pharaoh the estimated cost was presented as £500 (it would eventually cost twice that). Of the £500 the Portland club would find £150 themselves and raise the remainder by a bond issue. If by any chance the Portland Golf Club became defunct then outstanding bonds would be transferred to Troon Golf Club which had expressed itself content with this arrangement. The procedure of work would of course depend on securing some security of tenure.

Time was of the essence and Troon Golf Club Committee was approached for help. They were most willing to render what aid they could but pointed out that they were debarred from guaranteeing any money without the authority granted by a General Meeting.

Not for the first time the rescuing horseman on the charger wore a coronet. The Duke of Portland, ably prompted by his Agent, J. H. Turner, agreed to pay £25 per annum for four years as his contribution to the new building and also stated that during his own lifetime the feu duty would be a nominal five shillings a year.

In the event despite all efforts the Portland club came up several hundred pounds short. Troon Golf Club agreed to take responsibility for any deficit and this was to be regarded as a loan to be repaid as and when the Portland Club's circumstances allowed. It has to be said that the final Terms of Agreement show the Troon Club in a very generous light. The main Articles of Agreement were as follows:

i) Troon Golf Club would build the new clubhouse at a cost between £1,100 and £1,150.
ii) Portland Golf Club would give the Troon Golf Club any promised donations, pay £15 per year annual rent and hand over an additional subscription of five shillings per member.
iii) Troon Golf Club would pay all rates and taxes and be responsible for repairs to and the upkeep of the Clubhouse.
iv) Troon Golf Club would take over all debentures promised by members of the Portland Golf Club and pay 4% per annum on them.
v) The Troon Golf Club would grant the Portland Golf Club a lease which was concurrent with their own.
vi) The Clubhouse Management Committee would consist of three members from each club.

Before the clubhouse could be completed the First World War broke out and in fact it was 1915 before the club could take possession of the new building. The Portland Club ran into difficulties which would be accentuated in the Second World War. These were two-fold.

In general terms, the Portland membership was younger and therefore more caught up in the volunteering which marked the heady early days. Then again, the senior club could compensate for the loss of members to the Colours simply by creating new members. Since Portland was controlled in this by Troon however extraordinary recruiting was not a policy open to them. The elder club, so generous in much else, showed themselves curiously unaware that there was a real emergency here.

The Portland Clubhouse, 2000

Sometimes the Portland Club could play the role of junior partner to its own advantage. In January 1916, at one of the most despairing times of the war, the War Department let it be known that it might well want to use the clubhouse – a modern, commodious building – as an Explosives Store. The committee by return wrote a hasty letter, which declared that they "were only tenants of part of the premises" and that all such questions should be referred to Troon Golf Club.

By the end of the war it was, for the Portland Golf Club, a *"damn close-run thing"* as another Duke (Wellington) had observed of Waterloo. By 1919 the Portland membership was down to a skeletal 48 paid-up members and Troon Golf Club's offer to forego the annual rent of £20 was most gratefully taken. In May 1924 it was officially decided that the course should be called the Portland Course although habit and custom kept the terms 'New' and 'Relief' on the tongues of members for some time yet.

In its new guise the course bade farewell to Willie Fernie who had been both professional and member. Seeing him everyday in his normal avocations, it was easy to forget what a giant he had been. He thwarted Bob Ferguson of four Opens in a row when he won at Musselburgh in 1883. Alone of the leading finishers he had never seen the course before, never so much as played a practice round on it. Perhaps much of the spade work had been done before his arrival, noticed thus in the local press:

"After being one year at Ardeer, Fernie has been engaged by what has now (1891) become the important course at Troon".

The tastes of the Portland Club changed with the years, or at least in music they did so. In the first few years of the century the members are described as having repaired to the Portland Arms Hotel after the Annual General Meeting where they listened to gramophone records of Caruso, Tettrazini and Harry Lauder. Scarce twenty years later they were availing themselves of the Rhythm Syncopation Band for the Christmas Dance. The Rhythmic Syncopaters seemed a bargain with their fee a modest four guineas and their only expenses fifteen shillings for the taxi fare home. The choice of band perhaps denotes a hidden economy, for the year before the strains were those of the Zinovic Orchestra and the price of their labour was six guineas.

Throughout the 1930s the standard of golf at the Portland Club was very high although the membership remained comparatively low at 133. Quality rather than quantity was the watchword and a three-man team of Robert Garson, J. B. Stevenson and James Wallace came second in the West of Scotland Team Championship. Robert Garson rendered incalculable service to both the Portland and Troon clubs. Playing for the former, he reached the final of the Irish Open Amateur in 1909 being beaten by the familiar figure of Charles Hezlet. Later he was a full Scottish internationalist and carried the whole administration of the Portland Club when acting as Secretary during the difficult early days of the First World War. From 1930-34 he was captain of Troon Portland and when he moved to Troon Golf Club he was equally influential, being Green

Convener for the Open Championship of 1950 and producing greens which earned the unstinting approval of the great Bobby Locke.

J. B. Stevenson, with sixteen caps for Scotland, has already been mentioned and the third member of the trio, James Wallace, was equally one of the best amateur golfers of his time. It was his misfortune to have encountered the American W. Lawson Little in the final of the Amateur Championship of 1934 played over Prestwick. There was great excitement locally at the prospect of an Ayrshire win but Little won a crushing victory by 14 and 13. One could say that the occasion was too big for the Ayrshireman but that would be grudging toward Little. He took only 23 holes to secure the title and for those 23 holes he was 10 under fours. His first round was a searing 66 which trimmed three strokes off McDonald Smith's previous best in the Open of 1925.

The players had shaken hands and walked off by ten minutes to two. Superfluously, as it turned out, there had been an early start to allow Little to catch the boat back to the United States that night. He lunched in the sybaritic comfort of 12 up and it is fair to say that he made the gangway with plenty to spare. Very properly the Portland Club showed its appreciation of Jim Wallace's efforts in the week of the Championship in a very tangible form. He subsequently turned professional and was attached to Shirley Park near Croydon. An easier letter to write was the one congratulating Mrs Helen Holm on winning the Ladies' Championship by beating Pam Barton 6 and 5 at Porthcawl.

The economic climate of the 1930s was no less severe for Troon than for anywhere else. Through these years there was an ongoing competition for unemployed members and by 1937 the financial position of the Portland Club was causing great concern. A five shilling increase in subscription was thought desirable but proved unattainable and the Committee had to settle for half. The Secretary nobly agreed that his honorarium should be reduced from twenty to fifteen guineas and henceforth the subscription would be thirty five shillings per annum.

The economy picked up in 1938 but only because of preparations for war. The club was soon in trouble, not so much from military call-up as from the fact that munitions factories and other war producers were working flat out and there was little time for civilians to play golf. By April 1941, there were only 95 active members (that would have further reduced to 75 before the war ended) and there was a real chance that an under-utilised course might be requisitioned by one or other of the Services. This was no fanciful notion for the Dundonald Golf Club was so requisitioned and did not survive.

Rescue came from an unlikely source. In 1942 the Troon Clubhouse was taken over by the Royal Navy and the members had to decamp to the Portland. This solved the problem of usage to some extent since Sir Alexander Walker set a good example by becoming a member of Portland.

The guests stayed a long time, five years in fact as they did not fold their tents until April 1st 1947. Hereabouts the Troon Club won many friends across the road. The Portland Clubhouse was shabby after the war and needed drastic refurbishment. In a truly cavalier gesture, Sir Alexander Walker asked that a list of the required furniture should be drawn up and the bills sent to him.

There was further good news about the same time when the Troon Committee agreed that the number of Portland members should be increased to 100. There

J. B. Stevenson and Alistair McKinnon with the Evening Times Trophy

was a real attempt to get back to the pre-war ways of doing things although occasionally wires appear to have been crossed. Thus the Portland A.G.M. of 1946 resolved that "the Committee should discuss how to revive the competitive spirit in the Club" but followed this up with the cryptic entry "it was agreed that no competitions should be held this season".

There was a backward look to the war in a local rule that a ball lying in tank tracks must be played as it lay. William Kelly, who had captained Portland from 1938 all through the war, resigned in 1948. The club had been mercifully spared heavy losses, only one member had died on service. Every club has its own little quirks and Portland had a rather unusual category of "resignation by death" which one supposes conveys a fixed intent and purpose. Somewhat surprisingly the Club Championship does not seem to have been formally inaugurated until 1951.

Distinction was being won on foreign fields, so to speak. One of the leading Scottish tournaments is the Glasgow Evening Times Foursomes which at one and the same time contrives to be one of the most sociable and one of the most fiercely contested Scottish events. In the years following the war, Troon Portland won this twice, their team being the same on both occasions – J. B. Stevenson and Alistair McKinnon. The victory in 1949 was at Barassie, that of 1951 was played over Royal Burgess in Edinburgh.

Matt Lygate had a distinguished golf career at all levels with perhaps the highlight a defeat of Peter Oosterhuis, a future Canadian Open Champion, in the Amateur Championship of 1968. He had a good record in that particular tournament reaching the last 16 on three occasions and he twice reached the same stage in the Scottish. He was capped for Scotland and was a Walker Cup Selector. In addition he was non-playing Captain of the Scottish team from 1984-1988.

The planning for the Troon Portland Centenary started as early as 1991 although the event itself would not be celebrated until 1994. Such a notable occasion would in these modern times require sponsorship and there were three categories of sponsors, Gold, Silver and Bronze. In this regard Royal Troon very helpfully made playing time available to sponsors on the course.

The sale of club mementos was aided by the attraction of the famous Portland Vase, there are few clubs whose crest reaches back to the Emperor Augustus! The Centenary Dinner at which the centenary captain Matt Lygate, presided afforded the chance to pay tribute to the many fine golfers produced by the Portland Club in the past, men such as J. B. Stevenson, Charlie Gibb, Minty Miller, Alistair McKinnon, Robert Garson and of course the captain himself.

Fittingly, the venue for the Dinner was the Marine Highland Hotel as the club's oldest and most prestigious trophy is the Marine Cup, presented by an early manager. The centenary programme contained the annual match against The Ladies' Club for the Greta Laird Salver. There was a new and coveted trophy, the Centenary trophy, remarkable both in appearance and the identity of the donor. It was presented by the famous Largs golfing teacher and father of the famous Sam, Bob Torrance. The trophy itself is a replica of the Open Championship Cup. It was won by the late Duncan Mackay who was then in his seventies.

Troon Portland Golf Club Crest

Clubhouse refurbishment proceeded both sides of the Centenary Year. The changes were radical, the large locker room undergoing a drastic change of use to become the lounge and bar. New lockers were installed and toilet and showering facilities improved. In the ongoing period since the early 1970s many of the Club's members contributed greatly to the success of these changes by giving generously of their time and individual skills.

Those members of Troon Portland not sufficiently fortunate to have been born with a classical swing can console themselves with a quick look at their blazers which are classical enough in all conscience. The design is the famous Portland Vase, more than 2000 years old and for long the property of the Dukes of Portland. The vase is awe inspiring, made of dark blue glass with the reliefs being in white opaque enamel. They tell the story of the sea goddess Thetis for whom Zeus and Poseidon carried a godly torch but whose heart was set upon the mortal Peleus. There may have been a touch of ill luck about the name Thetis. A submarine of that name foundered in Liverpool Bay in 1939 and the vase itself was the victim of a frenzied attack by a madman in the British Museum in 1845. By an astonishing work of reparation the vase was restored to something like its erstwhile splendour. Royal Troon and The Ladies' Club of Troon have imposing Latin mottoes, Portland has the vase supported by crossed golf clubs on a Cambridge blue background.

Clubmasters and Caddie Masters

Clubmasters

OVER the years catering at Royal Troon has become a much more sophisticated affair. Before the opening of the Ailsa Lounge to all intents and purposes it consisted of the provision of lunch on Saturdays for the Glasgow-based members and Afternoon Tea in the Smoke Room for the locals. Sometimes the Club Masters stayed for many years as for example the Whites who held the post for almost thirty years between 1909 and 1938. Sometimes the Clubmaster died untimely as was the case of Mr Dodds, killed in a car accident of 1969 along with his counterpart from Prestwick.

The arrival of the Bromley's – Mrs Bromley was Swiss-born – was the signal for a more imaginative style of catering, especially as the Ailsa Lounge was now available. The policy was carried on by the Rowans and the McIntyres and during the latter's tenure the package arrangement for Visitors was introduced which consists of a round of golf on both courses and a substantial Buffet Lunch.

Catering is tested to the limit in the week of an Open Championship. During that of 1997 over 2000 meals were served in the Dining Room and more than 4000 sandwiches and light snacks were provided in other areas of the Club House.

List of Clubmasters since 1878

Mr. Flemming (1st appointment)	1886 – 1893
Mr. & Mrs. J. Arminshaw	1893 – 1899
Mr. & Mrs. Bastin	1899 – 1909
Mr. & Mrs. D. White	1909 – 1938
Mr. & Mrs. C. Earl	1938 – 1939
Mr. & Mrs. W. J. Francis	1939 – 1942
Mr. & Mrs. A. Ferguson	1943 – 1944
Mr. & Mrs. J. Fisher	1944 – 1949
Mr. & Mrs. Thomson	1949 – 1952
Mr. & Mrs. Moir	1953 – 1955
Mr. & Mrs. McDonald	1956 – 1962
Mr. & Mrs. Sibbald	1962 – 1968
Mr. & Mrs. Dodds	1968 – 1969
Mr. & Mrs. Alexander	1970 – 1971
Mr. & Mrs. Bromley	1971 – 1976
Mr. & Mrs. F. Rowan	1976 – 1987
Mr. & Mrs. W. Browne	1987 – 1988
Mr. & Mrs. G. McIntyre	1988 – 1998
Mr. & Mrs. D. Maddison	1999 –

Mr & Mrs Graham McIntyre, 1997 Open Championship

Caddie Master James Manson at Gywas Cottage with caddies, circa 1900

Caddie Masters

The qualities required of a Caddie Master are rather different from those asked of the catering side. Caddie Masters in golf bear in general a martinet quality and Troon was no different. The following four Caddie Masters in particular made their individual marks.

R Manson 1947-64

He had lost one arm during the First World War but nevertheless cycled to work every day. He was described as "a very austere man who did not endear himself to strangers, nor had he a great deal of time for those who lived locally". Towards the minority of the world who remained he appears to have been perfectly civil.

J Wallace 1964-73

Manson's successor could hardly have been more different. Away from the course he had a certain amount of acclaim as a Scots comedian in shows given in the local Concert Hall.

Bobby Doig 1975-84

Bobby Doig was short sighted, a cigarette his constant companion. His great passion was horseracing and he fulfilled the role of Bookies' Runner for Members in the Smoke Room. This had been a most useful function in the days when off-course betting was technically illegal although new resorts followed Rothesay's example in having a one-legged Bookies' Runner.

Bill McKnight 1984-99

After a stirring career in the Scots Guards and the Police Force he became Caddie Master at Troon and his period in charge of the caddies encompassed two Open Championships. Even more impressively he saw off ten Captains, four Club Masters and three Secretaries. He left his successor Michael McCallum well grounded to take over and he is the youngest man to hold the position.

List of Caddie Masters

James Manson	– 1900
Andrew Fulton	1900 – 1904
Mr. Gale	1904 – 1911
Mr. Donald	1911 – 1911
George Manson	1911 – 1916
Mr. Finniegan	1917 – 1917
Alex Black	1918 – 1918
D. McMillan	1918 – 1920
W. Howie	1920 – 1947
R. Manson	1947 – 1964
J. Wallace	1964 – 1973
Thoman Buchanan	1973 – 1975
Bobby Doig	1975 – 1984
Bill McKnight	1984 – 1999
Michael McCallum	1999 –

THE 1990s

Across the years Bill McKnight looks back at his charges with affectionate exasperation, perhaps with exasperated affection.

"I have had in the ranks of caddies men from all walks of life; military men, labourers, miners and seafarers and, although they were from different backgrounds and social standing, they had a common bond – a bond the strength of which confused me. I wondered about this strength and to my mind this was their way of bridging the gap, but just where exactly would I fit in? Did I have the ability to control or guide the ranks of the people for whom I was responsible to achieve an end product suitable to all? Bearing in mind I had inherited a group of self-opinionated professionals who probably knew more about golf than I would ever learn, that was the situation and it was important to me and what drove me to try to understand the hearts and minds of those unique individuals.

During the next few months, I set about finding out what made them tick what made them seek the respect they craved and whether or not they deserved such respect. I wanted to know if they were loyal, if they were honest and, above all, if they were as good as they made out they were. Over the next few years I was to be surprised and humbled.

In our changing world, where there is a general lowering of standards, increasing uncertainty, indiscipline and, I have to say, civil disobedience, I was not to find this among these men. This surprised me for, as I have already said, they were from a wide social range and obviously had differing attitudes, differing beliefs and differing standards. Bit by bit, event by event and through circumstances which occurred, I learned to trust and respect each one of them. During the course of my learning, I hoped within hope that they were beginning to trust me and give me some of the respect I had extended to them. I realised that they were, in a manner, a family. They had a relationship among themselves which I had never found in any other group of individuals; a strength, a union. The problem for me was to ease myself into this union without appearing to intrude in the process and without making a fool of myself. Thus I had started on a journey during which I was to be both entertained and enlightened.

There are many reasons for a "nickname" or "nom-de-plume". It may be due to an individual's appearance or manner, or to fondly describe someone for an indiscretion, or it may just be that for one reason or another an individual wished to be anonymous! For whatever purpose, every caddie at Troon has a nickname and it was important to him that this was so. Let me explain. Bearing in mind I had in the legions of caddies, the most unkempt, half sober, quick witted group of humanity any one could inherit and if any one of them was excluded and addressed by his proper name he would feel left out, unloved and isolated and that would never do. Would it?

Bill McKnight, Caddie Master 1984-99

Within the pecking order for caddies at Troon was a group called "The Dirty Dozen", the creme de la creme so to speak, the top team, the proven. They were the best and they knew it. Each one of them. after two or three holes, could club a golfer to perfection, to lose a ball was unthinkable and every green to them was like the back of their hand. Their knowledge of the Rules of Golf was legendary and they took pride in their assessment of distance. When one of their number, for one reason or another, retired or took up another occupation, the selection process to fill the vacancy was akin to appointing a new Pope, only to them it was much more serious. He had to be that good. Man is intent on doing what he does best and it is no different for a caddie. He assesses his charge very much as though "the boot was on the other foot" or, if you prefer, "the club was in the other hand". Caddying is no different from many other demanding occupations and they are proud to be part of the team, more so if it is a winning team.

Of a morning within the caddyshack holding 40 or so caddies, a question concerning the Rules of Golf or some incident occurring locally or on the tour, would arise. The Rule or incident was debated at length with vigorous enthusiasm by the caddies who would each form their own opinion and decide what was proper and correct. When professional advice was eventually given, they were delighted that it was as they had decreed and the interest generated was encouraging. It showed that they were interested in what they were doing which was to their credit and a further step in the right direction for respect.

Above all, I learned that the future of golf is assured as long as the game is played by men and women, whatever their skill, with enthusiasm and in the spirit of fair play and there will always be caddies to complement the game, adding their humour and expert knowledge. They have existed since the beginning and I hope will prevail until the final putt is holed out on the last green.

I remember that lovely man Payne Stewart visiting the Ayrshire coast with three friends to play golf and relax. On arrival at Royal Troon he had some time in hand prior to teeing-off and we were chatting away on the putting green about golf in general and life in particular, when the subject of Scottish ancestry cropped up.

He confided that he thought he might be descended from the Royal line of the Stuarts. I explained that the spelling of his surname was different from Charles Edward Stuart. He asked if I thought that made much difference as alterations over the years did happen. I told him that was sometimes the case. This seemed to amuse him and it was about this time I thought I was being wound up.

His tee time became due and with a smile and a cheery wave he went over to join his friends who had been fortified by four of the dirty dozen.

Several months later I was browsing through a book in the history of Scotland when I came across a portrait of Charles Edward Stuart (Bonnie Prince Charlie) and I will swear there was a remarkable likeness to the man I had the privilege to have had a chat with at Troon."

Old Course Championship Guide

FEW men have played the Old Course at Royal Troon as often as the current Professional Brian Anderson. Here he offers sound advice on how to play the Championship Course. If it does not ensure a low score it should nevertheless provide a strong hope of damage limitation.

1 Seal – Par 4 – 364 yards

A relatively gentle opening hole, the shortest par four on the course. The drive should be slightly to the right to avoid the two bunkers that guard the left side of the fairway. The second shot is played with a lofted iron to a very slightly elevated green protected by bunkers to the left and right.

2 Black Rock – Par 4 – 391 yards

The test begins to stiffen, particularly if the wind has done likewise and is blowing from behind. Such conditions bring three cross-bunkers into play. Avoid them and the approach shot is played to a closely bunkered green.

3 Gyaws – Par 4 – 379 yards

Named after the burn crossing the fairway some 275 yards from the tee, the majority of players will lay up on this narrow hole. As on the first, the landing area is further limited by fairway bunkers to the left.

4 Dunure – Par 5 – 557 yards

The first of the par fives, the long fourth dog-legs to the right. A deep bunker positioned right in the neck of the dog-leg foils any attempt to cut the corner. The second shot should be positioned to give the best line to a split-level green.

5 Greenan – Par 3 – 210 yards

Lying immediately above the shoreline Greenan is a long and difficult par three. The green is large but is flanked by deep bunkers left and right. The key here is to take enough club to land the ball in the heart of the putting surface beyond the trouble.

6 Turnberry – Par 5 – 599 yards

The longest hole in Open Championship golf. The drive must be arrow straight to finish between the fairway bunkers to the left and right. Ideally the second should favour the left side to give the best line for the approach to a long narrow green protected by a bunker on the left edge.

The Gyaws Burn which crosses the 3rd and 16th fairways

7 Tel-el-Kebir – Par 4 – 402 yards

The seventh is a very attractive golf hole played from an elevated tee set among the dunes. An accurate tee shot is essential to avoid twin bunkers on each side of the fairway. The well-trapped green lies between two imposing sandhills.

8 Postage Stamp – Par 3 – 126 yards

Much has been written about the famous eighth hole at Royal Troon, aptly named the "Postage Stamp". The tee is on high ground and a dropping shot is played over a gully to a long but narrow green set into the side of a large sandhill. Two bunkers protect the left side of the green while a large crater bunker shields the approach. Any mistake to the right will find one of two deep bunkers with near vertical faces. No safe way to play this hole, the green must be found with the first shot. Many top players have come to grief at this, the shortest hole in Open Championship golf.

9 The Monk – Par 4 – 423 yards

No relaxing finish to the outward nine here, the drive should be positioned to the left side of the fairway but short of the two bunkers to allow a second shot to a two-tiered green through a narrow undulating gulley.

10 Sandhills – Par 4 – 438 yards

No bunkers on this tenth hole but still one of the toughest pars on the course. A blind drive over a high ridge of sandhills leaves a searching iron to a plateau green set into the side of a rise with plenty of gorse to the left and a sharp drop to the right of the green.

11 The Railway – Par 4 – 463 yards

A hooked drive here will almost certainly be lost in the thick gorse bushes while too far to the right will be out of bounds on the railway which runs parallel to the whole length of the hole. A long second is required to a slightly raised green protected by a bunker to the left front and out of bounds a few yards to the right. This was rated the most difficult hole in the 1997 Open Championship.

12 The Fox – Par 4 – 431 yards

The twelfth is a straightaway hole with the drive finishing in a narrow neck of fairway. The approach shot being played to a slightly raised two-tier green falling away down a bank to the left and bunkered on the right.

13 Burmah – Par 4 – 465 yards

This hole heads back into the prevailing wind and is the start of a famously difficult and long finishing stretch of six holes. Turning slightly left to right the hole demands two big shots over undulating ground to reach an elevated green.

14 Alton – Par 3 – 179 yards

A strong iron-shot is called for to carry over the three bunkers protecting the front and sides of the green.

15 Crosbie – Par 4 – 457 yards

Another long two shotter, the drive should favour the left side of the fairway to give a view of the distant green, which rests, in a hollow. This hole is well bunkered and the emphasis is on accurate play.

16 Well – Par 5 – 542 yards

The longest hole on the inward half, the tee shot however must finish short of the burn crossing the fairway around 280 yards out. The second shot should be placed in the left half of the fairway to obtain the best line into a well-bunkered green.

17 Rabbit – Par 3 – 223 yards

Rabbit is the most difficult of the short holes, where the tee shot can be as much as a driver depending on the wind. The plateau green falls away sharply on either side and is well protected by deep bunkers.

18 Craigend – Par 4 - 452 yards

A really challenging finishing hole, the drive must negotiate three bunkers guarding the left side of the fairway and one to the right. Cross-bunkers short of the green will catch a miss-hit second shot and the green itself is protected by three bunkers and an out of bounds pathway a few yards behind.

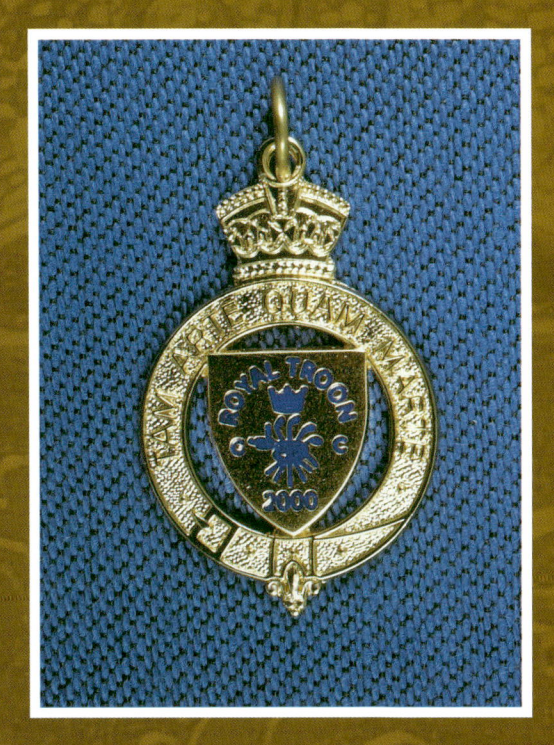

Millennium Monthly Medal

Chapter Seven

The New Millennium

The Millennium Year

IN common with many other Clubs and Associations across the land there was an expectation that special events would be organised to celebrate the new Millennium. During David Smyth's captaincy, a Sub-Committee was formed under the Chairmanship of Vice-Captain Boucher-Myers their remit being to suggest ideas for approval by Committee and subsequently organise appropriate events.

At an early stage it was agreed to hold few, but memorable, events for the enjoyment of the Members of Royal Troon. A range of merchandise bearing a new Millennium Logo was developed, with the Club commissioning a specially minted Millennium Medal to be awarded to the winners of both classes in the Monthly Medal Competitions, played over the Old Course.

Millennium Monthly Medal

The year started with the Annual Cocktail Party, which was attended by a larger number of members than normal. This was followed by the Club's Annual Dinner held on Friday 10th March, with the four winners of the Amateur Championship at Troon, Charlie Yates, John Beharrell, Michael Bonallack and Peter McEvoy being invited to join the celebrations on the evening. However, for health reasons Charlie Yates could not attend, but prepared a video message for the membership, which was played during the Top Table introductions. In his message Charlie apologised to John, Michael and Peter that he was unable to attend and make-up the fourball.

There were one hundred and fifty-nine Members in attendance with the Dining Room and Ailsa Lounge being utilised using close-circuit TV. The Toast to "Royal Troon Golf Club" was proposed by Sir Michael Bonallack OBE, Captain of the Royal & Ancient Golf Club of St. Andrews, responded to by the Captain Bryan Boucher-Myers, whose father Bill had been Captain in the Club's Centenary Year, a unique distinction for the Boucher-Myers family. Bob Crampsey, the author of this Club History, proposed the Toast to "The Game of Golf". The Toast to "Our Guests" was proposed by Vice-Captain Rait, which was responded to by Duncan MacLeod, Immediate Past Captain of Prestwick Golf Club. The

The Top Table, Annual Dinner, 2000
Left to right (Standing) P. McEvoy, Amateur Champion 1978; D. J. MacLeod, Past Captain, Prestwick Golf Club; J. P. Imlay Jnr. representing C. R. Yates, Amateur Champion 1938; T. O. M. Cordiner, Captain, Pollok Golf Club; P. W. Jamieson, Vice-Captain, Western Gailes Golf Club; J. C. Beharrell, Amateur Champion 1956; A. M. Duncan, Captain, Kilmarnock (Barassie) Golf Club.

Left to right (Seated) J. F. Rait, Vice-Captain, Royal Troon Golf Club; D. B. Fraser, Honorary President, Royal Troon Golf Club; B. J. Boucher-Myers, Captain, Royal Troon Golf Club; Sir Michael F. Bonallack, OBE, Captain, The Royal and Ancient Golf Club of St. Andrews and Amateur Champion 1968 and, R. A. Crampsey, Guest Speaker and Author, Royal Troon's Club History.

formal part of the evening concluded with Honorary Membership being conferred on Sir Michael Bonallack. This was in recognition of his victory in the 1968 Amateur Championship at Troon and his outstanding contribution to the game of golf, as a player, Secretary and now Captain of the R&A. When the lights went out, everyone present agreed it had been a memorable evening.

H.V.S Thomson Putter

Following the Annual Dinner, a few months elapsed before the focus of the Millennium events turned to the links, or close proximity to them. In conjunction with the Summer Meeting a new Competition for the H.V.S Thomson Putter had been organised. Through the good offices of the Club Professional, a Hickory shafted Nicol Gem Putter used to good effect by H.V.S. in his competitive amateur days was obtained. The putting green was organised for a series of activities, the winner of the inaugural event being Mr R. A. W. Johnston.

The H.V.S Thomson Putter is now mounted in a display case in the Smoke Room and will be played for on an annual basis.

The Grand Match

Held on Saturday 15th July, The Grand Match involved Members of Royal Troon, The Ladies' Club and Portland, one hundred and seventy-six players in total. The format required teams of four, two members from Royal Troon and one each from the Ladies' and Portland Clubs.

The competition was played as a Texas Scramble under handicap, where each player hits their own tee-shot, the team members selecting the best tee-shot from where they all play their second shot. Each team Member then plays a ball from that position with the process continuing until they reach the green. The best putt, possibly not the shortest, is selected and each player then attempts to hole out from this location. The process continues until the team holes out. One wonders what the Club's founding fathers would have thought of this format of play?

To conclude an enjoyable day, team members enjoyed a Buffet Lunch in the Dining Room, followed by refreshments and the prize giving. The Competition was won by Mr R. A. W. Johnston and Mr W. S. Laing of Royal Troon, Mrs J. Tucker of the Ladies' Club and Mr B. Clark of Portland, with a net score of 63.

The 2000 British Mid-Amateur Championship

In 1997, the Club were approached by the Royal and Ancient Golf Club of St. Andrews with a request to host the 2000 British Mid-Amateur Championship. The R&A were keen that their key supporting Clubs should participate in hosting one of their events in the Millennium Year and the Club were delighted to accept the invitation.

As a relatively new Championship on the Amateur circuit, the Mid-Amateur is targeted at players over twenty-five years of age, the objective perhaps being to find the true Amateur Champion. The young hopefuls will probably have turned professional by that time. The Championship inaugurated at Sunningdale New in 1995, is open to players having a handicap of three or less, the field restricted to 144 players. Given the standing of Royal Troon in the world of golf over three hundred and fifty entries were received by the R&A, which resulted in players with a handicap of greater than 0.4 being balloted-out. The growing popularity of the

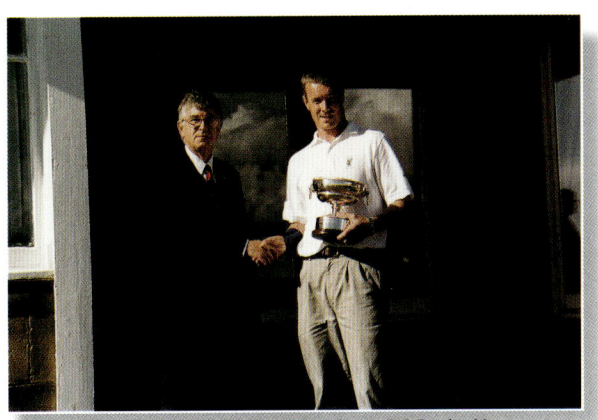

Andrew Farmer receives the Trophy from Captain B. J. Boucher-Myers, 2000 British Mid-Amateur Championship

competition, coupled with the venue was demonstrated by the large overseas entry, in particular the American entry of 57 competitors, which was reduced to one by the semi-final stage.

The Championship format, was thirty-six qualifying holes played over the Old Course, with the leading 64 players taking part in the match-play stages.

Mixed weather greeted the players on the qualifying days, with a stiff prevailing wind bidding welcome to those from foreign shores. The quality of golf displayed was reflected in the splendid scores of the leading qualifiers Richard Walker (Walton Hall) and Giles Legg (Dudsbury) each with 36 hole totals of 143. The title-holder John Kemp (John o'Gaunt) eased into the match-play stages with a two round total of 151.

Kemp's game sharpened in the cut and thrust of the match-play and he proceeded to the final to meet 26 year old Andrew Farmer from Kilmacolm. In the semi-final match the Scot took the honours against the surviving American Don Baker, having set out on the first day simply to beat the cut. It was the Kilmacolm man who won the Championship, when he finally prevailed at the 18th hole taking the title by a narrowest of margins.

The Cross Country Match

Before discussing the Match held on Sunday 10th September, it is worthwhile recounting the history of this unique fixture. The match is played on the same day across the links of two Clubs who between them have hosted thirty-one Open Championships, namely Prestwick and Royal Troon Golf Clubs.

There are many stories about unofficial matches being played in the 1920s, 30s, and 40s but it wasn't until the late sixties, early seventies that the match became an annual event, but still an unofficial fixture. The match in those days was given the seal of approval as the Captains of both Clubs were invited to compete. The Match organisers were John Leburn for Royal Troon and Tim Morrison for Prestwick. In those days it was normally twelve or fourteen a-side but for the Millennium Year it was increased to forty-eight a-side.

The format of the match is Foursomes match-play with points being awarded for the match, the bye, the bye-bye and any other eventuality. Play normally commences at 9:00am from the 1st Tee at Troon, playing Troon's front nine, then after a short trek cross-country to the 9th Tee at Prestwick, would complete the morning round of nineteen holes. All players would then partake of the famous "Prestwick Lunch" quenching their thirst and partaking in a Kummel or two, re-appearing on the 1st Tee some hours later. With the pairings re-drawn for the afternoon matches, players would then play the first eight holes at Prestwick, followed by Troon's testing back nine. The combatants would then return home somewhat wearier. The following year the match would commence at Prestwick playing to Royal Troon for lunch and back again.

The match requires a considerable amount of planning and the assistance of the Clubs' Caddiemasters who transport the players' clothing from the starting Club to their near neighbour to enable players to change for lunch. The procedure is then reversed to ensure that players had a change at conclusion of play. It goes without saying that there have been some mishaps over the years. To bond the friendship between the players a Black Tie Dinner was introduced in 1992 and is held every two years on the Friday preceding the match. There is also a cross-country tie available to members who have played in the match.

Cross Country Challenge Cup

THE NEW MILLENNIUM

In 1999 both John Leburn and Tim Morrsion requested that responsibility for organising the match should be taken over by the Clubs, who could increase the number taking part and more importantly make it an official Club Fixture. Both Clubs agreed to this request and to herald the new dawn a forty-eight a-side match was organised as part of the Millennium activities. However, one major change was required to enable the match to be completed on the one day. Half of the matches would commence at Troon and the other half at Prestwick, lunch being served in both Clubhouses. As the first match of the new format, it was agreed that the day should be concluded with a Black-Tie Dinner involving all the participants and this would be held at Royal Troon.

To herald this new beginning, a new trophy was played for which would be known as the "Cross Country Challenge Cup". The new trophy had been presented to the Clubs for annual play by Keith Martin, whose uncle Dick Smith is a Member of both Clubs. Dick has the unique distinction of having played for both Clubs in the early matches and had won the new trophy in 1945 at the Royal Calcutta Golf Club. The trophy is inscribed "Amateur Golf Championship of India – Challenge Cup".

The match itself was a keenly contested affair and, at lunch Royal Troon were twenty points ahead and in the words of their Captain, "were clear favourites". However, he failed to take account of their neighbour's hospitality at lunch, which added a degree of fluidity to the players' swings for the afternoon matches and may have contributed, to the final result. After a number of recounts and at the end of an excellent dinner to mark the occasion, Prestwick Golf Club was victorious by the smallest of margins – three points.

The Members' Christmas Luncheon

In 1983, the Thursday Group of retired members led by Willie Millar, Jim Morton, Leslie Hardie and Jim Donald decided to hold an end of season Christmas Luncheon, which was attended by thirty members.

The following year the Club's first Christmas Luncheon took place with approximately forty members in attendance. The event has grown in popularity and by 1996 had outgrown the capacity of the Dining Room with the Ailsa Lounge also being required to seat the one hundred and ten members who wished to attend. In 1998 one hundred and thirty members attended, which was surpassed by the 1999 Luncheon, which also marked the retirement of Bill McKnight, the Club's Caddiemaster.

The Members' Christmas Luncheon is now one of the highlights of the Members' year and is a pleasant entrée to the Festive Season. It also brought to an end a successful and enjoyable Millennium Year for the Club.

Members' Christmas Luncheon, 2000

Might I Suggest

THE Suggestions Book is seldom the preferred reading of the committee and it is true that in its pages the Club wit, the Club bore and the Club paranoiac often seek refuge. But at its best, the Suggestions Book reveals what the thinking is out there in the bazaars and just occasionally the committee is legitimately sent homeward to think again.

In the following excerpts from the Royal Troon Suggestions Book the names of those making the suggestions have been reduced to initials to protect the guilty. A feature of any golf club's Suggestion Book is the surpassing knowledge of retail prices in shops, shops with which the Golf Club itself almost always compares unfavourably. Thus this entry of March 1908 from J.B.P.:

"That Three Castle cigarettes be supplied by the Club at nine pence and not one shilling as sold elsewhere".

The emollient answer was that the matter had the attention of the House Committee. G.M. was similarly pacified in January 1911 when he made the not exorbitant demand that the hot water taps should provide hot water. In September of that same year J.M.S. was one of the few members who raised a point directly connected with the actual playing of the game:

"That: As was the case some years ago, a chalk line be drawn between the two plates on the tee as some people are inclined, quite unintentionally, to tee before the line and a mistake of this kind in a medal round means disqualification".

His plea was rebutted and despite his use of 'unintentionally' the reader is left with the uneasy impression that J.M.S. knew exactly who teed off where and would not hesitate to invoke the appropriate penalty. F.K. had more luck with his criticism of the rudimentary telephone service provided to the clubhouse:

"That the Secretary be instructed to make strong representations to the Telephone Company regarding the bad service. A mere puff of wind puts the instrument out of order and the club is entitled to a new up-to-date instrument".

The club thought so too and the desired improvement was speedily effected. Coming to 1913, J.M.C. was more prolix in his complaint;

"That notice boards be not erected in bunkers or such places where by removing them a player would lose the hole. This applies particularly to the notice at the last green. Also, that garden implements be kept out of the bunkers on the Relief (Portland) course, five were found in a bunker at Siberia on Monday last".

One has to admit that five seems a touch excessive.

There were requests from G.F. and P.D. that China tea and lager beer respectively should be available in the clubhouse. Occasionally it was the timing of the suggestion rather than the actual request which was inclined to strike a jarring note. Take this one on the ever-vexed question of caddying:

"The subscribers hereto ask the Committee to take immediate steps to engage an efficient Caddy Master who will be able to exercise discipline and anticipate the requirements of the members by procuring the attendance of sufficient boys or, if need be, girls. Anticipating an objection to the proposal (by the committee) on the grounds of economy, the Subscribers' desire to express their emphatic opinion that, if any economy be essential, the very last direction in which it should be operated is in regard to the Caddy Master on whose work if efficiently performed, so much depends for the enjoyment of golf. As an example of what the members have suffered in recent years we record that today three members had to carry their clubs on the morning round while six boys were present but refused to caddy."

Very vexing, to be sure and normally nothing to

take offence about, but the date, November 1st 1918 uncomfortably reminds us that precisely at that time several scores of Troon members were undergoing hardships which did put the lack of a caddy well down the great league table of suffering.

Playing conditions did loom large and over the years committees have been prompt to respond to reasonable suggestions. The 7th, 10th 13th, 14th and 15th holes all had greens where the exact position of the pin was difficult to see. Long bamboo poles as used at Machrihanish were found to be the answer. W.W.M. wished the greens to be watered later rather than the six o'clock of the evening which was the norm but here optimum timing did conflict with the hours that greenkeeping staff could reasonably be expected to work.

J.McN. had been checking up on the food situation and made this suggestion:

"I beg to suggest that tea and toast should be 6d the same as all the other clubs rather than 8d".

Down came the price.

The Portland members were agriculturists at heart, no fewer than 20 of them signing a 1926 suggestion that worm casts be cleared from the greens on Sunday mornings as the effect of their being trampled into the greens was deleterious. This omission may simply have been a hangover from the days of Sunday closing.

Occasionally a proposal went rather deeper. Towards the end of the twenties there was a feeling among the membership that the Club was becoming an over-cosy, self perpetuating oligarchy. J.L.C.J. (guess who!) was successful with his plea that no member of committee should propose or second any candidate for membership of the club.

The price of meals was a perennial. The members fondly quoted lower prices elsewhere, the Steward and Mrs Steward mused on the impossibility of making a profit from the catering. J.McN. was among the signatories to this suggestion of June 1929:

"We beg to draw to the attention of the Committee the exorbitant profit from catering in a non-commercial proposition. This club should be seen to cover expenses with a small profit not an enormous profit of £800 or over. The cost of lunch here is much more than in the neighbouring club of Prestwick and we beg to suggest that an inclusive charge of 2/6d for a two course lunch, plus sixpence for each additional course, is ample. We also suggest that the profits from drinks be shown separately in the annual accounts from those obtained from the supply of meals."

Robert Louis Stevenson once wrote in his poem 'The Vagabond': *"Not to autumn will I yield, not to winter even"* The members belonged to this school and would not compromise over winter conditions. D.G.R. had a thing about teeing grounds:

"That the teeing greens be improved during the winter time. It should not be necessary to play off such bad teeing greens as are in use at present. In many instances the fairway is better than the teeing greens."

J.W. in almost the last entry for a while seems to have been unsure whether he was referring to vandalism or mere self-expression when in October 1941 he suggested that:

"Steps should be taken to have the mural decoration in the hut adjacent to the 10th tee removed with the utmost despatch".

This was not quite the last entry for in the same month G.P.B. showed a laudable desire to help the war effort:

"To economise in service it is suggested that a large whiskey (sic) be served to a member at the equivalent price of two small whiskies".

It is hard not to draw the inference that a member insisting on a small whisky might have been deemed lacking in patriotism.

With more serious matters occupying minds, the Suggestion Book was closed in 1941 and did not resurface until 1952. War had not coarsened the mind since bidding re-opened with a plea for serviettes in the dining-room but this was vetoed on grounds of expense. From time to time a suggestion had the power to really surprise, as this of October 1959:

"That consideration be given to the instigation of a Club Championship. It is suggested that 16 qualifiers be obtained from the May Medal and Spring Meeting."

The surprise of course is occasioned by the fact that so comparatively late in the history of a venerable golf club, no attempt had been made hitherto to formalise a championship. R.H.C.'s plea was not uttered in vain and happily the event was introduced just in time to accommodate some of Troon's most famous names on the winner's board.

The use of caddy-cars was always going to evoke strong feelings and the anti-car lobby thought they saw their chance in the immediate wake of the Open Championship of 1962. They did not hold back:

"That the use of caddy-cars should now be allowed on the Old Course seems completely ludicrous. We have already experienced the type of damage caused by caddy-cars and that we now face this immediately after the course has taken the greatest pounding in its history seems wrong.

Apart from the slowing of play caused by these vehicles it is suggested that only good can come by continuing to ban the use of caddy-cars."

The Committee was not won over:

"While the Committee have agreed to permit the use of caddy-cars over the Old Course at present, they will again restrict their use whenever conditions demand it".

Fruit machines were another bone of contention. Many did not want them at all, some would have them if unobtrusively placed. Was a clubhouse a place to relax in friendly conversation with a drink or were livelier discussions essential? And what place had television as big sporting events became more frequent and accessible? Well, perhaps not all that accessible at the outset:

"On certain very special occasions, the T.V. set should be set up in the Smoke Room (Lounge). This would save 90 per cent of the present members sitting on beer crates and others watching through the bothy window."

Modest proposals – double the sweep money to 20p in 1969 to take account of inflation – had a chance where more ambitious schemes e.g. floodlighting for winter practice, failed dismally.

Toast reared its singed head again in 1978 with a puzzled query from G.B.S.T. as to why he could get toast in the Smoke Room but that sanctum did not provide him or anyone else with toasted cheese. Governments have fallen on smaller issues and he was assured that a new Smoke Room menu was even now in preparation.

We end on a rather macabre note, which begins when an indecipherable member vents his feelings thus:

"While I appreciate the Committee's wish to pander to each and every whim of the members, I think that the retention of the appurtenance in shower cubicle number three is carrying this ideal too far. Normally of phlegmatic nature I was nearly driven to use it today after a particularly horrendous medal round and I fear others may not be able to exercise the same self-control. Foreign guests may be thought to be particularly susceptible. Is it not time that we got rid of the noose?".

The Committee's reply was inspired and deserves to be recorded in its entirety:

"This matter has been duly executed".

Envoi

IT would be marvellous to be granted the position of Celestial Starter at Royal Troon on one of those long grey April evenings which are such an individual feature of the West Coast of Scotland. Let us assume those powers. First on the tee is a young lady who has already made her mark in lawn tennis. Lottie Dod, for it is she, has a swing comparatively unburdened by the cumbersome gear which aspiring female golfers then perforce had to wear. She makes her way down the first to the spectral accompaniment of Francis Thompson's "soundless clapping host".

Allowing her to play her second with almost palpable reluctance, James Jenkins bustles onto the tee, combativeness positively oozing from him. Great skill allied to a superb match-play temperament has brought him the Blue Riband of amateur golf and he remains the Club's only Amateur Champion to date.

Two on the tee after him and the cut of their jib is vaguely un-British, in an indefinable way. One is of medium height, the other perceptibly smaller but with an engaging grin which belies the notion that small men must necessarily be pugnacious. The small man, Gene Sarazen, has little cause to remember his debut at Troon with any great affection but he does and his links with the Club will span a period of seventy years. He will be the Open Champion and his partner, Walter Hagen, already has been. Without fuss each hits a more than adequate drive and together they pass into the mist and into history.

They are followed by a self-effacing tall Englishman, Arthur Havers, whose popularity will be diminished by the merest trifle when he mentions how glad he is to have kept the premier golfing trophy in England.

By now the crowd round the first tee has grown somewhat and volleys of applause come from what is clearly a swelling crowd out there. Two ladies have just left the tee. The swing of Miss Joyce Wethered is a thing of beauty. Bobby Jones will say that he has never seen one more graceful and her opponent, Cecil Leitch, has tenacity stamped upon every feature.

In no particular order the golfers roll up. This is Tom Burrell who for fun entered the Scottish Amateur Championship as a Troon member and won it. Booked for a later tee time are Jimmy Armour and Stewart Wilson who will each bring the Boy's Championship to the Ayrshire Coast.

Here following we have two golfers who have adorned the course by reason of their charm and skill. The lady is Helen Holm, a golfer of world ranking and yet another who proves with every swing that watching golf can be an aesthetic experience. On the tee with her a young Atlantan, laconic and ever threatening to burst into song, Charlie Yates, who will win the 1938 Amateur, play in the Walker Cup and become a most-cherished Honorary Member of the Club.

By now Lottie Dod must be out about the fourth but still the golfers come thick and fast. Here in a clutch are the Open winners, the smooth, imperturbable Bobby Locke who always seemed to proceed inexorably to victory and a young American who has brought his fan club with him. Smile on him for he is Arnold Palmer and he more than any other man has fought to preserve the Open as a major tournament.

Troon will be Tom Weiskopf's greatest week of his golfing career and he, above anyone else, will remember this old links course with particular affection. Tom Watson too, although he did make a habit of acquiring Open championships on assorted Scottish courses.

The Celestial Starter gives an approving nod as he recognises Mark Calcavecchia, a man who kept his head in a crisis. He is with Jack Nicklaus and Tiger Woods, the illustrious past and astonishing present of the game. By simple thought transference the C.S. is able to refresh his memory as to the extent to which Greg Norman dominated the course for one fateful day. Norman, the swashbuckler, appears to be partnered today by the Method Man par excellence, Justin Leonard.

Here's a threesome of Amateur Champions, John Beharrell, who had the thing won at 18 years of age, Michael Bonallack who for almost ten years was unbeatable in top amateur circles and Peter McEvoy who was good enough to play through the Masters at Augusta.

The Starter's notion that the standard of amateur golf is pretty high down Ayrshire way is reinforced as he watches a group of Scottish Amateur Champions. Dr F. W. G. Deighton, R. D. B. M. Shade, J. M. Cannon and Alan Brodie, Each won their title over Troon and the Celestial Starter allows himself a quiet smile of satisfaction at the quality of the crop.

And finally, bringing up the rear and in no way intimidated by the calibre of those out front, here comes a fourball of Royal Troon members bickering amiably as they make their way over the weel-kenned ground. They are at one and the same time the least illustrious and yet the most important of all those who have teed off today. It is good that famous golfers have brought glory to themselves and great renown to the Club of which they have either been members or played there at the very top level. It is good that Royal Troon is a name which is recognised and respected wherever the game is played. If any further proof were needed the allocation of the Amateur Championship for 2003 and the Open Championship of 2004 would certainly furnish it.

Yet pre-eminently it must be a club for members which provides keen competition and a happy social ambience. It was for this that James Dickie and John Highet worked so assiduously all those years ago. It is for this that their present successors in office must continue to strive.

Appendix I

Honorary Presidents

1901 – 43   His Grace William John Arthur Charles James, 6th Duke of Portland
1943 – 77   His Grace William Arthur Henry, 7th Duke of Portland
1971 – 87   F. D. Black
1988 – 93   A. H. Galbraith
1994 – 96   W. G. Macfarlane
1998 –   D. B. Fraser

Captains

1878 – 1882	J. Dickie	1942 – 1945	J. A. McAra
1882 – 1883	R. Easton	1945 – 1948	J. L. C. Jenkins, MC
1883 – 1887	W. A. Robertson	1948 – 1951	J. W. G. Wyllie, MC
1887 – 1890	W. Morison	1951 – 1953	J. Laird
1890 – 1893	W. J. Anderson	1953 – 1956	F. D. B. Black
1893 – 1897	A. Wood	1956 – 1959	H. G. Hendry
1897 – 1899	D. Fullarton	1959 – 1962	N. S. Smith
1899 – 1901	J. B. Wilson	1962 – 1964	T. C. Currie
1901 – 1904	W. Law	1964 – 1966	A. H. Galbraith
1904 – 1906	R. G. Ross	1966 – 1968	J. E. Dawson
1906 – 1908	Col. J. Smith Park	1968 – 1970	H. M. McMaster
1908 – 1910	J. Wishart	1970 – 1973	D. K. Henderson
1910 – 1912	R. Dunlop	1973 – 1975	A. N. Smith
1912 – 1915	R. Dickie	1975 – 1977	W. G. Macfarlane
1915 – 1919	Sir Frederick Henderson, KBE	1977 – 1979	Major B. W. S. Boucher-Myers, DSO
1919 – 1921	W. M. M. Turner	1979 – 1981	D. B. Fraser
1921 – 1922	J. G. Clark Millar	1981 – 1983	Sir Robert Fairbairn
1922 – 1923	Sir Alexander Walker (Acting), KBE	1983 – 1985	T. L. Holden
1923 – 1925	W. P. Stewart	1985 – 1986	G. B. Heaney, CBE OStJ
1925 – 1927	G. Clark	1986 – 1987	R. Kirkland
1927 – 1929	A. C. Robertson	1987 – 1989	D. H. D. Forsyth
1929 – 1931	J. Dundas	1989 – 1990	J. H. Greene
1931 – 1934	W. Forbes	1990 – 1992	Prof. J. Armour, CBE
1934 – 1936	Brigadier-General J. W. Walker, CMG DSO	1992 – 1994	M. G. F. Houston
1936 – 1937	G. Newton	1994 – 1997	I. B. Valentine
1937 – 1941	W. L. Carlow	1997 – 1999	D. S. Smyth
1941 – 1942	Sir Alexander Walker, KBE	1999 –	B. J. Boucher-Myers

	Honorary Secretary		**Secretaries**
1878 – 1893	Dr. J. Highet MB	1893 – 1909	W. Mackie
		1909 – 1929	H. R. Coubrough
	Honorary Treasurers	1929 – 1942	W. H. Johnson
1878 – 1887	Dr. J. Highet MB	1942 – 1966	A. G. Brander
1887 – 1890	J. Andrew	1942 – 1970	Miss E. L. Dawson (Assistant)
1890 – 1892	G. Morton and R. Lyn (Joint)	1966 – 1972	A. Sweet
1892 – 1893	W. Mackie	1972 – 1973	W. R. McCreath and A. H. B. Alexander (Joint)
		1973 – 1980	A. H. B. Alexander
		1973 – 1989	Mrs. M. H. Millar (Assistant)
		1980 – 1984	Wing Commander D. Graham (Rtd)
		1984 – 1987	J. A. Sword
		1987 – 1997	J. D. Montgomerie
		1997 –	J. W. Chandler

Appendix II

Origin of Hole Names: Old Course

1. SEAL

The Chain of Rocks named Seal lie only a few yards from the high water mark of the Spring Tides. It is not unusual some 100 years after the hole being given this name to view seals basking on the reef.

2. BLACK ROCK

Given this name after the reef lying offshore between the second and third tees.

3. GYAWS

This is an old Scot's word meaning furrow or a drain. The burn, which traverses the 16th and 3rd fairways, is so called.

4. DUNURE

The village of Dunure and its ruined Castle sits proudly overlooking the sea south of Ayr.

5. GREENAN

The old Kennedy Castle ruin just south of Ayr lends its name to the short fifth hole.

6. TURNBERRY

The point at Turnberry can be seen from Troon. The lighthouse marks the site of Turnberry Castle childhood home of the Bruce.

7. TEL-EL-KEBIR

Named after a battle fought in 1882 just before the hole was created

8. POSTAGE STAMP

Originally called "Ailsa" because there is a perfect view of the rocky islet of that name, from the tee. The smallness of the putting surface accounted for the current name when Willie Park writing in "Golf Illustrated" said, " A pitching surface skimmed down to the size of a Postage Stamp".

9. THE MONK

Faces towards the village of Monkton.

10. SANDHILLS

Large Sandhills face the Tee shot from the Championship Tee. In recent years part of the Sandhills have been lowered to afford the player a view of Sandhills House.

11. THE RAILWAY

Named after the railway line, which runs parallel with the 11th hole.

12. THE FOX

At one time a wooded area inhabited by a number of foxes. However, the woods have mostly gone and only the occasional fox remains.

13. BURMAH

The hole was designed shortly after Burmah was taken over in 1886 by Britain. The Country is now a Republic called Myanmar.

14. ALTON

Named after part of the Fullarton estate, to the north side of the railway.

15. CROSBIE

The name given to a small fortification near Alton, which was the home of the Fullartons for centuries.

16. WELL

A fresh water well was situated not far from the house of the Course Manager

17. RABBIT

A popular location for members of the Leporidae family. Clearly the passing of one hundred years has not diminished the rabbit's enthusiasm for the Links.

18. CRAIGEND

The name of the old farm demolished at the turn of the century has given its name in perpetuity to the closing hole. The Old Course and the Portland Course are formed on the Craigend grazings.

Origin of Hole Names: Portland Course

1. DANDERIN' INN
The hole was in close proximity to the Inn of this name. The correct name for the Shepherd's Cottage was Bogend, however locals thought Danderin' Inn more appropriate.

2. KYLE
The view to the south from the second tee encompasses the district of Kyle.

3. WHINS
This hole has the beauty of the scent and colour of whin bushes, which line the hole.

4 WRACK
Named after the Wrack Road, which runs behind the green and was used to bring seaweed from the shore to the local farms.

5. WARREN
Named after an area of land close to the golf course.

6. THE WOOD
The sixth hole runs parallel with the South Woods

7. SPRING
A spring, which was located mid-way along this hole, gives rise to the name.

8. GRAVEL
There used to be a gravel pit located at this hole.

9. PIERSLAND
Called after Piersland House, the home of Sir Alexander Walker, which can be seen from the hole.

10. DUKE
Named after the Duke of Portland

11. SKELDON
Skeldon House is situated in Dalrymple and is on the Skeldon Estate. This was part of the domain owned by the Duke of Portland and the residence was for a time occupied by the Duke's factor.

12. GOAT
From the old Scot's word meaning ditch or burn. A ditch crosses this hole some hundred yards from the tee and was known as the Goat Burn.

13. SIBERIA
At one time there was a wooded area known as Siberia between the 12th Tee on the Old Course and the Portland Course. This area was inhabited by a number of foxes however only scrub and bramble bushes remain.

14. PUDDOCK
A damp area of the course favoured by frogs and hence the Scot's word Puddock.

15. THE ROAD
The continuation of the Wrack Road across the 15th fairway prompted this name

16. TITCHFIELD
The hole name was taken from the title of the Duke of Portland.

17. FULLARTON
Troon was part of the estate of Fullarton, which was owned by the Duke of Portland, whose residence in Troon was Fullarton House.

18. HOME
Appropriately enough the final hole.

Appendix III
Course Records
Old Course

Amateur

1926	C. Gibb	68
1935	H. Thomson	68
1950	F. Stranahan	66
1961	J. M. Cannon	71*
1961	W. D. Smith	71*
1968	A. M. B. Sym	69
1972	H. B. Stuart	71*
1974	C. W. Green	70
1975	J. Harkiss	70
1989	R. Claydon	70*
1991	D. W. Hawthorn	70
1997	D. B. Howard	70*

Professional

1923	M. Smith (USA)	69
1923	J. M. Kirkwood (Australia)	69
1950	F. van Donck (Belgium)	65
1962	A. D. Palmer (USA)	67*
1973	J. W. Nicklaus (USA)	65*
1989	P. Stewart (USA)	65*
1989	G. Norman (Australia)	64
1997	E. Woods (USA)	64*

Course altered

Portland Course

Amateur

1931	J. Wallace	68
1975	I. R. Harris	66
1975	J. H. McKay	66
1990	G. S. Reynolds	65

Professional

1979	W. G. Cunningham	65

Appendix IV

The Club's Principal Medals and Trophies with their Winners

Hillhouse Cup
Presented to the Club in 1882 by Major McKerrill of Hillhouse, to be played for as a Scratch competition, amongst Members of Ayrshire Clubs.

		Club	*Score*
1883	J. Kirk	Ardeer	88
1884	R. Adam	Ardeer	90
1885	D. Thomson	Prestwick St. Nicholas	87
1886	D. Bone	Prestwick St. Nicholas	83
1887	D. D. Robertson	Troon	81
1888	A. Morison	Troon	84
1889	A. Morison	Troon	79
1890	W. Morison	Troon	85
1891	J. A. Shaw	Troon	83
1892	D. D. Robertson	Troon	78
1893	E. D. Prothero	Prestwick St. Nicholas	83
1894	T. Anderson	Prestwick	81
1895	R. Adam	Ardeer	83
1896	A. Boon	Prestwick St. Nicholas	87
1897	J. Thompson	Prestwick St. Nicholas	87
1898	R. Fullarton	Troon	77
1899	J. G. MacFarlane	Glasgow	76
1900	J. Robb	Glasgow	81
1901	J. Thomson	Prestwick St. Nicholas	76
1902	J. Robb	Prestwick St. Nicholas	80
1903	T. H. Walker	Troon	72
1904	R. Andrew	Prestwick St. Cuthbert	76
1905	J. Black	Troon Portland	76
1906	R. Andrew	Prestwick St. Cuthbert	75
1907	J. L. C. Jenkins	Troon	76
1908	R. Garson	Troon Portland	73
1909	H. F. McNeal	Western Gailes	79
1910	J. Shannon	Troon Portland	77
1911	G. Lockhart	Prestwick St. Nicholas	77
1912	G. Lockhart	Prestwick St. Nicholas	74
1913	G. V. M. Boyd	Troon	75
1914	R. Garson	Troon Portland	78

1915 – 1919 The Great War

1920	G. Lockhart	Prestwick St. Nicholas	79
1921	J. Wilson	Prestwick St. Nicholas	78
1922	J. Wilson	Prestwick St. Nicholas	74
1923	J. Wilson	Prestwick St. Nicholas	79
1924	J. L. C. Jenkins	Troon	76

		Club	*Score*
1925	J. L. C. Jenkins	Troon	73
1926	C. Gibb, jun.	Troon Merchants	68
1927	J. Brock	Western Gailes	75
1928	A. Boon, jun.	Prestwick St. Cuthbert	76
1929	J. Brock	Troon	73
1930	J. E. Dawson	Troon	75
1931	J. Brock	Troon	76
1932	W. Armstrong	Troon St. Meddans	77
1933	C. J. Lowdon	Ayr Belleisle	72
1934	J. Brock	Troon	73
1935	H. Thomson	Troon Burgh	68
1936	J. M. Dykes, jun.	Troon	73
1937	J. B. Stevenson	Troon Burgh	69
1938	J. B. Stevenson	Troon Burgh	74
1939	J. E. Dawson	Troon	72

1940 – 1946 World War II

1947	J. B. Stevenson	Troon Portland	74
1948	R. Neill	Troon	77
1949	J. B. Stevenson	Troon Portland	74
1950	J. E. Dawson	Troon	74
1951	A. McKinnon	Troon Portland	75
1952	J. B. Stevenson	Troon	70
1953	J. B. Stevenson	Troon	70
1954	J. B. Stevenson	Troon	73
1955	J. B. Stevenson	Troon	75
1956	J. B. Stevenson	Troon	71
1957	S. C. Wilson	Troon Burgh	72
1958	W. Alexander	Prestwick St. Nicholas	75
1959	J. Wilson, jun.	Kilmarnock Barassie	76
1960	J. R. McKay	Troon Portland	71
1961	J. M. Cannon	Bogside	71
1962	J. M. Cannon	Bogside	76
1963	D. J. R. Andrew	Troon Portland	79
1964	M. Lygate	Troon Portland	73
1965	I. D. Hamilton	Belleisle	77
1966	K. H. Martyn	Troon Portland	80
1967	D. J. R. Andrew	Troon Portland	77
1968	I. Cannon	Bogside	76

Hillhouse Cup (continued)

		Club	Score			Club	Score
1969	W. D. Smith	Troon	74	1985	J. Spiers	Annanhill	77
1970	G. D. Spence	Ravenspark	77	1986	S. Cox	Loudon Gowf	79
1971	G. B. Cosh	Troon	76	1987	D. Bruce	Ravenspark	75
1972	J. M. Cannon	Bogside	76	1988	B. S. Leburn	Royal Troon	80
1973	A. G. Neil	Ravenspark	78	1989	R. McCaig	Ardeer	77
1974	R. L. Crawford	Caprington	76	1990	J. Graham	Loudon Gowf	79
1975	J. Harkiss	Prestwick St. Cuthbert	70	1991	D. W. Hawthorn	Prestwick St. Nicholas	70
1976	I. D. Hamilton	Troon	72	1992	C. R. Savala	Prestwick St. Nicholas	78
1977	A. M. B. Sym	Troon	76	1993	G. Sherry	Kilmarnock Barassie	75
1978	N. J. Angus	Prestwick	79	1994	F. Hall	West Kilbride	74
1979	D. Andrews	Troon Portland	73	1995	G. Bryden	Girvan	74
1980	A. M. B. Sym	Royal Troon	76	1996	G. C. McKelvie	Royal Troon	76
1981	N. J. Angus	Royal Troon	74	1997	D. Orchiston	Ballochmyle	75
1982	D. Bruce	Ravenspark	76	1998	L. Kydd	Welbeck	71
1983	R. L. Crawford	Kilmarnock Barassie	75	1999	J. Callaghan	Largs	77
1984	J. Muir	Loudon Gowf	72	2000	B. Crawford	Kilbirnie	75

The Jenkins Trophy

Presented in 1960 by J. L. C. Jenkins, Amateur Champion 1914, Captain of the Club 1945-48, the Winner being the Club Champion.

1960	H. V. S. Thomson	1971	S. C. Wilson	1982	J. F. Rait	1993	M. Hamilton
1961	H. V. S. Thomson	1972	A. M. B. Sym	1983	H. D. McQuiston	1994	J. N. Rowberry
1962	H. V. S. Thomson	1973	A. M. B. Sym	1984	A. M. B. Sym	1995	D. S. Smyth
1963	H. V. S. Thomson	1974	J. R. W. Walkinshaw	1985	G. B. Cosh	1996	A. D. Kelly
1964	J. F. Snodgrass	1975	J. R. W. Walkinshaw	1986	M. C. Armour	1997	K. E. Brown
1965	A. G. Gordon	1976	I. D. Hamilton	1987	D. S. Smyth	1998	P. Convery
1966	S. C. Wilson	1977	I. R. Harris	1988	J. A. Barclay	1999	P. Convery
1967	C. C. Bird	1978	A. M. B. Sym	1989	J. L. Hastings	2000	G. A. Johnston
1968	S. Alexander	1979	A. M. B. Sym	1990	B. J. Boucher-Myers		
1969	J. Armour	1980	A. M. B. Sym	1991	D. S. Smyth		
1970	J. B. Stevenson	1981	A. Sinclair	1992	N. M. Bain		

The Dickie Cross

Presented in 1878 by Club's first Captain James Dickie. Played for annually, the winner having the lowest Scratch Score in the Spring Meeting.

		Hcp.	Score			Score			Score
1878	A. Yates	36	102	1922	J. L. C. Jenkins	77	1964	M. A. Holm	75
1879	D. McCulloch		126	1923	J. L. C. Jenkins	74	1965	R. P. Thomas	77
1880	T. McCulloch	12	105	1924	T. M. Burrell	79	1966	W. D. Smith	72
1881	A Yates	38	70	1925	J. C. L. Jenkins	76	1967	W. D. Smith	75
1882	T. G. Young	24	89	1926	I. G. Collins	80	1968	S. C. Wilson	74
1883	J. Balsillie		100	1927	W. G. Sweet, jun.	76	1969	S. Alexander	80
1884	A. Porteous		113	1928	J. Brock	77	1970	J. B. Stevenson	76
1885	A. Morison	20	87	1929	J. Brock	71	1971	J. H. Morrison	73
1886	T. Johnston	16	78	1930	J. M. Dykes, jun.	79	1972	W. A. Millar	73
1887	E. L. Dunlop	20	80	1931	J. E. Dawson	69	1973	J. Armour	74
1889	W. J. Anderson	24	77	1932	R. Neill	74	1974	J. B. Brown	76
1890	W. Morison		83	1933	J. E. Dawson	69	1975	J. R. W. Walkinshaw	75
1891	W. Milne		87	1934	H. G. McCallum	74	1976	J. R. W. Walkinshaw	75
1892	E. D. Prothero		86	1935	J. M. Dykes, jun.	72	1977	A. M. B. Sym	78
1893	J. A. Shaw		88	1936	A. W. Whyte	73	1978	G. McSherry	77
1894	E. D. Prothero		82	1937	J. E. Dawson	75	1979	G. C. Miller	78
1895	D. Dundas	5	80	1938	S. P. Morrison	70	1980	I. D. Hamilton	79
1896	W. Laidlaw	2	82	1939	H. G. McCallum	73	1981	I. R. Harris	76
1897	C. H. Herbertson	2	80	1940	J. N. Reynard	77	1982	A. M. B. Sym	72
1898	W. Fleming	2	81	1941	J. E. Dawson	73	1983	I. D. Hamilton	72
1899	W. G. Stewart	Scr.	78	1942	R. Garson	79	1984	W. D. Smith	75
1900	G. Miller	3	84		1943 – 46 World War II		1985	G. Foster	75
1901	A. Johnston	Scr.	81	1947	R. Neil	75	1986	N. M. Bain	76
1902	R. G. Ross	6	81	1948	C. Gibb	72	1987	D. S. Smyth	76
1903	W. Fulton	3	78	1949	J. N. Reynard	74	1988	D. S. Smyth	76
1904	T. H. Walker	+6	84	1950	J. M. Dykes, jun.	76	1989	W. B. Buchanan	71
1905	J. A. Shaw	Scr.	78	1951	J. B. Stevenson	78	1990	I. D. Hamilton	72
1906	C. A. Lauder	6	81	1952	J. B. Stevenson	72	1991	P. Convery	75
1907	J. Sturrock, jun.	6	80	1953	R. D. R. Walker	72	1992	B. J. Boucher-Myers	76
1908	W. B. Laird	Scr.	82	1954	A. E. McLeod	76	1993	R. C. Hood	75
1909	M. Laird	3	80	1955	W. S. McLeod	72	1994	K. E. Brown	78
1910	J. A. Shaw	+2	75	1956	J. H. Morrison	72	1995	G. McSherry	76
1911	G. V. M. Boyd	+2	77	1957	H. McMaster	79	1996	I. R. Harris	74
1912	W. B. Laird	Scr.	78	1958	J. C. Donald	73	1997	A. M. Fraser	74
1913	D. H. Buchanan	Scr.	77	1959	R. D. R. Walker	76	1998	B. J. Boucher-Myers	74
1914	W. Forbes	6	83	1960	J. B. Stevenson	74	1999	G. C. McKelvie	74
	1915 – 1919 The Great War			1961	W. Hogg	77	2000	G. C. Miller	78
1920	J. L. C. Jenkins		77	1962	H. V. S. Thomson	70			
1921	J. L. C. Jenkins		79	1963	R. R. Campbell	82			

Turner Cup

Presented by J. H. Turner, The Duke of Portland's Estate factor, in 1883 and is played for under handicap in the Spring Meeting.

Year	Name	Hcp.	Score
1883	J. F. Longmuir	24	86
1884	M. Laird	14	91
1885	W. Morison	8	88
1886	T. B. A. McMichael	22	75
1887	J. Guthrie		-
1888	W. Findlay	24	84
1889	C. Aird	24	89
1890	T. B. A. McMichael	6	89
1891	A. Johnston	12	82
1892	W. M. Paton	12	82
1893	W. Renwick	6	84
1894	W. Law	10	81
1895	W. P. Stewart	12	73
1896	D. Templeton	10	75
1897	R. Brownlee, jun.	8	83
1898	P. Robertson	11	75
1899	J. Meek	9	82
1900	D. G. L. McLure	8	85
1901	C. A. Lauder	7	81
1902	J. L. C. Jenkins	9	76
1903	F. Kufeke	9	74
1904	J. C. C. Miller	12	80
1905	G. D. Deuchar	8	81
1906	H. Beckett	10	82
1907	J. S. Eadie	8	87
1908	W. McLintoch	7	80
1909	M. W. Struthers	11	85
1910	R. Howie	8	86
1911	J. MacGill	10	77
1912	W. McNair	10	78
1913	S. Jackson	12	74
1914	W. T. Law	12	82
1915 – 1919 The Great war			
1920	J. Laird	6	76
1921	J. W. Jeffrey	Scr.	83
1922	W. Forbes	10	72
1923	F. A. Wilson	12	74
1924	G. L. Ogg, jun.	14	70
1925	J. Forest, jun.	11	71
1926	D. A. Liddell, jun.	3	77
1927	J. O. Lang	14	67
1928	D. McAlister	24	70
1929	J. E. Dawson	Scr.	75
1930	E. Lilburn	12	69
1931	J. N. Reynard	2	72
1932	J. M. Brown	12	73
1933	J. W. Penman	10	69
1934	J. Laird	3	75
1935	R. H. Scott	12	71
1936	K. M. Millar	8	71
1937	H. G. Brodie	15	69
1938	H. Waddell	11	69
1939	H. G. Brodie	10	68
1940	F. C. Comery	7	71
1941	W. C. H. Gray	10	78
1942	R. G. Gray	14	75
1943 – 46 World War II			
1947	D. McColl	1	79
1948	J. M. Burnet	9	72
1949	V. Gerstenberg	7	73
1950	A. B. S. Young	12	73
1951	A. Cleland	14	71
1952	W. G. MacFarlane	11	70
1953	J. C. Young	18	67
1954	R. A. Ogg	16	70
1955	D. S. M. Eadie	14	68
1956	G. B. Davie	11	67
1957	G. H. N. Reid	18	67
1958	J. Wilson	15	64
1959	G. A. Montgomerie	6	72
1960	J. B. Neil	16	68
1961	J. E. Snodgrass	13	72
1962	R. P. Burnet	8	68
1963	J. A. Dow	17	71
1964	D. M. J. Henderson	7	70
1965	R. Morton	15	67
1966	W. Duncan	11	69
1967	T. Symington	11	70
1968	J. W. Fisher	9	67
1969	B. R. Johnston	10	70
1970	J. C. Donald	4	72
1971	P. A. Martin	17	68
1972	J. R. Heugh	15	70
1973	J. G. Ogg	23	69
1974	J. A. Gemmell	14	71
1975	W. G. Hood	17	71
1976	A. Taylor	21	71
1977	A. M. B. Sym	2	76
1978	J. Duvoisin	18	71
1979	S. F. Johnston	7	72
1980	J. D. Millar	12	72
1981	G. C. Miller	4	73
1982	G. Easton	11	80
1983	W. D. Smith	5	69
1984	J. G. Paton	13	62
1985	J. G. McVey	20	68
1986	N. M. Bain	6	70
1987	B. Boland	21	68
1988	A. R. Grant	6	71
1989	B. R. Johnston	11	69
1990	J. S. Grant	14	69
1991	F. M. Watson	24	66
1992	D. Bancewicz	8	71
1993	N. McColl	16	70
1994	W. Neil	11	67
1995	P. D. Crumlish	17	65
1996	T. G. Church	7	70
1997	G. D. Ness	16	69
1998	R. L. Dunlop	9	70
1999	G. R. G. Andrew	11	68
2000	K. M. Sim	12	72

Duke of Portland Gold Medal

This was presented by His Grace The 6th Duke of Portland in 1881 for Scratch Competition and is played for in the Summer Meeting.

		Score			Score			Score
1881	J. R. Motion	95	1923	J. L. C. Jenkins	74	1964	J. F. Snodgrass	77
1882	R. Morison	97	1924	J. E. Dawson	78	1965	J. B. Stevenson	79
1883	J. Kirk	89	1925	J. L. C. Jenkins	73	1966	J. B. Stevenson	76
1884	J. J. W. Deuchar	97	1926	H. R. Orr	76	1967	M. A. Holm	80
1885	W. Morison	84	1927	D. A. Liddell, jun.	75	1968	A. M. B. Sym	70
1886	D. D. Robertson	93	1928	J. M. Symington	73	1969	A. M. B. Sym	73
1887	D. D. Robertson	92	1929	K. B. Symington	72	1970	A. M. B. Sym	69
1888	H. S. C. Everard	81	1930	J. W. G. Wylie	74	1971	A. M. B. Sym	73
1889	W. Morison	82	1931	J. E. Dawson	74	1972	T. W. Bryson	73
1890	H. S. C. Everard	83	1932	J. E. Dawson	74	1973	J. B. Gordon	75
1891	H. S. C. Everard	85	1933	J. M. Dykes, jun.	70	1974	A. M. B. Sym	72
1892	E. D. Prothero	83	1934	J. E. Dawson	72	1975	H. V. S. Thomson	79
1893	E. D. Prothero	86	1935	H. G. McCallum	70	1976	A. M. B. Sym	75
1894	A. Rowland	84	1936	H. G. McCallum	71	1977	W. D. Smith	77
1895	W. M. Paton	85	1937	J. E. Dawson	71	1978	A. M. B. Sym	73
1896	R. Fullarton	84	1938	J. E. Dawson	75	1979	I. D. Hamilton	72
1897	C. E. Dick	78	1939	J. E. Dawson	70	1980	S. F. Johnstone	75
1898	D. Templeton	78	1940	H. G. McCallum	75	1981	I. D. Hamilton	76
1899	W. G. Stewart	79	1941	J. E. Dawson	74	1982	D. J. Cotter	74
1900	W. G. Stewart	84	1942	J. Brock	76	1983	G. B. S. Thomson	76
1901	W. G. Stewart	86	*1943 – 1946 World War II*			1984	I. D. Hamilton	72
1902	J. A. Shaw	78	1947	R. D. R. Walker	74	1985	A. M. B. Sym	73
1903	J. L. C. Jenkins	80	1948	W. C. H. Gray	72	1986	D. S. Smyth	75
1904	J. L. C. Jenkins	78	1949	W. C. H. Gray	72	1987	C. S. Montgomerie	72
1905	J. A. Shaw	81	1950	J. M. Dykes, jun.	71	1988	N. Angus	72
1906	J. L. C. Jenkins	80	1951	J. B. Stevenson	72	1989	D. S. Smyth	72
1907	J. L. C. Jenkins	77	1952	A. W. Whyte	75	1990	N. M. Bain	76
1908	J. L. C. Jenkins	77	1953	J. B. Stevenson	72	1991	I. D. Hamilton	77
1909	R. G. Jenkins	75	1954	J. B. Stevenson	75	1992	I. R. Harris	75
1910	J. L. C. Jenkins	77	1955	J. B. Stevenson	74	1993	I. D. Hamilton	75
1911	G. V. M. Boyd	77	1956	W. G. Sweet	75	1994	N. M. Bain	75
1912	J. V. C. Jenkins	78	1957	M. D. Dawson	73	1995	J. N. Rowberry	75
1913	J. R. Beckett	77	1958	S. P. Morrison	73	1996	A. Reid	75
1914	J. W. Jeffrey	81	1959	J. E Dawson	70	1997	A. A. McLarty	77
1915 – 1919 The Great War			1960	J. B. Stevenson	70	1998	R. H. Calderwood	78
1920	K. B. Symington	76	1961	W. A. Millar	77	1999	G. McSherry	78
1921	K. M. Millar	77	1962	J. B. Stevenson	75	2000	G. C. McKelvie	76
1922	J. L. C. Jenkins	74	1963	W. S. McLeod	73			

Edinburgh Medal

In September 1881, several Edinburgh gentlemen got together, and donated the medal to the Club, to be played for on handicap, in the month of September. It is now played for under handicap in the Summer Meeting.

Year	Name	Hcp.	Net Score
1881	G. White	16	85
1882	J. M. Lipscomb	24	90
1883	W. A. Robertson	20	85
1884	A. T. Arthur	24	91
1885	J. M. Stewart	18	87
1886	J. Guthrie	18	84
1887	J. Clark	24	80
1888	F. G. Tulloch	-	-
1889	A. C. Robertson	-	-
1890	N. D. Michael	12	82
1891	S. Foulis	10	84
1892	W. Renwick	8	84
1893	W. P. Stewart	12	86
1894	A. Rowland	6	78
1895	R. Shaw	11	82
1896	G. K. Fullarton	8	77
1897	R. M. Clark	6	75
1898	H. Bishop	9	82
1899	J. C. Ure	8	81
1900	G. Rome	5	85
1901	A. Walker	4	86
1902	W. P. Nicholson	6	79
1903	G. Drummond	5	80
1904	R. Guthrie	7	80
1905	N. Glen	9	79
1906	R. G. Campbell	4	79
1907	H. W. Smith	5	76
1908	R. Guthrie	7	79
1909	R. G. Campbell	3	76
1910	F. D. Morton	3	74
1911	J. Y. Morrison	7	75
1912	A. N. Hunter	9	75
1913	R. Dickie	5	82
1914	H. W. Smith	6	80
1915 – 1919 The Great War			
1920	J. Laird	4	74
1921	J. M. Dykes	6	73
1922	R. Ballantine	16	77
1923	R. J. C. Clark	4	71
1924	H. G. Hendry	6	72
1925	I. H. Reeve	14	62
1926	T. L. Burnside	10	69
1927	S. P. Morrison	4	71
1928	W. D. Lang	13	69
1929	J. G. Wishart	18	66
1930	A. E. Howell	15	71
1931	W. S. Colville	3	73
1932	R. J. Shanks	12	74
1933	K. B. Symington	8	67
1934	W. Forbes	15	66
1935	J. S. Eadie	14	70
1936	A. Marr	5	69
1937	R. G. Jenkins	5	73
1938	D. M. Martin	8	71
1939	A. W. Whyte	2	68
1940	A. T. Hendry	5	72
1941	J. E. Forest	4	73
1942	R. G. Gray	14	77
1943 – 1946 World War II			
1947	D. McColl	1	79
1948	A. Sweet	4	75
1949	D. Williams	12	72
1950	T. L. T. Burnside	8	71
1951	A. C. Smith	10	72
1952	W. F. C. Smith	10	69
1953	R. J. G. MacDonald	14	67
1954	A. Lunan	5	72
1955	W. R. McCreath	8	71
1956	N. F. Robbie	19	67
1957	H. H. Pinkerton	12	61
1958	J. O. Lang	20	71
1959	J. A. Robertson	11	66
1960	A. W. L. Galbraith	6	65
1961	A. M. Brown	15	71
1962	G. M. Frame	12	67
1963	E. H. B. Sharp	12	69
1964	W. R. Houston	19	72
1965	J. Aitken	16	74
1966	W. Johnston	12	72
1967	C. W. F. Low	21	72
1968	J. G. Brown	12	67
1969	J. E. Murray	23	70
1970	D. C. Spence	4	71
1971	R. W. Jenkins	4	69
1972	J. F. Snodgrass	4	72
1973	D. J. S. Wilson	14	67
1974	E. H. B. Sharp	7	70
1975	J. M. R. Rennie	8	77
1976	R. A. Hardie	13	70
1977	R. A. Stevenson	16	73
1978	J. Armour	6	70
1979	J. G. Hunter	14	67
1980	T. L. Holden	13	66
1981	J. A. G. Winter	13	72
1982	D. J. Cotter	8	66
1983	J. Dunn	15	67
1984	T. C. McKeith	24	66
1985	J. M. Johnston	5	69
1986	W. Westbrook	14	68
1987	A. H. Galbraith	21	65
1988	E. C. Ecrepont	6	69
1989	J. Pauling	19	69
1990	A. H. Galbraith	19	69
1991	D. Mitchell	7	71
1992	G. W. Mowat	18	68
1993	G. W. Andrew	11	67
1994	P. W. Thomson	12	68
1995	D. B. Murphy	16	67
1996	R. L. Dunlop	11	69
1997	A. G. Sweet	14	67
1998	F. M. Watson	16	71
1999	B. A. Sugden	17	68
2000	S. J. McKelvie	9	67

Morison Medal

Presented in 1890 by Wm. Morison, Captain of the Club 1887-90 for Scratch Competition to be played for in the Autumn Meeting.

Year	Winner	Score	Year	Winner	Score	Year	Winner	Score
1890	A. McMurray	88	1929	H. G. McCallum	72	1967	H. V. S. Thomson	81
1891	H. S. C. Everard	-	1930	J. Brock	72	1968	W. A. Millar	77
1892	W. Milne	84	1931	W. G. Sweet, jun.	76	1969	S. C. Wilson	75
1893	E. D. Prothero	81	1932	J. M. Dykes, jun,	76	1970	Dr. J. L. Hastings	79
1894	E. D. Prothero	81	1933	A. C. J. M. Anderson	76	1971	Dr. J. L. Hastings	77
1895	J. A. Shaw	81	1934	J. Brock	73	1972	A. M. B. Sym	72
1896	J. A. Shaw	80	1935	J. M. Dykes, jun.	72	1973	J. D. S. Leburn	74
1897	C. E. Dick	77	1936	J. E. Dawson	76	1974	D. B. Fraser	75
1898	D. Templeton	84	1937	R. Neill	75	1975	A. M. B. Sym	71
1899	W. G. Stewart	83	1938	S. P. Morrison	77	1976	J. L. Hastings	76
1900	W. G. Stewart	74	1939	J. Laird	73	1977	J. Armour	78
1901	W. G. Stewart	83	1940	J. L. C. Jenkins	75	1978	I. D. Hamilton	72
1902	J. A. Shaw	77	1941	J. N. Reynard	70	1979	I. D. Hamilton	72
1903	J. L. C. Jenkins	80		*1942 – 1946 World War II*		1980	G. C. Miller	76
1904	J. Shaw	84	1947	J. E. Dawson	75	1981	R. S. Pringle	75
1905	J. W. Walker	81	1948	J. A. Lang	75	1982	A. R. G. Grant	74
1906	J. A. Shaw	79	1949	W. C. H. Gray	73	1983	A. M. B. Sym	81
1907	J. L. C. Jenkins	79	1950	J. B. Stevenson	77	1984	I. D. Hamilton	71
1908	J. L. C. Jenkins	75	1951	J. Armour	77	1985	J. C. Donald	75
1909	J. L. C. Jenkins	79	1952	J. C. Donald	75	1986	I. D. Hamilton	75
1910	J. A. Shaw	81	1953	J. B. Stevenson	74	1987	I. R. Harris	74
1911	J. L. C. Jenkins	78	1954	J. B. Stevenson	67	1988	I. D. Hamilton	78
1912	J. L. C. Jenkins	77	1955	J. B. Stevenson	73	1989	B. B. MacDonald	76
1913	J. L. C. Jenkins	72	1956	J. B. Stevenson	70	1990	N. M. Bain	79
1914	A. Drew	87	1957	H. V. S. Thomson	81	1991	I. D. Hamilton	72
	1915 – 1919 The Great War		1958	J. B. Stevenson	73	1992	J. M. Johnston	76
1920	J. L. C. Jenkins	75	1959	R. R. Campbell	68	1993	G. C. McKelvie	73
1921	J. Laird	78	1960	H. V. S. Thomson	72	1994	M. Hamilton	76
1923	H. R. Orr	76	1961	W. D. Smith	72	1995	G. McSherry	76
1924	K. B. Symington	74	1962	H. V. S. Thomson	74	1996	T. H. Webster	77
1925	H. G. McCallum	76	1963	H. V. S. Thomson	74	1997	G. A. Johnson	78
1926	J. Crawford	80	1964	J. F. Snodgrass	76	1998	J. N. Rowberry	77
1927	J. L. C. Jenkins	71	1965	D. H. McIvor	73	1999	J. M. Johnston	77
1928	J. E. Dawson	71	1966	H. K. Paton	76	2000	K. E. Brown	74

St. Andrew's Cross

First played for in 1890 under handicap, it is now played for under handicap in the Autumn Meeting.

Year	Winner	Hcp.	Net Score
1890	J. Wilson	20	86
1891	T. B. A. McMichael	6	85
1892	S. Foulis	6	83
1893	H. W. Mackie	7	81
1894	A. Porteous	6	77
1895	W. Fulton	9	80
1896	J. A. Patrick	8	74
1897	J. M. Bishop	2	79
1898	R. G. Ross	6	85
1899	J. G. Ure	7	81
1900	Dr. Roxburgh	8	82
1901	J. W. Walker	5	88
1902	W. Fulton	6	77
1903	G. Drummond	5	79
1904	J. Muir	8	82
1905	R. Stevenson	2	85
1906	H. J. Howie	6	74
1907	G. Morton, jun.	3	86
1908	D. Rintoul	2	79
1909	T C. Smith	1	80
1910	N. D. McMichael	6	83
1911	J. H. D. Allison	6	84
1912	R. H. Ballantine	8	83
1913	K. B. Symington	3	75
1914	J. Walker	8	81
1915 – 1919 *The Great War*			
1920	W. Lindsay Carlow	5	78
1921	P. W. Hopper	16	76
1923	J. W. G. Wyllie	4	75
1924	D. Young	18	76
1925	D. Young	16	72
1926	J. Dickie	12	75
1927	H. M. Hodgart	11	71
1928	J. Brock	Scr.	73
1929	G. V. Stewart	9	69
1930	Dr. J. W. MacFarlane	8	71
1931	A. M. Brown	8	89
1932	J. L. C. Jenkins	2	78
1933	A. Sweet	5	68
1934	W. Lindsay Carlow	4	70
1935	J. W. G. Wylie	5	73
1936	R. G. Jenkins	7	72
1937	H. Waddell	11	74
1938	A. W. Harrington, jun.	7	72
1939	D. Cameron	8	73
1940	J. M. Eadie	9	75
1941	R. Garson	Scr.	72
1942 – 1946 *World War II*			
1947	W. W. Deakin	12	68
1948	E. S. Brown	5	76
1949	F. R Rait	12	73
1950	M. J. G. Wylie	11	75
1951	G. B. Davie	14	69
1952	A. F. McFadzean	6	70
1953	H. Waddell	13	68
1954	A. W. L. Galbraith	12	68
1955	D. S. Young	6	69
1956	I. M. Brown	11	69
1957	J. R. Hendry	10	75
1958	I. M. Kennedy	8	69
1959	W. G. C. Gillies	2	66
1960	A. F. McFadzean	9	68
1961	G. F. Urquhart	17	69
1962	J. R. Lundie	10	71
1963	W. Ross	16	73
1964	R. P. Burnet	8	71
1965	C. G. Taylor	18	70
1966	J. F. Morton	15	70
1967	J. W. Fisher	10	77
1968	J. F. Morton	12	69
1969	W. G. Macfarlane	12	65
1970	W. A. Millar	4	75
1971	G. C. Miller	9	73
1972	T. Jack	19	77
1973	J. D. S. Leburn	3	71
1974	R. B. McColl	10	71
1975	A. M. B. Sym	2	69
1976	B. B. MacDonald	6	72
1977	A. Waldron	10	72
1978	J. Easton	10	69
1979	J. McNee	7	83
1980	G. C. Miller	4	72
1981	A. Murdoch	10	70
1982	A. R. G. Grant	5	69
1983	B. B. MacDonald	9	76
1984	D. C. Kennedy	10	67
1985	J. C. Donald	6	69
1986	J. D. S. Leburn	6	71
1987	J. Jardine	20	65
1988	B. R. Johnston	11	73
1989	B. B. MacDonald	7	69
1990	D. Johnston	11	69
1991	W. L. Wilkinson	12	66
1992	N. M. Bain	5	74
1993	J. Jardine	19	66
1994	A. M. Fraser	8	69
1995	D. Ferguson	11	81
1996	R. McKinlay	7	70
1997	R. B. McColl	12	74
1998	P. W. Thomson	10	68
1999	H. H. Kelly	11	70
2000	A. G. Sweet	11	67

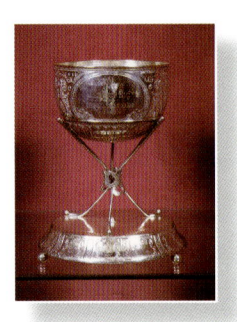

John Wood Cup

Presented by John Wood to the Club in 1882 and is played for as a Stableford Competition.

1882	W. I. Duncan	1906	J. O. M. Clark	1978	S. C. Wilson
1883	A. Porteous	1907	G. P. McIndoe	1979	K. I. McLeod
1884	J. Merry	1908	A. McCredie	1980	A. R. MacWilliam
1885	R. G. Ross	1909	R. J. C. Clark	1981	J. D. Thomson
1886	J. Robertson	1910	G. Hart	1982	R. A. Hamilton
1887	L. Robertson	1911	J. Donaldson	1983	G. M. Cameron
1888	L. Robertson	1912	R. H. Ballantine	1984	J. McNee
1889	W. C. Mitchell	1913	J. McD. Brown	1985	I. R. Harris
1890	A. Adams	1914	G. Findlay	1986	A. M. Lackie
1891	G. Drummond	1915 – 1919 *The Great War*		1987	W. J. Campbell
1892	J. Hutchison, jnr.	1920 – 1964 *No Competition*		1988	J. Ferguson
1893	A. Raeside	1965	W. D. M. Johnston & H. K. Paton	1989	B. Boland
1894	D. C. L. McLure	1966	*No Competition*	1990	W. Mackay
1895	W. Colvil	1967	*No Competition*	1991	R. Carter
1896	W. W. Bishop	1968	J. M. Cran	1992	K. Sim
1897	A. W. Harrington	1969	J. M. R. Rennie	1993	R. MacDonald
1898	J. F. Brown	1970	W. Duncan	1994	R. C. Sharman
1899	J. Salmon	1971	J. Armour	1995	D. C. Kennedy
1900	A. Gilmour	1972	D. B. Fraser	1996	J. C. Boland
1901	W. G. McBeth	1973	J. B. Stevenson	1997	P. A. Martin
1902	J. S. Wyper	1974	H. V. S. Thomson	1998	I. F. Penman
1903	D. G. Cunningham	1975	J. B. Stevenson	1999	N. McColl
1904	R. Harrington, jnr.	1976	J. Watson	2000	P. Muirhead
1905	W. Stevenson	1977	R. G. C. Gibson		

Blackrock Cup

Presented by A. Fraser in 1936, to be played for under handicap by Members over 40 years of age.

		Hcp.	Score
1936	H. G. McCallum	Scr.	71
1937	J. B. Lang	6	72
1938	F. C. Comery	11	66
1939	J. D. Hunter	16	71
	1940 – 1946 World War II		
1947	R. Garson	Scr.	77
1948	H. Waddell	10	70
1949	J. E. Dawson	Scr.	74
1950	R. B. More	16	75
1951	J. B. Jamieson	11	70
1952	A. N. MacFie	12	65
1953	A. H. Galbraith	17	70
1954	H. Paterson	19	70
1955	N. Y. Keanie	15	71
1956	A. H. Galbraith	16	68
1957	G. H. N. Reid	14	67
1958	S. A. Ballantyne	18	66
1959	J. B. Jamieson	16	68
1960	Dr. T. Semple	24	65
1961	J. N. Lang	18	69

		Hcp.	Score
1962	N. J. Capper	20	69
1963	R. Forrest	4	77
1964	R. R. Campbell	5	69
1965	T. Symington	14	66
1966	J. Morton	9	70
1967	A. B. S. Richardson	20	72
1968	J. B. Stevenson	1	72
1969	T. Jack	19	69
1970	D. C. Spence	9	70
1971	A. Hawley	15	70
1972	W. L. Laird	13	70
1973	D. J. S. Wilson	14	67
1974	J. D. Millar	12	65
1975	J. P. Linklater	12	70
1976	A. N. Smith	17	71
1977	T. L. T. Burnside	19	69
	J. A. Myers	11	69
1978	J. A. G. Winter	15	72
1979	R. H. B. Lowe	22	71
1980	W. A. G. Burnet	5	70

		Hcp.	Score
1981	M. W. Thomson	17	73
1982	G. I. Hervey	12	73
1983	B. W. S. Boucher-Myers	19	68
1984	W. D. Smith	4	68
1985	K. M. Sim	15	68
1986	J. Tinley	14	70
1987	D. K. Terras	13	68
1988	R. G. C. Gibson	16	64
1989	D. B. Murphy	20	68
1990	J. C. Hart	10	67
1991	A. M. Lackie	21	69
1992	D. J. C. Watson	7	69
1993	J. Jardine	21	65
1994	A. Waldron	9	70
1995	A. Ewart	9	68
1996	J. W. Gorman	12	70
1997	J. S. Westwater	6	64
1998	M. G. F. Houston	11	69
1999	N. M. Bain	5	75
2000	J. M. Clark	11	72

John Martin Cup

This was presented by John Martin in 1930, to be played for under Stableford by Members over 55 years of age.

1930 A. A. Martin	1953 H. G. McCallum	1970 A. M. Barr	1987 J. G. Mann
1931 A. A. Martin	1954 W. W. Galbraith	1971 J. B. Stevenson	1988 W. Roy
1932 S. Bell	1955 A. M. Brown	1972 C. C. Deurden	1989 W. S. P. Doodson
1933 W. Shaw	1956 H. G. McCallum	1973 W. W. Cowan	1990 W. G. Lundie
1934 A. Ballantine	1957 A. McIntosh	1974 T. M. Kennedy	1991 J. G. Craig
1935 D. McAlister	1958 A. McIntosh	1975 I. H. Paterson	1992 R. H. Morton
1936 J. McFadzean	1959 W. W. Galbraith	1976 I. H. Paterson	1993 W. L. Wilkinson
1937 K. M. Millar	1960 G. H. N. Reid	1977 H. White	1994 J. G. Craig
1938 J. G. McCutcheon	1961 L. Goldman	1978 W. Westbrook	1995 R. H. M. Scoular
1939 R. A. McKinlay	1962 J. G. Brown	1979 I. T. G. Tulloch	1996 M. McN. W. Hare
1940 – 1946 World War II	1963 W. G. Sweet	1980 J. L. Shaw	1997 J. Armour
1947 R. G. Gray	1964 L. Goldman	1981 N. F. Robbie	1998 W. H. Beaton
1948 J. L. C. Jenkins	1965 L. Goldman	1982 W. R. McCreath	1999 M. A. Cameron
1949 H. G. McCallum	1966 W. M. Brown	1983 H. V. S. Thomson	2000 P. W. Thomson
1950 J. W. MacFarlane	1967 A. Hawley	1984 W. R. Houston	
1951 J. Laird	1968 S. Dow	1985 W. R. Houston	
1952 J. O. Lang	1969 W. G. Sweet	1986 I. R. Harris	

The Trophy Cabinet

THE CLUB'S PRINCIPAL MEDALS & TROPHIES

Anderson Cup

Presented in 1893, by W. J. Anderson, Captain of the Club 1890-93, for match-play under handicap.

1893 P. Gouldie	1920 R. Paul Steward	1951 R. M. Easdale	1977 W. A. G. Burnet
1894 R. G. Campbell	1921 G. L. Millar	1952 H. C. MacLaine	1978 D. S. Smyth
1895 R. Fullarton	1922 K. B. Symington	1954 J. T. Lang	1979 W. D. M. Johnston
1896 A. Dunlop	1923 J. E. Dawson	1955 S. W. McInnes	1980 A. N. Sturrock
1897 J. Muir	1924 W. S. Colville	1956 A. Garson	1981 A. N. Sturrock
1898 W. W. Clark	1925 C. B. Symington	1957 R. S. Waddell	1982 J. K. S. Leburn
1899 Dr. Cowan Lees	1926 F. Caldwell Ker	1958 J. E. Murray	1983 I. R. Harris
1900 A. Gilmour	1927 J. E. Dawson	1959 J. T. Shaw	1984 R. Catterson
1901 W. P. Nicholson	1928 J. E. Dawson	1960 S. C. Wilson	1985 A. Barclay
1902 C. W. Rowat	1929 A. H. Anderson	1961 G. B. Davie	1986 P. W. Thomson
1903 R. Stevenson, jun.	1930 J. W. Tait	1962 J. C. Donald	1987 I. R. Harris
1904 C. W. Rowat	1931 J. Laird	1963 A. M. B. Sym	1988 D. S. Smyth
1905 F. Abbott	1932 A. J. Carlow	1964 J. C. Donald	1989 G. C. Miller
1906 J. O. M. Clark	1933 W. Beattie	1965 S. P. Morrison	1990 J. S. Westwater
1907 M. W. Struthers	1934 J. E. Dawson	1966 H. K. Paton	1991 W. A. G. Burnet
1908 A. McCreadie, jun.	1935 K. B. Symington	1967 J. C. Donald	1992 A. Waldron
1909 A. McNair	1936 D. McColl	1968 J. D. Sharp	1993 D. Mitchell
1910 J. Dundas and D. Dundas, finalists - *Tie not played*	1937 R. Neill	1969 A. Garson	1994 P. W. Thomson
	1938 H. G. Hendry	1970 R. B. McColl	1995 A. C. Simpson
	1939 J. G. Moffat	1971 J. M. R. Rennie	1996 I. R. Harris
1911 W. G. MacBeth	*1940 – 1946 World War II*	1972 R. A. W. Johnston	1997 D. J. Hervey
1912 C. W. Rowat	1947 A. Lunan	1973 N. W. Watson	1998 C. A. J. Watson
1913 W. A. Collins	1948 R. M. Easdale	1974 W. D. M. Johnston	1999 A. C. Simpson
1914 J. Y. Morrison	1949 A. Marr	1975 W. S. P. Doodson	2000 S. Leonard
1915 – 1919 The Great War	1950 T. Black	1976 A. R. G. Grant	

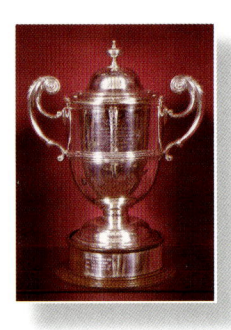

Lord Ashton Cup

Presented by Lord Ashton in 1906, the winner being the holder of the aggregate best 4 net scores in the season's competitions.

1908 J. O. MacNiven	1934 R. Neill	1960 R. R. Campbell	1980 D. H. D. Forsyth
1909 K. B. Symington	1935 K. B. Symington	1961 R. O. Whiteford	1981 I. R. Harris
1910 R. J. C. Clark	1936 J. N. Reynard	1962 R. P. Thomas	1982 J. Wilson, jnr.
1911 J. L. C. Jenkins	1937 A. W. Whyte	S. C. Wilson (tie)	1983 W. A. R. Cook
1912 W. Morrice	1938 R. Neill	1963 A. M. B. Sym	1984 I. Dunlop
1913 J. L. C. Jenkins	1939 R. Neill	1964 C. W. F. Judge	1985 S. C. Wilson
1914 J. L. C. Jenkins	1940 – 1946 World War II	1965 S. C. Wilson	1986 S. C. Wilson
1915 – 1919 The Great War	1947 D. McColl	1966 D. S. Campbell	1987 B. Boland
1921 K. B. Symington	1948 A. T. Hendry	1967 A. M. B. Sym	1988 R. Carter
1922 K. B. Symington	1949 W. C. H. Gray	1968 J. C. Donald	1989 S. Doak
1923 H. G. Hendry	1950 A. W. Whyte	1969 W. A. G. Burnet	1990 H. Osborne
1924 J. L. C. Jenkins	1951 W. C. H. Gray	1970 I. Gordon	1991 J. E. Palmer
J. W. G. Wyllie (tie)	1952 M. A. Holm	1971 L. A. Hardie	1992 W. L. Wilkinson
1925 J. Laird	1953 J. B. Stevenson	1972 S. C. Wilson	1993 A. A. McLarty
1926 J. W. G. Wyllie	1954 W. G. Hood	1973 W. A. Millar	1994 R. C. Sharman
1927 A. R. Anderson	1955 J. B. Stevenson	1974 J. B. Brown	1995 P. J. Lawrence
1928 E. S. Brown	1956 R. H. Patterson	I. Gordon (tie)	1996 G. C. McKelvie
1929 J. Brock	1957 N. F. Robbie	1975 A. M. B. Sym	1997 J. A. Jones
1930 J. Brock	1958 M. D. Dawson	1976 J. G. Hunter	1998 R. H. Calderwood
1931 R. G. Finlay	H. V. S. Thomson (tie)	1977 I. D. Hamilton	1999 P. W. Thomson
1932 J. Brock	1959 J. C. Donald	1978 A. R. Brown	B. A. Sugden (tie)
1933 J. H. Robb	R. J. Y. Wilson (tie)	1979 D. H. D. Forsyth	2000 R. J. Livingston

THE CLUB'S PRINCIPAL MEDALS & TROPHIES

J. A. Shaw Cup

Presented in 1948 by J. A. Shaw for competition in Winter Foursomes match-play.

1949 – 50 J. C. Donald & J. T. Shaw
1950 – 51 A. N. Smith & J. Wilson
1951 – 52 G. H. Blain & S. Halliday
1952 – 53 Dr A. P. Walker & R. D. R. Walker
1953 – 54 J. McQueen & A. C. Taylor
1954 – 55 J. E. Dawson & J. R. Hendry
1955 – 56 R. Neill & M. D. Dawson
1956 – 57 G. B. Davie & G. I. Ogg
1957 – 58 W. G. Davidson & R. S. Waddell
1958 – 59 W. W. Galbraith & W. C. H. Gray
1959 – 60 H. V. S. Thomson & S. GIlmour
1960 – 61 R. S. Waddell & W. G. Davidson
1961 – 62 K. I. McLeod & W. A. McAlpine
1962 – 63 S. C. Wilson & J. D. Thomas
1963 – 64 S. C. Wilson & J. D. Thomas
1964 – 65 R. R. Campbell & T. M. Brown
1965 – 66 I. T. G. Tulloch & A. G. Gordon
1966 – 67 L. Goldman & J. Laing
1967 – 68 C. S. Brown & J. T. Lang
1968 – 69 K. D. Fraser & J. C. Donald
1969 – 70 W. Hogg & S. R. Wood
1970 – 71 L. A. Hardie & A. S. Burns
1971 – 72 A. N. Smith & H. V. S. Thomson
1972 – 73 K. D. Fraser & J. C. Donald
1973 – 74 J. Cran & C. G. Taylor
1974 – 75 J. M. R. Rennie & P. J. Lawrence

1975 – 76 J. G. Mann & A. D. Chirnside
1976 – 77 R. J. T. Glen & W. L. Wilkinson
1977 – 78 A. E. Smith & W. Neill
1978 – 79 C. S. Waters & T. C. Cotter
1979 – 80 D. B. Fraser & D. C. Spence
1980 – 81 M. A. Cameron & S. C. Wilson
1981 – 82 J. M. Johnston & J. R. B. Penny
1982 – 83 H. V. S. Thomson & J. L. Hastings
1983 – 84 A. Gow & W. B. Milligan
1984 – 85 S. C. Wilson & M. A. Cameron
1985 – 86 I. Gordon & J. D. Thomson
1986 – 87 W. A. G. Burnet & M. G. F. Houston
1987 – 88 R. G. T. Glen & W. L. Wilkinson
1988 – 89 T. Gilchrist & I. S. Ruthven
1989 – 90 J. G. Craig & J. S. Westwater
1990 – 91 J. Easton & J. H. Greene
1991 – 92 W. A. G. Burnet & M. G. F. Houston
1992 – 93 D. Banciewicz & A. Waldron
1993 – 94 A. Reid & J. Sanderson
1994 – 95 G. McSherry & R. L. Dunlop
1995 – 96 D. C. Kennedy & G. D. Ness
1996 – 97 S. J. McKelvie & G. McKelvie
1997 – 98 T. H. Webster & J. F. Morman
1998 – 99 D. C. Kennedy & G. D. Ness
1999 – 00 D. M. Richmond & W. A. Cameron

Design and Origination By Thomson Print Services (Glasgow) Ltd,
Printing and Binding by Lithoprint (Scotland) Ltd

PLAN
OF
TROON GOLF LINKS.
1888.

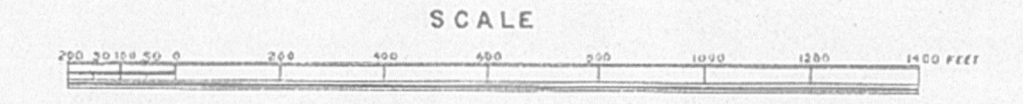

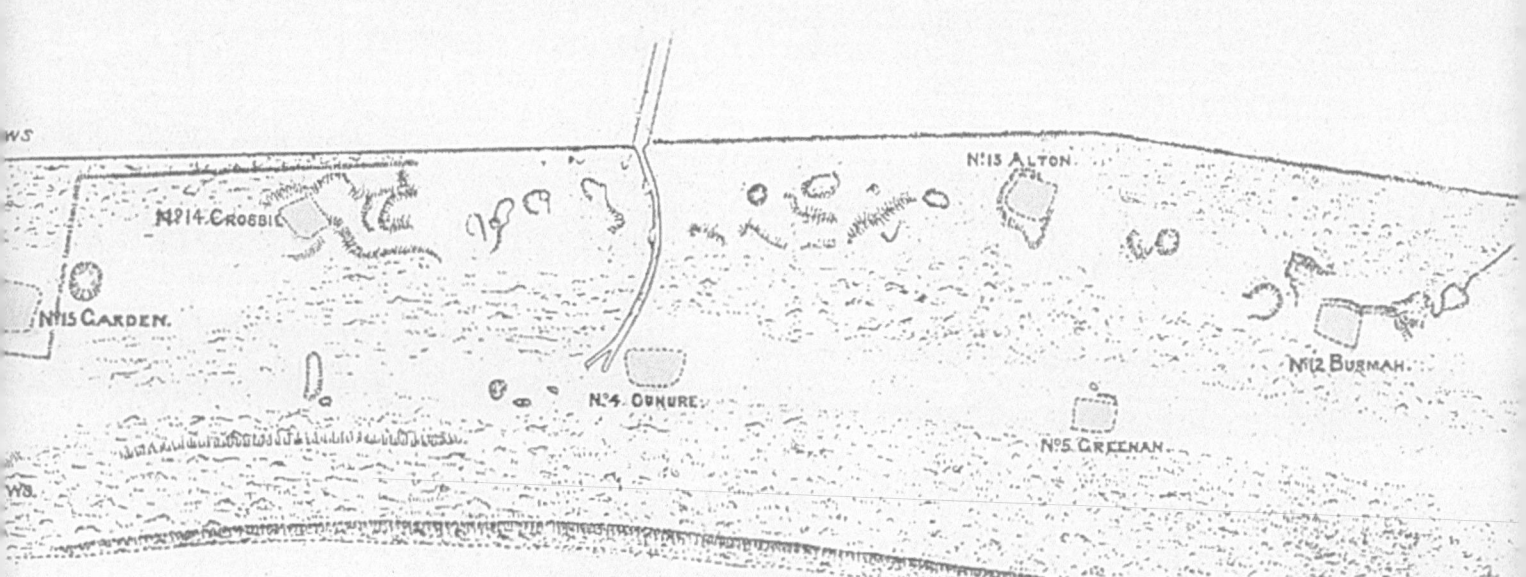

SCALE

Nº 14 CROSBIE
Nº 13 ALTON
Nº 15 GARDEN
Nº 12 BURMAH
Nº 4 DUNURE
Nº 5 GREENAN

High Water Mark of Ordinary Spring Tides